The Atum-Re Revival

Ancient Egyptian Wisdom for the Modern World

The Atum-Re Revival

Ancient Egyptian Wisdom for
the Modern World

Mélusine Draco

AXIS MUNDI
BOOKS

Winchester, UK
Washington, USA

First published by Axis Mundi Books, 2013
Axis Mundi Books is an imprint of John Hunt Publishing Ltd., Laurel House, Station Approach,
Alresford, Hants, SO24 9JH, UK
office1@jhpbooks.net
www.johnhuntpublishing.com
www.axismundi-books.com

For distributor details and how to order please visit the 'Ordering' section on our website.

A CIP catalogue record for this book is available from the British Library.

Design: Stuart Davies

Printed and bound by CPI Group (UK) Ltd, Croydon, CR0 4YY

We operate a distinctive and ethical publishing philosophy in all
areas of our business, from our global network of authors to
production and worldwide distribution.

CONTENTS

The calendar compilation and exercises used in the text of *The Atum-Re Revival* have been reproduced with the kind permission of the Temple of Khem and taken from their Year One foundation study course for the Egyptian Mystery Tradition. www.templeofkhem.com

Part One

The Egyptian Revival

Already in antiquity, there was an opinion that the land of the Nile was the fount of all wisdom and the stronghold of hermetic lore. Thus began a tradition that is still alive today ... Alchemy, astrology, and other secret sciences have Egyptian roots, and films, popular fiction, and comic books frequently draw upon Egyptian themes ... Modern-day esoteric endeavours find an endlessly renewable intellectual reservoir in ancient Egyptian culture ...
[*The Secret Lore of Egypt: Its Impact on the West,* Erik Hornung]

'*Was there ever a civilisation more in love with the cult of the dead and the afterlife than the ancient Egyptians?*' asked travel writer Bob Maddams in the *Daily Telegraph* [29th January 2011]. He was observing that a 12ft scroll detailing the perilous adventures awaiting the spirits of the departed on their journey through the underworld, and containing spells to help them towards their final judgement, reads more like a storyboard for a Hollywood horror movie than a religious text.

But were the Egyptians obsessed with death? What of the Egyptian gods themselves? Those strange anthropomorphic creatures, half-man, half-animal, that would have appeared to Renaissance Europeans as demons from the darkest corner of Dante's *Inferno*. Could anyone today take seriously a civilisation that worshipped cats and baboons? Or mummified the remains of sacred bulls and crocodiles? And what about all the tales of myth, magic and arcane wisdom? Why does this ancient civilisation continue to fascinate people from all over the world? **And how can any of it be relevant in today's cosmic computer age?**

Despite all its apparent remoteness, the Mystery of ancient

Egypt lingers on in what Jung described as the collective unconscious. And we must use an upper case 'M' when referring to the
Egyptian Mysteries because this is *exactly* what has endured for
over six millennia, inspiring adventurers, architects and artists,
not to mention an assortment of esoteric communities, down
through the centuries. The Egyptian gods still reach out from
beyond the grave to communicate to today's living, the relevance
of their ancient wisdom in our modern world.

We must, however, be mindful that both the social and
magico-religious development of Egypt underwent some drastic
internal changes during its long history, and so it would be
unwise to attempt to compartmentalise the attributes of deities
who appear in their extremely powerful primitive guise in pre-
dynastic times, with those diluted forms from the much later
Graeco-Roman period. Even the earliest texts record the dual
purpose of local gods and goddesses; deities whose worship also
waxed and waned with changing fashion, and the development
of various cults during 3,000 years of pharaonic rule.

As with all other civilisations, the earliest Egyptian gods
metamorphosed and merged with deities of other regions as the
shift of power moved from centre to centre. As always, however,
the enormous time-span of Egyptian history complicates matters
even further when identifying with a particular deity or period.
For example: a pre- or early dynastic Egyptian may not have a
clue who Isis or Osiris were if they did not live in that particular
province or *nome*, **of which these were merely localised deities
of the time.** Conversely, a New Kingdom priest may possibly
have looked upon Neith as simply a minor funerary goddess,
when in her hey-day she was the mighty hunter-warrior goddess
of pre-dynastic Egypt.

Let's make no bones about it, today's Egyptian interpretation
of the Mysteries belongs to a revivalist tradition **and should not
claim to be anything else.** Nevertheless, the magical application
needs to be as close as it can get to the beliefs of ancient Egypt,

without falling into the trap of lumping all the gods together in one ageless pantheon … and expecting their *heka* to work for us! In order to follow the Old Ways, it is easier to understand if we use three separate approaches:

- The Stellar Path that deals with the primeval/primordial forces of the universe usually aligned with ritual magic and inner temple working; pre-dynastic and Old Kingdom.
- The Solar Path that offers a more intellectual, spiritual or mystical approach; Middle Kingdom.
- The Lunar Path, which concentrates on the purely devotional aspects and the ability to move between the worlds, i.e. different planes of consciousness. New Kingdom.

And a fundamental understanding of Egyptian history *is* necessary because not everyone works magically or mystically at the same level. Some take longer to realise that an intimate knowledge of Egyptian myth and its attendant politics *is* essential for the effective practice of magic/mysticism at higher levels of awareness. This knowledge has to extend beyond the stereotypical deities of popular Egyptomania, to embrace a wider and loftier range of supernatural beings; and to accept that the deities are *not* real 'divine beings' at the seeker's beck and call. This is why it becomes so important to successful magical/mystical working to be able to differentiate between the subtle levels of magic, historical influence and religious emphasis that mark the shift between these different Paths.

And to do so safely and successfully.

On the surface, it may appear that this is merely massaging a system that purports to be all things to all men: but this is not the case. The original Egyptian religion *was* stellar based. Early texts refer to the stairway to heaven, and the alignment of the mortuary temples situated toward the north (the direction of the circumpolar stars) reveal the importance of the Imperishable Stars within the Mysteries. According to Egyptologists, the architectural changes in pyramid design actually reflect this shift *from a stellar cult* to one that was fully solar, as the religious ideology changed and a new priesthood gained power. And as each new centre became the focus of priestly power, so the religion altered and a new set of myths were created to attest to the local gods' supremacy over the Old Ones – with Isis eventually supplanting the 'Great God Thoth' in the magical stakes.

These shifting influences on Egyptian history meant that ancient reference texts fall roughly into two separate categories.

- Firstly, actual magical, religious and mythological sources written by the early indigenous priesthood *for* the Egyptian people;
- Secondly, later accounts of magic, religion and mythology translated by Greek and Roman historians and philosophers, who recorded information as told to them by latter-day priests (since they were unable to read the texts for themselves) *about* the Egyptian people.

And by the time of the Graeco-Roman invasions the priesthood were themselves extremely vague and uncertain about the early beliefs of their own ancestors. Subsequent translations indicate that the native priesthood no longer understood the rudimentary principles of their archaic religious antecedents, the primitive stellar-cult, or the nature of its symbolism, **despite continuing to use its imagery in their temples and texts right up until the end of the empire.**

Unfortunately, many present-day writings on the Egyptian Mystery Tradition make no attempt to unravel this tangled skein of magico-religious evolution. Rather, this imposes some oversimplified form of order on the chaos created by the multitude of dual-purpose gods from different periods of history. But there is no way of simplifying this complicated tapestry because of that immense time-span from pre-dynastic times to the Battle of Actium, which sealed the fate of the last ruling Great House of Egypt. Cleopatra, in terms of historical dating, was nearer to man landing on the moon than to the building of the Great Pyramid at Giza.

Thus, the religion developed over thousands of years, with each deity assuming many forms under the influence of the different religious movements and/or foreign invasions. Each form also developed its own positive and negative aspects, which responded in various ways to a wide variety of magical applications, and so it is impossible to be dogmatic about how the gods of those different theologies relate to, and blend with, each other. It is also important to keep in mind that the original religion was never an earth-bound concept since the priesthood explored mysticism on a cosmic scale: their spirituality extending to the stars and beyond. The Egyptian civilisation took over 3,000 years to fully evolve and a further 2,000 years to decay, which is why the Egyptian Mystery Tradition cannot be encapsulated into convenient modern packaging.

Magic – Charm, Spell and Taboo

Archaeological evidence for Egyptian magic spans about 4,500 years, and there were two basic forms: *heka* and *akhu*. Both involving recognition of some kind of supernatural force that could influence or change the course of events. This force was not an independent power; it was thought of as residing in natural objects, or invoked by actions and/or words. This concept, which is generally considered by archaeologists to be more primitive superstition than religion, manifests itself in different ways: in the supernatural power of objects, the practice of magic, and in the recognition of the 'forbidden'.

The Egyptians used the term *heka* to refer to magical power, in the sense of a divine force [sometimes personified as the god Heka] that could be invoked both by deities and humans to solve a problem or crisis. In modern times there is a clear distinction between prayers, healing and magic, but for the Egyptians these were overlapping and complementary. As we learn from the *BM Dictionary of Ancient Egypt*, a single problem might be solved by a combination of magical rituals or treatments (*seshaw*), medicinal prescriptions (*pekhret*) and religious texts (*rw*). Geraldine Pinch, in *Magic in Ancient Egypt*, gives us the word for the magical power used for deities and stars as *akhu*, which is sometimes translated as enchantments, sorcery or spells, and is primarily associated with the Ancestors.

The most common form of protective magic came in the form of amulets, which were subsequently copied all over the ancient world. Huge numbers survive and those found in humbler graves are more likely to be those actually worn by the deceased in life. They could go on helping and protecting the owner in the afterlife, and were probably considered too valuable (in magical terms) to be passed on to someone else. An amulet or talisman is generally defined as a powerful or protective object worn or carried on a person; some (talismans) were used on a temporary basis in crisis situations, while others (amulets) were worn on a regular basis for permanent protection or benefit.

Pinch also suggests that permanent amulets were likely to be worn in the form of personal adornment. *'It is hardly an exaggeration to say that most Egyptian jewellery has amuletic value. How conscious the wearers were of the symbolism of their ornaments is a more difficult question ...'* Amulets can be natural or manmade, and *heka* was believed to reside in rare or strange objects. Natural shells, claws and river pebbles were common, as were imitations in faience, silver or gold. And it wasn't just the object itself that was protective since an amulet may also consist of the cord on which the items were strung, the bag that contained them, and the words needed to activate the protective charm. The word for

6

an amulet (*sa*) refers to all these things, and the hieroglyphic sign used to write the word is a looped cord.

The *ankh* is one of the oldest religious symbols in the world, although Egyptologists are still not sure as to the precise interpretation of the image. The symbol itself means 'breath of life' and was common from the beginning of Egyptian writing. In religious images the gods hold the *ankh* in one hand, or offer it to the king. The sign was eventually adopted by the Coptic church as its unique form of cross, and is one of the most common Egyptian images worn today as jewellery, even by those with no particular interest in Egyptian beliefs.

How to Make a Simple Egyptian Amulet

Cowrie shells were considered to be a powerful amulet against the evil eye, and are still worn as such by modern day Turks and Arabs. A cowrie (or cowroid) shell-shaped amulet is frequently inscribed and serves a similar purpose to that of the scarab. The cowrie shell amulet was known as early as pre-dynastic times and its shape was believed to mimic the female genitalia; girdles made from them were used to symbolically protect women. From the 6th Dynast the shells were imitated in faience, and later in cornelian and quartz.

Method: Obtain either a single cowrie shell for inclusion in a pouch, or a collection to be made into a bracelet, girdle or necklace.

- The single cowrie (actual or imitation) should be magically cleansed in cold running water and anointed with an appropriate oil before placing in a small fabric pouch to protect from the evil eye. This can be carried in a bag or briefcase, and should not be handled by

anyone else.
- A collection of shells can be strung on nylon thread, with coloured beads in between to make an attractive bracelet, girdle or necklace that can be worn without anyone being aware that this piece of jewellery has a protective nature.

Egyptologist Geraldine Pinch cites the definition of magic given by Sir James Frazer in *The Golden Bough*, as being the *'manipulation of supernatural beings by a human who expects that the correct sequence of words or actions will automatically bring about the desired result'*. He did acknowledge that the same individuals might be involved in both magic and religion, but looked upon magicians and priests as belonging to rival groups. In fact, Egyptian priests were master magicians who were paid specialists of ritual rather than being mere guardians of morality. As Pinch points out, however, the theory that magic is always an unorthodox and subversive part of religious and political counterculture, does not seem to apply in Egypt, where ritual magic was practiced on behalf of the State for at least 3,000 years.

> *Some Egyptian priests used magic for private purposes, even when it involved practices that might seem blasphemous from a religious [i.e. modern] view point. Egyptian spells may plead with and command a deity to carry out the magician's desire. Other spells go as far as threatening the gods with sacrilegious acts and cosmic catastrophe.*
> [Magic in Ancient Egypt, Geraldine Pinch]

Curses were also the province of the priesthood, and it was the mortuary priests who resealed Tutankhamun's tomb with the words: *'May death come on swift wings to him who disturbs the rest of the Pharaoh'.* The newly discovered tomb of a Dynast IV man named Petety had on either side of the entrance examples of hieroglyphic curses to protect it. Petety's well-known threat spell reads:

> *Listen all of you! The priest of Hathor will beat twice any one of you who enters this tomb or does harm to it.*
> *The gods will confront him because I am honoured by his Lord.*
> *The gods will not allow anything to happen to me.*
> *Anyone who does anything bad to my tomb, then (the) crocodile, (the) hippopotamus, and the lion will eat him.*

'The Cursing Litany', translated by Egyptologist Margaret Murray, is probably the most deadly of all, because it is not only aimed at the living, but also the obliteration of a person's spirit and memory after death. For the Egyptians, to deprive someone of their Name was to rob them of a continued existence in Amenta (Otherworld). This particular curse required the participation of two or more people: one to speak the curse, the other(s) to repeat the refrain: *'Mayest thou never exist'.*

Mayest thou never exist, may thy ka never exist,
may thy body never exist.
Mayest thou never exist.

May thy limbs never exist.	*Mayest thou never exist.*
May thy bones never exist.	*Mayest thou never exist.*
May thy words of power never exist.	*Mayest thou never exist.*
Mayest thou never exist.	*Mayest thou never exist.*
May thy form never exist.	*Mayest thou never exist.*
May thy attributes never exist.	*Mayest thou never exist.*
May that which springs from thee never exist.	
	Mayest thou never exist.
May thy hair never exist.	*Mayest thou never exist.*
May thy possessions never exist.	*Mayest thou never exist.*

May thy emissions never exist.	*Mayest thou never exist.*
May the material of thy body never exist.	
	Mayest thou never exist.
May thy place never exist.	*Mayest thou never exist.*
May thy tomb never exist.	*Mayest thou never exist.*
May thy cavern never exist.	*Mayest thou never exist.*
May thy funeral chamber never exist.	*Mayest thou never exist.*
May thy paths never exit.	*Mayest thou never exist.*
May thy seasons never exist.	*Mayest thou never exist.*
May thy words never exist.	*Mayest thou never exist.*
May thy enterings never exist.	*Mayest thou never exist.*
May thy journeying never exist.	*Mayest thou never exist.*
May thy advancings never exist.	*Mayest thou never exist.*
May thy comings never exist.	*Mayest thou never exist.*
May thy sitting down never exist.	*Mayest thou never exist.*
May thy increase never exist.	*Mayest thou never exist.*
May thy body never exist.	*Mayest thou never exist.*
May thy prosperity never exist.	*Mayest thou never exist.*

Thou art smitten, O enemy.

Thou shalt die, thou shalt die.

Thou shalt perish, thou shalt perish, thou shalt perish.

One of the original, most magical of acts of all, however, must surely be in that most solemn of all ceremonies: the rites of purification, which in later dynastic times would have been wholly religious; classic writers refer to the daily ritual performed in the temples to 'animate' divine statues, as an exalted form of magic. Temple magic, however, was believed to be a Great Work performed for the benefit of all Egyptians, with one esoteric text claiming that the land of Egypt was indeed 'the temple of the whole world'. In fact, we would not be wrong in presuming that many of those early rites of purification *were* originally magic spells to protect against evil (negative) forces.

Another primitive survival in Egyptian ritual is in the special category of magic custom which anthropologists have conveniently designated as 'taboo' (from the Polynesian *tabu*, meaning 'unclean'), or religious prohibition. The analysis of the traces of 'taboo' surviving in the customs of the ancient religion reveals that, though some have obviously characteristic Egyptian developments and extensions (as in the 42 Negative Confessions), the majority are ideas common to most primitive peoples.

The accepted code of social behaviour, and the distinction between right and wrong during the pharaonic period, also tend to be closely intertwined with funerary beliefs and various cultural requirements. The Pyramid Texts (Old Kingdom), Coffin Texts (Middle Kingdom) and the Book of the Dead (The Coming Forth by Day of the New Kingdom) all contain magical spells (or 'Utterances') to help the deceased navigate the perils of the Underworld; often using archaic language indicating the predynastic origins of the ideas. *'Indeed some of these magical utterances seem to be referring to aspects of the funerary cult that were no longer current at the time that the pyramids were built,'* observes the British Museum *Dictionary of Ancient Egypt*.

The concept of *ma'at* (often translated as 'truth' or 'harmony') was also central to ancient Egyptian ethics, representing the original state of tranquillity at the moment of the Creation of the universe. And it was the feather of the goddess Ma'at that was weighed against the heart of the deceased to determine whether he or she was worthy of resurrection in the afterlife. The so-called 'negative confession' – a list of sins that had *not* been committed by the deceased – was intended to be recited in the Hall of Judgement in order to ensure a successful outcome.

Summary:

In *Liber Ægyptius* it is pointed out that personal honesty and integrity remains an import facet of the modern Egyptian Mystery Tradition since it will be the Adept *alone* who takes responsibility for his or her own actions when called upon to stand before the 42 Assessors in the Hall of Judgement. This aspect of the religion has remained intact since the beginning of recorded history, and should not be dismissed as part of the mythos. Neither should the Adept practice self-delusion in trying to ignore this very basic tenet of all magical traditions that has existed from ancient times, right up to the present day – **self-regulation and responsibility.**

The Spirits – Belief and Worship

The basis of the old Egyptian religion and the greater part of its beliefs and practice *'before its extension, which was also its contamination'*, belongs to the phase that anthropology has given the name 'animism'. The word was first invented by Sir Edward Burnett Tylor (*Anthropology*) to express the attribution of a spirit to natural objects and phenomena, and which has been taken to be the source of all primitive religious development.

Rosalie David, however, in her Introduction to Christian Jacq's first edition of *Egyptian Magic* wrote that all elements of life, whether divine, human, animal or inanimate, were considered to be imbued with magical power, and animated by a spiritual force that could be manipulated.

> *Essentially, the spiritual and material were believed to be woven from the same substance, and it was considered possible, by using magic, to control the order of the cosmos, and to modify individual destiny by combating negative trends.*

It goes without saying that the most powerful natural 'object' that was regarded with awe was the Nile – itself the longest river in the world – since without its waters and fertile floodplain, it is highly unlikely that the Egyptian civilisation would have developed and endured in the way it did. The study of the topography and geology of the Nile valley by the Egypt Exploration Society (*EES Egyptian Archaeology*) has also revealed a complex sequence of phases, whereby the river gradually changed its location and size over the course of a million years. Even in recent millennia, the course of the river continued to shift, but from the earliest times the waters flooded over the surrounding countryside every year between June and September, thereby fixing the start of the Egyptian year.

The sky-goddess (Nut) and her relationship with the earth-god (Geb) is undoubtedly one of the oldest of Egyptian concepts of deity. Their parents were Shu the god of (dry) air and sunlight, and Tufnut, goddess of moisture or corrosive air. It was Shu's role to support the outstretched figure of Nut, thus effectively separating the sky from the earth and this image appeared on countless inscriptions throughout the whole of the dynastic era. And although various localised deities grew to prominence, it has been suggested that man's earliest conception of actual spirits was of malign and maleficent powers that thwarted the normal progress of life, and that fear created the first gods in the world: the principal malevolent being the snake-god Apophis, who symbolised the forces of chaos and evil.

As with all developing civilisations in the ancient world, transition from early spirit beliefs, on which magic was an integral part, to those of organised religion was a natural transition, since much of the external form of the magic spell was retained in the formulae of prayer to the spirits/gods. By the time the days of the State cult were reached, the primitive beliefs would have fallen into the background and prayer would be made rather for the prosperity of Egypt and protection from its enemies, rather than family or community rites.

Summary:

Much of Egypt's early magico-religious rites would have been what we now refer to as shamanic in nature, and one of the most evocative images is that of a masked or hooded man from the early Naqada I period. Depicted as conveying an eerie sense of menace, figures with these same enveloping hoods are occasionally depicted on early palettes. As Billie Walker-John described them in *The Inner Guide to Egypt*: *'It is a form which is bland enough to accept a huge range of emotional, religious and psychic associations. Devoid of any personality through their grab, they are the men and women who once became pure channels for communication with the worlds, linking life and death, matter and spirit, past and future.'* **These are the ancestral images of the cowled figures present in the modern magician's or witch's Circle.**

The Gods – Anthropomorphism

In the very early days of Egyptian antiquity many of the gods were abstract concepts rather than the actual anthropomorphic god-pictures familiar to us today. Many of the later, fully-morphed deities were originally purely theological concepts represented by a distinctive hieroglyph, very similar to sigils used in modern Western ritual magic. But, as the need for a controlling religion grew, so did the spiritual need for more tangible forms on which to focus the common people's devotions.

Needless to say, the common man's mind dwelt on the concrete, not the abstract, and so the gods took on those easily recognisable animal-human shapes to satisfy a religious *'Wallace and Gromit'* style of teaching-by-pictures demands of less scholarly folk. The images recorded in tomb paintings, bas-relief and statuary were intended to represent living forms of the gods themselves, or Pharaoh as a god – and there was a simple reason behind this. Egyptian life, magic and religion were inextricably intertwined, one simply could not, and did not, exist without the other. God, or a male/female/multiple concept of that god, was manifest in Nature.

By the Middle Kingdom, the attributes of the major gods were extended to create a whole pantheon of relatives, extended families and helpers. For example, the concept of *ma'at* – that symbolic terminology for cosmic order, and earthly truth and justice, was depicted in the Pyramid Texts by an ostrich feather. This concept later metamorphosed into a beautiful woman, who sat in judgement on those in the Underworld; she was sometimes shown as the wife of Thoth, or the female embodiment of the god himself. In fact, the popular form of Egyptian religion, as most people know it today, is fundamentally a complete Greek interpretation.

An Appeal for Justice

Egyptian law was based on the concept of *ma'at* – the common-sense view of right and wrong as defined by the social norms of the day. As we have seen, during the early period of history, *ma'at* was an abstraction represented by the hieroglyph for an ostrich feather. The white ostrich feather suggesting the idea of lightness, and associated by the Egyptians with everything to do with levity and imponderability. Therefore, to them it was the only possible comparison that a pure and guiltless heart should have in facing judgement after death.

It was not until the New Kingdom that Ma'at became a goddess in human form with her own cult following. The ostrich feather was worn as a plume on her headdress, while magistrates and high priests wore the figure of the seated goddess in lapis-lazuli or gold around their necks. The British Museum exhibits a small gold Ma'at on a gold chain that could be an example of such a symbol of office. In religious or magical observance, the feather is the perfect offering since it represents the honest and personal integrity of the person performing the ritual as well as being the symbol of the goddess by which we swear. Her name is used in an oath or promise that can never be broken, especially as she is often seen as the female embodiment of

Tahuti (Thoth), the Great Scribe, who records our actions in the *Registers of Doom*.

The following is an appeal to the goddess for justice for which you will need a soft, curled feather, a small square of white paper/papyrus, four white candles, an appropriate incense and, if possible, a white linen robe. Your Circle should be free of all other adornment with the white candles marking the four quarters. On the square of paper write the cause for requesting judgement and/or the name of the offender. This is particularly appropriate if you suspect you're under psychic attack or ill-wishing, but you're not 100% sure of the sender. Cast your Circle and, sitting on your heels in the centre, hold your hands out with the paper cupped lightly in the palm of your right hand and the feather in your left. Invoke the goddess, saying:

Lady Ma'at, Goddess of Truth and Justice
Balance me in harmony that I might
Know and hear my own true self

State your case clearly and concisely. Ask that you be given a sign and if there is a case to be found against your enemy; then request that his/her malice/evildoing be returned to them in accordance with the law of balance and harmony. This method allows for retribution without any excessive use of spite on the petitioner's behalf.

I ask for justice to be done according to thy wisdom.

Open your hands and if the feather is blown from your palm it means that the message has been received loud and clear. If, on the other hand, the paper blows from your palm, it may mean that you're blaming the wrong person; that your request is unreasonable; or that you need to re-examine the case again.

Summary:

In religious iconography, the animal chosen to represent a particular deity or aspect of divinity was selected for the qualities (not necessarily beneficial) it embodies. A further idea in Egyptian magic and theology was 'fighting like with like'. Therefore an animal that embodied a particular undesirable characteristic, or whose behaviour adversely affects humans, was chosen as the image of the deity to guard against such eventualities. These sigils or hieroglyphics representing deity in whatever form, can be thought of as the forerunner of **what modern magical practitioners refer to as 'correspondences'**.

The Gods – The State Cult

The alterations in worship that were brought about when the localised cults of the *nomes* became united in the State religion (following the Unification of the Two Lands), obviously had their ongoing psychological effects. The main changes were the inevitable unreality caused by the transference of localised rites and festivals to the town-based community. [*Here we have echoes of modern paganism. MD*]. The other was the 'deadening of religious instinct' in the common people as a result of the development of an institutionalised cult in the hands of an organised priesthood. The transition from the provinces to the town mean that the calendar was still based on the assumption that everything remained the same, and where the festivals continued to be performed with the meaningless tenacity of the old rural rites.

It is obvious that such irrational clinging to old customs must have led to a sense of unreality, which only increased as time went on. And the more the rites were performed as a convention by State officials and the priesthood, the more the common people became disenfranchised. Often the meaning of the rite was altogether lost; sometimes even the character and function of the deity concerned vanishing behind a veil of confusion. Ultimately these rustic and domestic festivals could not provide adequately for the expanding urban life, and consequently there are festivals in the calendar that belong essentially to the city stage of civilisation, and which cannot have existed before the city-communities were formed. From this thumbnail sketch of the State religion of Egypt and its organisation, it will be seen that the impact of its establishment and development was to withdraw it from the religious experience of the ordinary people; and that the religion in the hands of the priesthood left the common man disenfranchised from his personal gods.

Pharaoh, by his character as the supreme protector of Egypt and the *'consequent universality of his functions, and the commanding position of the temple was the supremacy of unchallenged dignity; and his Majesty was the majesty of Egypt itself'* [*The Religion of Ancient Rome*]. And as soon as religion ceases to be purely personal and individual, it is inevitable that there must be organisation and some form of religious institution. In the days of the *nomes*, it was enough that the family should pray for the prosperity of their own household; they could join with their neighbours in a common festival, but even so it was largely their own *personal interests* that dominated the simple rites.

Magic *was* regarded as an exact science and, in its highest form, its secrets were revealed only to the highest orders of the priesthood, *'who thus had the ability to control and regulate events and actions,'* observed Rosalie David. The actual worship of the State gods was performed by this professional high priesthood with two main functions: the god's daily offering ceremony (which was a private affair), and the periodic public festivals. This daily service was performed in the inner sanctuary of the temple before the image of the god, which was concealed in a special shrine. The image was anointed and symbolically clothed while offerings of food and incense were made.

The organisation of temple ritual was designed to cement the relationship between Pharaoh and the god, and was therefore an intensely personal form of worship at the highest level.

Traditionally, Pharaoh performed this daily ritual, but for practical reasons he would not be in a position to carry out the rite in every temple in the land, and so his place would be taken by a priest-delegate, or the high priest of that particular temple. At the next level there were the lower ranks of the priesthood who performed other tasks within the temple precincts at different levels of importance: men and women of letters who maintained order within the establishment.

On a popular level, the seasonal festivals commemorated various events in which the people could participate, i.e. New Years Day, the sowing and the harvest, and the Inundation of the Nile. Ordinary people only participated in temple ritual if it linked their destiny or wellbeing with that of Pharaoh or State (which was one and the same), but no doubt they all turned out in force at the great temples when Pharaoh fulfilled his obligations on the principle feast days. Historical records show that even the poorest were given to celebration and feasting whenever the opportunity allowed, although neither the public nor the lesser priesthood were admitted within the precincts of the inner temple.

Summary:

To overcome this exclusion ordinary people set up their own sacred areas for worship, which have been found on the periphery of the temples, in their homes and tombs. These rites, whether celebrated in the outer courts of the temple, or in a private personal space, were all considered divine acts of worship in favour of their particular god. If they required a spell-casting or a magical talisman made, they went along to the appropriate temple and the priest provided whatever was necessary. **For today's seeker, the practice of having a sacred area at home is still the norm, although s/he is more likely to be able to produce a spellcasting or talisman without the aid of another.**

Emotion and Mysticism

In Roman Catholic theology, *transubstantiation* means the change during the Eucharist, of the substance of wheat bread and grape wine into the substance of the Body and Blood of Jesus, while all that is accessible to the senses remains as before. The Catholic Church holds that the same change of the substance of the bread and of the wine occurs at the consecration of the Eucharist when the words are spoken. In other words, that by speaking the 'words of power' and making the offering of food and wine, the priest is performing a magical ritual and bringing the essence of 'god' down into the human domain. The Anglican Church, on the other hand, only accepts the presence of Christ in a 'heavenly and spiritual manner' and performs the rite in token – i.e. symbolically.

These rites are reminiscent of those performed in ancient temples along the Nile Valley and, by the end of the Roman Republic, Egypt had made several religious contributions destined to have a wide ranging influence. Tradition places the introduction of the worship of Isis into Rome, first as a private and secret cult; and a long and interesting story might be told of the struggles of the Roman State against it! Finally, during the reign of Caracella, Isis was admitted among the State gods of Rome and established in a temple on the Capitol. She attained a position of supreme importance and in the in the syncretism of the neo-Platonists, became the 'one goddess of many names' displacing many of the mighty gods (male and female) of Egypt in power and stature. The holy image of Mother and Child is first seen as Isis nursing the infant Horus (the Younger) in Egyptian iconography.

According to *Egypt's Making*, the sensitivity of the Egyptians to the world around them and their capacity for *'synthesizing disparate phenomena into a single poetic image'* is nowhere better demonstrated than in their celebration for the first light of dawn. The Egyptians were, according to Rice, in a quite literal sense, enchanted by the band of light that appears at the eastern horizon heralding the appearance of the sun each day. They told themselves that the god was returning after surviving the perils of the Night, but as Rice continues: *'As they were pragmatists as well as poets it is not essential to think that the Egyptians actually believed this, or, indeed, any of their engaging myths.'*

Initiation, of course, played a prolonged part in the Egyptian Mysteries, and among the initiated there was a hierarchy with distinct grades and true religious significance. The public part of the Osirian Mysteries dramatised the well-known myth of Osiris and Isis; the hidden part taking place within the depths of the temple. All public emphasis in the Mysteries were on Osiris, i.e. his undying nature and the promise of eternal life. Yet anyone able to see behind the surface images would have perceived a far more subtle Mystery being enacted, as Billie Walker-John revealed in *The Setian*. The unique appeal to the common man, however, was that in the Osirian Mysteries there was a sense of morality with a theological and religious basis. It inspired the individual with the desire to live the good life because in doing so he was giving the right service to his god – and rewarded with eternal life.

Summary:

The Egyptian were also staunch advocates of 'dualism' – the constant linking of apparent opposites in everything – where one is never separated from the other. This remarkable preoccupation with dualism, where everything has its counterpart or opposite, is apparent throughout Egyptian belief and nowhere more so than in the identification of Pharaoh with the 'two-dwellers-in-the-palace; that is Horus and Set'. Here the ruler appears to be accepted as the personification of the two eternal opposites, the two perpetually warring ancient divinities who are only reconciled in his person. **Dualism has played an important part in the development of modern esoteria,**

including Gnosticism and Western ritual magic.

Philosophy

Being a highly practical people, philosophy (in the Greek sense) had little appeal for the Egyptians, but they nevertheless were fearful of the 'unknown' on two separate levels. The first arose from the belief in the action of the gods in the government of the world and in the affairs of men, and the risk of returning to Chaos. This was derived from the contemplation of the heavenly bodies, moving in their orbits in regular order and system, and from the more obvious terrifying phenomena of storm and tempest, lightning and thunder, earthquake and eruption.

The second was the dread of the punishment of the 'soul' after death for sins committed in the present life. We still speak of death as one of the great rites of passage, but the Egyptians occupy a unique position with regard to their approach to death and the possibility of resurrection.

> *As to the time of deeds on earth,*
> *It is the occurrence of a dream;*
> *One says: 'Welcome safe and sound'.*
> *To him who reaches the West.*

Although a great deal of Egyptian belief has survived in the form of funerary texts, little survives concerning the supreme god of the Egyptians, the Undifferentiated One, the All-Seeing One, the Being Who Loves Silent Prayer, the Bornless One. The idea of the one, all-pervading divinity, the First Cause, was however, deeply ingrained in Egypt, having its origins in times long before the XVIIIth Dynasty and Akhenaton's monotheism, and having its roots in the pre-dynastic culture.

As Wallis Budge pointed out, no attempt has been made in any texts to describe the form and likeness of the Being, who was regarded as invisible, and no artist or sculptor ever made any representation of Him. That his inscrutability, omnipresence and omniscience are assumed is demonstrated by the following extract quoted in *Osiris & the Egyptian Resurrection, Vol I* and directed to Atum-Re:

Alone, without a second.
One, the maker of all things,
the Spirit, the hidden spirit, the maker of spirits.
He existed in the beginning, when nothing else was.
What is he created after he came into being.
Father of beginnings, eternal, infinite, everlasting.
Hidden one, no man knoweth his form,
or can search out his likeness;
he is hidden to gods and men,
and is a mystery to his creatures.
No man knoweth how to know him;
his name is a mystery and is hidden.
His names are innumerable.
He is the truth, he liveth on truth, he is the king of truth.
He is life, through him man liveth; he gave life to man,
he breathed life into his nostrils.
He is the father and mother,
the father of fathers,
the mother of mothers.
He begeteth, but was not begotten;
he bringeth forth, but was not brought forth;
he begat himself and gave birth to himself.
He created, but was not created,
he made his own form and body.
He himself is existence;
he neither increaseth nor diminished.
He made the universe,
the world, what was, what is, and what shall be.
What his heart conceived came to pass forthwith;

when he speaketh what resulteth therefore endureth forever.
He is the father of the gods.
He is merciful to his worshipper,
he heareth whom calleth on him,
he rewardeth his servants,
those who acknowledge him he knoweth,
he protecteth his follower.

Summary:

As S G Brandon observed in *Man, Myth & Magic*:

*The 'dawn of conscience' has been located, with good reason, in ancient Egypt. Already in the Old Kingdom the concept of ma'at, which denoted the qualities of truth and justice, was associated with the 'Great God' as the basic principle of an ordered universe. From this period, too, emerge the beginnings of the belief so important to the evolution of ethics and morality, that the dead would be judged on their conduct in this life. This concept of judgement after death is unique in the ancient world and, by the New Kingdom, the process of the weighing of the heart against a feather was developed into **one of the most impressive scenes in the religious iconography of the ancient world.***

Syncretism and Superstition

The last phase of religion in Egypt is difficult to grasp and still harder to describe. The complexity is almost baffling, for we are confronted with the amalgamation of all the streams of thought, belief and practice that were shown in the earlier phases, and with various interpretations.

On the one hand it might be regarded as a time of religious advancement, for the various elements, religious and philosophic, were tending to unite in something like a higher monotheism, while the conception of the relation of the individual man to god was becoming more definite and more effective. On the other, it may be pictured as a period of decadence, for reason was tending to give way to emotion, debased mysticism and magic, to superstition. These elements frequently mingled together where there was no clearly marked borderline; although the old rites were still performed, most of the ritual had become mere routine.

Not far removed from magic, but later considered more respectable both in origin and in practice, was the development of astrology. Astrology was the invention of the Chaldeans of Babylon, the first astronomers of the ancient world; the astronomy of the Chaldeans *was* scientific, but its offshoot – astrology – working on a principle of inverted sympathetic magic, assumed that the movements of the known planets influenced the fate of man. And in Egypt, the stars which now ruled the destiny of man, had always been worshipped as divine...

In the Hellenistic world, astrology spread rapidly after the conquests of Alexander, and in Egypt, Alexandria became the home of astrological learning and the birthplace of many treatises on it. After the death of Cleopatra, Isis, who in a celestial capacity became 'the queen of the sky' and 'the mother of the stars', and even identified with the moon – suggests the reconciliation of her cult with that of the male syncretistic sun-god. In the *Metamorphoses*, Isis, in whom the other gods are united, becomes the 'saviour' (*sospitatrix*), sometimes of the individual in time of trouble, sometimes of the whole human race. By the end of the Roman Empire the old Roman religion counted for little and it was these oriental cults that were the focus of popular enthusiasm, with Osiris-Serapis in his dual capacity as god of the upper and lower worlds, spreading throughout the empire

Summary:

In considering the survival of magical practices in Egypt, a sharp line must be drawn between private and public rituals. In private life there can be little doubt that magical practice was in vogue right through the history of the Egyptian people: magic is the most persistent part of superstition and even in highly civilised communities it is rarely wholly eradicated. **And so the beliefs and magical knowledge of ancient Egypt passed into the modern world...**

Why Has This Fascination Endured?

For the answer we must return to Carl Jung and his collective unconscious – the repetition of identical or directly related symbols in different ages and cultures – and a truly 20th century concept. As Michael Rice observes in *Egypt's Making*, Jung seems to have understood that there was a deep and very special stratum of experience underlying the familiar stereotypes of ancient Egypt.

Jung saw the collective unconscious as constituting a common psychic substrate of a suprapersonal nature which is present in every one of us. He demonstrated that the concept of a collective unconscious casts light on many of the less rational or otherwise inexplicable apprehensions and motivations of the human psyche at its most profound level. In a pristine society such as Egypt's it should be possible to see it at work in a way quite different from the experience of later cultures. The collective unconscious is the fountain from which the archetypes flow. The collective unconscious in Egypt would, in this view, be especially powerful and as pristine a phenomenon as the society itself.

According to Rice, the creation of the Egyptian State and the extraordinary psychic forces which it released, produced a rich tapestry of archetypal images. The gods themselves being archetypal, *'both as abstractions and, in their latest form, as humans writ large'*. The Egyptians also invented the idea of the Divine King and in keeping with their obsession with dualism, the Pharaoh was linked with the Magus, the High Priest, Master of Mysteries.

The Egyptian experience of those early times is what links us to the collective experience; it is this which gives the whole its often mystical, faintly uncanny, but enduring character.

To understand this psychic heartbeat of Egypt, what we need to do is begin at today – rather like the popular BBC television genealogy programme *Who Do You Think You Are?* – and get to grips with exactly where we are placed in this esoteric scheme of things. On the surface it may appear that ancient Egypt is merely a fascinating hour's entertainment on the Discovery channel; a luxury cruise along the Nile on SS Misr; or a visiting museum exhibition, but its impact on the very culture of Europe has been immense and ongoing.

Our first point of reference is that intriguing book, *The Egyptian Revival* by James Stevens Curl, who reminds us that the Revival has had a longer life than most people suppose; that it was not a 'short-lived aberration' following the Napoleonic campaigns in Egypt, or the aftermath of the discovery of Tutankhamun's tomb in 1922. Dr Curl takes us on a journey that goes back to the 'booty' taken back to Rome by Octavian to demonstrate how successfully mighty Egypt had been subdued.

> *The worship of Isis, Serapis, and of other gods and goddesses, together with the fashion for collecting Egyptian objects d'art, ensured that not only a steady export of Egyptian antiquities to the cities of the Roman Empire, but that such antiquities would be copied by craftsmen working in Europe.*

The Egyptian style, such as obelisks, lions, sphinxes and pyramids, were incorporated into Imperial Roman architecture and decoration to such a degree that eventually the motifs ceased to be recognisable as having any Nile origins at all. Nevertheless, the real key to the remarkable earlier spread of Egyptian belief was Alexander the Great. When *he* conquered Egypt, the ancient deities gained a new and potent influence throughout the Greek world and, on his death, his successor Ptolemy, transformed Alexandria into that splendid metropolis and centre of learning. Plutarch wrote that during his visit to Alexandria in 48BC Julius Caesar 'accidentally' burned the library down when he set fire to his own ships to frustrate Achillas' attempt to blockade his fleet.

But it is not just in the spheres of romanticism and revivalism that the world reflects on the splendours of Egypt. The Revival spans a much greater length of time, and leads us from the Present age to the furthest reaches of Time ... both in the Past and in the Future ...

Part Two

The Book of Days

The crucible for the development of astronomy and mathematics, the calendar has always been a measure of how the world is understood and evaluated, and the object of fascination for the greatest scholars. It has existed as long as time itself, but the story of its reckoning is a tale of human will, vanity, experimentation and endeavour ...
[*The Calendar*, David Ewing Duncan]

All civilised societies introduced a calendar as a form of measuring time: we still celebrate Easter, Passover and Ramadan on pre-arranged dates just as our ancestors did centuries ago, and as we expect the following generations will do for centuries to come. For thousands of years the need to create a workable table of months, days and seasons, obsessed anyone who needed to count the days until the next harvest, to calculate when taxes were due, or perform an annual religious ceremony. As a result, all these calendar compilations show that the year 2000AD of the Christian calendar corresponded with the year:

 2753 according to the old Roman calendar
 2749 according to the ancient Babylonian calendar
 5760 according to the Jewish calendar
 1420 according to the Moslem calendar
 1716 according to the Coptic calendar
 2544 according to the Buddhist calendar
 and 5119 in the current Mayan great cycle

For the Egyptians, however, it corresponded to year 6236 according to the reckoning of their *first* calendar [4236BC], and revealed that the lives of the people, like those of all ancient civilisations, revolved around the cycles of the year. The predictability of the annual flooding of the Nile provided pre-dynastic farmers with a simple device – the Nilometer, which gave them the most accurate calendar in the ancient world. This crude piece of wood marking each year's water level calculated the seasons. Later, during the Pyramid Age, the rising of the 'Dog Star', Sirius, gave the priesthood a more accurate method by which to align their calendar. At the New Year, this brightest of stars appeared in the dawn sky in a direct line with the rising sun; which also happened to coincide with the annual flooding at the Summer Solstice.

The Egyptians were also among the first of the ancients to recognise that the solar year was very close to the 365 days still used today, but as David Ewing Duncan observes, how these Neolithic farmers figured out so close an approximation to the true year remains a mystery. Egyptian science was advanced very early, but they were never really renowned for their astronomy, like the Babylonians, or for a keen interest in mathematics, like the Greeks – despite the precision with which they calculated the movement of the stars (for magico-religious purposes) and the precise, geometric construction of the pyramids.

This calculation, in turn, led to the creation of a calendar with three seasons: 12 months of 30 days each and an additional five 'epagomenal days' – the birthdays of the gods Osiris, Isis, Horus, Nephthys and Set. While later astronomers did calculate the solar year to be one-fourth of a day longer than 365 days, the priesthood refused to alter the sacred calendar and, as a result, the disparity between the civil and astronomical calendars produced some strange anomalies. These differences brought about some extremes of dating since they only coincided once every 1,460 years!

An inscription from Dynasty XII records an official visit in what was (according to the civil calendar), the third month of winter. In reality the actual weather conditions were those of high summer because by then the civil and sacred reckonings were some seven months out of alignment. A papyrus from Dynasty XIX states: *'Winter is come in Summer, the months are reversed, the hours in confusion.'*

For thousands of years, the Nile flood would have reached Aswan by the last week in June (Summer Solstice) and reached its full height near Cairo by September. The floods would begin to subside about two weeks later to allow for the first crops planted in October and November to ripen in March and April when the river was at its lowest level. Another complication caused by six thousand years of precession (the gravitational pull by the sun and moon), meant that the Egyptian New Year now fell around 19th July (according to the old Julian calendar). Also, as a result of modern developments in Egypt, the annual flooding of the Nile has not happened since the completion of the Aswan High Dam in 1971.

Both the British and Cairo Museums have authentic calendars that were used by the people of the Nile Valley, which means that today, those with a committed interest in following the Egyptian religion can celebrate feast days taken from genuine texts. In the same manner, a Buddhist, Muslim, Hindu or Jew living in a foreign land still observes the religious calendar of his or her ethnic or cultural roots, which might also be at odds with the seasonal cycle of his adopted country. The Egyptian gods have their own festivals to observe that need not be aligned with any European 'wheel of the year' purely for the sake of convenience, or due to a lack of information.

This *Books of Days* has been compiled from the Greek and Demotic *Magical Papyri* lodged in the British Museum; the Bibliothéque Nationale in Paris; the Staatliche Museum in Berlin; the Rijksmuseum in Leiden; and the *Sallier Papyrus IV* (No.10184) and *The Cairo Calendar* (No.86637) currently lodged in the British and Cairo Museums. The latter, (translated into English by Abd El-Mohsen Bakir, a former Professor of Egyptian Philology at Cairo University), shows that although the document itself was made during the time of Rameses II (Dynasty XIX), it was a 'reprint' of much earlier material. Parts of all the documents are missing because the texts are riddled with *lacunae* (probably caused by white ants burrowing into the papyrus).

The papyri list the names of the gods and goddesses whose anniversaries take place on every day of the year including special spells that were devised for protection on the 'Epagomenal Days'. Every day was considered to have some magical significance, which caused it to be 'good, bad, or partly good and partly bad' and the *Book of Days* was compiled for purposes of religious observance. By consulting these lists of lucky and unlucky days, each individual could protect himself and his family against the danger of the day. The Egyptians also had a more liberal attitude to death and the Otherworld, believing that, *'To speak the name of the dead is to make them live again. It restoreth the breath of life to he who hath vanished'*, and consequently there are numerous feast days dedicated to the Ancestors.

That unknown and long-dead scribe who compiled *The Cairo Calendar* alluded to the 'mythological entries' as being *'collected by Thoth in the great house in the presence of the Lord of the Universe'*. *'They were,'* he added, *'an introduction to the manifestation feasts of every god and every goddess on their fixed days'*. Also, in strict conformity with *'what has been found in the writings of ancient times'* which, *'have been deposited in the library in the rear house of the Ennead[†],'* etc. The texts were principally based upon the beliefs of Memphis and Heliopolis – older traditions so firmly implanted in the minds of the people that they had survived the religious revolution of Dynasty XVIII.

The original calendar entries were arranged, first according to chronological sequence, and second according to the deities and divine objects or sacred place names in the text. They give us (in the

---

[†] Ennead: The grouping of nine gods – the most significant being the Great Ennead of Heliopolis referred to in this text as comprising of Atum, his children Shu and Tefnut; his grandchildren Nut and Geb and four grandchildren Osiris, Isis, Set and Nephthys.

words of that ancient scribe), an introduction to *'the beginning of infinity and the end of eternity which the gods and goddesses of the shrine and the assembly of the Ennead have made and which the Majesty of Thoth has gathered together in the great house in the presence of the Lord of the Universe. Which has been found in the library in the rear-house of the Ennead. House of Re, House of Osiris, House of Horus* [i.e. temples or shrines of the gods].' Professor Bakir adds this footnote to his translation:

> At first sight it seems surprising, in view of the fact that this is originally a Memphite composition, that Ptah does not figure in this basic introductory formula. One is tempted to interpret the roles of Re, Osiris and Horus in the light of the well-known statement where **Re is equated with tomorrow**, Osiris with yesterday, and where Horus is the successor of Osiris and is so equated virtually with today. **The relevance of the triadic concept to the calendar lies in the fact that the fate of people in the present and in the future is related to the experiences of the gods in the past, and the suggestion is that the calendar is applicable to all future ages.'** [Author's emphasis in bold. MD]

Nevertheless, *The Book of Days* provides an insight into both the religious and everyday aspects of ancient Egyptian life. It also introduces the seeker to genuine religious texts (in the form of prayers or invocations), and offers a general overview of Egyptian belief that makes it possible to see a living, breathing people – not just exhibits in a museum

Lucky and unlucky days:
The calendars generally appear to be in agreement over which days are auspicious and which are inauspicious. In some instances a 'lucky day' may not be considered suitable for prayer or divination. Translations from the original text and god-names are given in italics.

Aket-Season (Inundation)
First Month: Dhwty

Day 1 – 19th July: *The Opening of the Year and the Feast of every god. The birth and feast of Re-Harakhte; ablution* [purification] *throughout the entire land in the water of the beginning of the High Nile* [Inundation] *which comes forth as fresh as Nun* [the Chaos of Creation, or beginning]. *And so, all gods and goddesses are in great festivity on this day and everybody likewise. Do not navigate ships or anything that goes on the water on this day.*

This was the national New Year celebration which coincided with the annual inundation of the Nile and, as the land either side of the river would eventually be flooded to a depth of several feet with black, muddy water, there was little else to do but party. The floodwaters brought about the purification of the land prior to it emerging anew [fertile] as it did from the primordial waters of Nun on the Day of Creation. From the lowliest peasant to the mightiest of gods, everyone played a part in this important festival of celebration and feasting. The warning not to venture out onto the river was pure common sense, since the turbulent waters would be extremely hazardous for shipping. Prayer or divinatory time: dawn.

Re-Harakhte: R'-Hr-3hty

Horus (the Elder) was the sky-god whose eyes symbolised the sun and the moon. Old Kingdom texts frequently describe him as 'God of the East' and the sunrise. Harakhte means 'Horus of the Horizon' and merged with Re, he became Re-Harakhte – a name linked with Pharaoh in the Pyramid Texts since he was the great solar god of Heliopolis, sovereign Lord of Egypt and Lord of the Universe. He is usually depicted in human form with a falcon's head, crowned with the solar disc, encircled by the

---

cobra *uraeus*. He would be petitioned for success in new undertakings or for protection.

Prayer or Invocation:
The gods who are in the sky are brought to you,
The gods who are on earth assemble for you,
They place their hands under you,
They make a ladder for you that you may ascend on it into
*   the sky,*
The doors of the sky are thrown open to you,
The doors of the starry firmament are thrown open for you.
[Pyramid Text PR 572]

Day 2 – 20th July: The feast of Shu, son of Re. *It is the feast which Re made for Shu when he seized for him the Eye of Horus. If you see anything it will be good on this day.* Prayer or divinatory time: noon.

Day 3 – 21st July: *The feast of Sekhmet which Re made for her when he pacified her. Do not do anything on this day; do not go out on any journey on this day.* Prayer or divinatory time: do not observe – not a suitable day.

Day 4 – 22nd July: The feast of Hathor, mistress of Byblos. *Do not do anything on this day.* Prayer or divinatory time: dawn.

Day 5 – 23rd July: Feasts of Horus the Elder and Hathor. *Do not do any work on the land on this day. If you see anything, it will be good on this day.* Prayer or divinatory time: dawn.

Day 6 – 24th July: The Feast of Mnevis, the sacred bull of Heliopolis. Sun rises in Leo. Prayer or divinatory time: do not observe – not a suitable day.

Mnevis: Mwr

The sacred bull regarded as the physical manifestation of Atum-Re, the sun god. Each bull was totally black and depicted with the solar disk between its horns. When the animal died it was buried with great ceremony and the priesthood sought a new bull, with similar markings. Because of the creature's association with the sun-god, Mnevis was one of the few traditional deities acknowledged by Akhenaten's solar cult during the New Kingdom. His energies should be drawn upon when sheer physical strength is needed. [Mnevis should not be confused with the Apis bull, which was the living manifestation of Ptah at Memphis.]

Prayer and Invocation:
Homage to thee O Bull of Re with the four horns.
Thy horn is in the West, thy horn is in the East,
thy horn is in the South, thy horn is in the North.
The meadow of thy horn is the Amenti of the deceased,
set thou him on his way
[Unas funerary temple inscription invoking the gods of the four cardinal points]

Day 7 – 25th July: The Feast of Sobek, the crocodile god. The Feast of Anubis. *It is a day of welcoming the river* (i.e. in its state of inundation) *and offering to the gods. If you see anything it will be good on this day.* Prayer or divinatory time: noon.

Day 8 – 26th July: Feast of every god and goddess. *Do not do any work in the entire land.* A public holiday. Prayer or divinatory time: throughout the day.

Day 9 – 27th July: The Feast of Khumn, the ram-headed god of creation, Re and Sobek. *If you see anything it will be good on this day.*

Do not do anything on this day. Do not walk by darkness. Prayer or divinatory time: do not observe – not a suitable day.

Day 10 – 28th July: The Feast of Tefnut. *Do not eat honey or sugar cane on this day. As to anyone born on this day they will die as an honoured one in old age. Do not do anything on this day.* Prayer or divinatory time: throughout the day.

Day 11 – 29th July: Feast of Re and Sobek. *It is the day of the going forth of the great flame.* [Wedjet of Buto, the fire-spitting cobra goddess whose image was incorporated in the royal crown.] Prayer or divinatory time: in the afternoon.

Day 12 – 30th July: Feast of Kenty-khtay [Horus of Athribis]. Feast of Satet in Elephantine. *Do not eat any meat. Do not do anything on this day. Spend the day until Re sets in his horizon in meditation.* Prayer or divinatory time: throughout the day.

Day 13 – 31st July: Feast of Nut. *Do not do anything on this day.* Prayer or divinatory time: throughout the day.

Day 14 – 1st August: Feast of Khonsu-Osiris. Feast of Meskhetyu [name of the constellation of Ursa Major]. Feast of Ptah. *If you undertake any errand, it will be accomplished immediately.* Prayer or divinatory time: dawn. Khonsu-Osiris is Osiris identified with the moon so pay special attention to the lunar aspects tonight.

Day 15 – 2nd August: Feast of Sepa-Osiris who rules in Heliopolis. [Sepa was originally a centipede deity who prevented snakebite.] *Do not eat fish. Do not start anything (new).* Prayer or divinatory time: throughout the day.

Day 16 – 3rd August: The Coming Forth of Neith. *It is favourable to do anything on this day.* Prayer or divinatory time: do not observe – not a suitable day.

Day 17 – 4th August: Feast of Sobek-Re. *Do not eat fish on this day. Do not do anything on this day.* Prayer or divinatory time: do not observe – not a suitable day.

Day 18 – 5th August: Feast of Osiris. *If you see anything it will be good on this day. It is the day of magnifying the Majesty of Horus more* *than his brother.* Prayer or divinatory time: dawn and in the afternoon.

Osiris: Wsir

Originally a fertility god, Osiris is always shown with the green skin that he inherited from his father Geb. It would appear, however, as early as *The Pyramid Texts*, that he was considered primarily a god of the dead. It was not until much later (when the priesthood had re-attributed some of Re's functions) that he, Isis and Horus (the Younger) became the chief deities with which the later Pharaohs identified themselves. From a very different viewpoint, Osiris's early fertility associations acquired an even greater importance – re-birth. He is best petitioned in his guise as an Otherworld deity.

Prayer or Invocation:
Praise be to Osiris!
Adorations be given unto him!
Smelling of the earth to Un-Nefer!
Prostrations to the ground to the
Everlasting Self-Created Sun-God!
[Book of the Dead]

Day 19 – 6th August: Feast of Thoth. *A happy day in heaven in front of Re, the Great Ennead is in great festivity. Burn incense on the fire. It is the day of receiving. It is the day of going forth of Thoth.* Prayer or divinatory time: dawn.

Day 20 – 7th August: Feast of Hathor. *Do not do any work. It is the day when the great ones are well disposed.* Prayer or divinatory time: dawn.

Day 21 – 8th August: Feast of Osiris. *Take a holiday on this day; offer* *to the followers of Re on this day. It is a day to be cautious.* Prayer or divinatory time: in the afternoon.

Day 22 – 9th August: Creation of the world. *Re calls every god and goddess, and they await his arrival.* Feast of Wp-wat. Prayer or divinatory time: in the afternoon.

Day 23 – 10th August: Feast of Anubis. *Do not burn any incense on the fire for the god on this day. Do not listen to singing or dancing on this day.* Prayer or divinatory time: dawn.

Day 24 – 11th August: Feast of Osiris. The Sun's journey in the Otherworld. *The Majesty of this god sails with a favourable wind peacefully. Behold, he settles down, his heart especially. As for anyone born on this day they will die as an honoured one in old age.* Prayer or divinatory time: dawn.

Day 25 – 12th August: The Going Forth of Sekhmet. *Do not go out of your house on any road at the time of night.* Prayer or divinatory time: do not observe – not a suitable day.

Sekhmet: *Shmt*

The most difficult and unpredictable deity in the whole Egyptian pantheon, whose name means 'powerful'. When mankind rebelled against Re, the gods called down retribution in the form of the mighty lioness-goddess who began to systematically massacre the human race. At the sight of so much spilled blood, Re relented, but could only stop her by causing the land to be covered with beer, stained with pomegranate juice. Thinking it was blood, the angry Sekhmet stopped to drink and became so intoxicated that she could not continue the slaughter. By contrast, she is also the patron of doctors and healers, and although plagues were believed to have been brought by the 'messengers of Sekhmet', she was also hailed as the 'lady of life'. She is usually depicted as a lioness-headed woman; her emblem is

---

the rosette of shoulder-knot hairs on lions. She can be petitioned in cases of serious illness, particularly those involving surgery. The image of a lion is a common theme in early Egyptian symbolism; lions being considered to be the guardians of the eastern and western horizons, the places of sunrise and sunset. The dual lion-god Aker guarded the gateways to the underworld, while goddesses Tefnut and Sekhmet were depicted as lion-headed women.

Prayer or Invocation:
We shall keep [Name] safe from Sekhmet and her son,
We shall keep [Name] safe from the collapse of a wall
And from the fall of a thunderbolt.
We shall keep [Name] safe from leprosy, from blindness ...
Through the whole of [his/her] lifetime.
[BM Papyrus No. 10083]

Day 26 – 13th August: Feast of Heka, god of magic. *Do not do anything on this day. It is the day of Horus fighting with Set.* Prayer or divinatory time: in the afternoon.

Day 27 – 14th August: Feast of Nekhbet, the vulture goddess. *Peace on the part of Horus and Set. Do not kill any* **nhy**-*reptile on this day* [the serpent was sacred to Set]; *make a holiday.* Prayer or divinatory time: throughout the day.

Day 28 – 15th August: *The gods are happy on this day when they see the children of Nut peaceful* [Horus and Set]. *If you see anything, it will be good on this day.* Prayer or divinatory time: throughout the day.

Day 29 – 16th August: Feast of Khumn. *Do not kindle fire in the house on this day. Do not burn incense; do not go out by night on this day.* Prayer or divinatory time: throughout the day.

Day 30 – 17th August: Feast of Osiris. *If you see anything it will be*

good on this day. **House of Re, House of Horus, House of Osiris.**
Prayer and divinatory time: in the afternoon.

Second Month: Phaophi

Day 1 -18th August: The Opet Festival dedicated to Amun, Mut
and Khonsu at Karnak. The Marriage of Isis and Osiris. The birth
and feast of Re-Harakthte. The Feast of Wedjet. *Jubilation. The
Great Ennead is in festivity on this day. Do not do anything on this
day.* A public holiday or celebration. Wedjet, the cobra goddess of
Lower Egypt was bound up with the regenerative forces.
Traditionally, Pharaoh, or his high priest, would undergo
extensive purification rituals during the two to four-week
festival. Prayer or divinatory time: dawn.

On the eastern bank of the Nile at modern Luxor, is a vast
enclosure containing the Great Temple of Amun; the Great
Hypostyle Hall is 6,000 square metres with 134 columns built by
Seti I and Ramesses II in Dynasty XIX. Religious processions in
honour of Amun, carried in state in a shrine, aboard his sacred
boat, or personal confrontations between the Pharaoh and his
god cover every column and every inch of wall space as a
testament to the piety of the royal family. The Opet Festival is
one of the best-known religious festivals that took place at
Thebes from the early Dynasty XVIII onwards. Occurring
annually in the second month of the season of *Akhet*, and lasting
for a period that varied from two to four weeks, the main event
was the ritual procession of the divine images of Amun, Mut and
Khonsu from Karnak to Luxor. The Temple of Luxor was largely
constructed as a suitable architectural setting for the Festival of
Opet.

Amun: 'Imn

Almost unknown outside the Theban area at the time of the Old Kingdom, Amun's cult grew during Dynasty XII and rose to even greater prominence under the great Pharaohs of Dynasty XVIII. With Thebes now the capital of Egypt, Amun with his consort Mut became the great divinity of the entire country. He is usually depicted in human form with a crown supporting two straight, tall parallel plumes. He was also represented with the head of a ram with curled horns and styled Amun-Re as the great sun-god. He can be petitioned for the invigorating energy brought by the sun.

Prayer or Invocation:

This holy god, the lord of all the gods, Amun-Re,
The lord of the throne of the two lands.
The governor of Apt;
The holy soul who came into being in the beginning;
The great god who liveth by Ma'at;
The first divine matter which gave birth unto subsequent
*   divine matter!*
The being through whom every other god has existence;
The One who hath made everything which hath come into
existence since primeval times when the world was created.
[Book of the Dead of Nesi-Khonsu, priestess of Amun]

Day 2 – 19th August: Feast of Thoth. *The proceeding of the Majesty of Sais* – Neith. *Offer to all the gods. It is important to hear what I say to you.* Prayer or divinatory time: noon.

Day 3 – 20th August: *Thoth is in the presence of Re in the inaccessible shrine. If you see anything, it will be good on this day.* Prayer or divinatory time: do not observe – not a suitable day.

Day 4 – 21st August: *It is the day of the Going Forth of Anubis for the inspection of the amulet for the protection of the body of the god.* Prayer or divinatory time: dawn.

Day 5 – 22nd August: Feast of Osiris. *Do not go out of your house on this day. Do not copulate with a woman. It is the day of offering in the presences of Montu* [the falcon-headed war god] *on this day.* Prayer or divinatory time: dawn.

Day 6 – 23rd August: Feast of Nekhbet. *A happy day for Re in heaven, and the gods are pacified in his presence. The Ennead is making glorification in front of the Lord of the Universe.* Prayer or divinatory time: do not observe – not a suitable day.

Day 7 – 24th August: Feast of Horus. *Do not do anything on this day.* Sun rises in Virgo. Prayer or divinatory time: noon.

Day 8 – 25th August: *If you see anything on this day, it will be good. Favourable is to do everything on this day.* Prayer or divinatory time: throughout the day.

Day 9 – 26th August: Feast of Khnum. *Jubilation in the heart of Re. His Ennead is in festivity, all enemies are overthrown on this day. Anyone born on this day will die at a good age. Favourable is to do everything.* Prayer or divinatory time: do not observe – not a suitable day.

Khnum: *Hmnnw*

Ancient statues of this ram-headed god, who created the human race from clay fashioned on a potter's wheel, can be seen from his image as a flat-horned ram, which became extinct around 2000BC. His worship can be traced back to the early dynastic periods when he had three consorts: Heqet (represented as a frog), Anukis (a parrot) and Saris (a gazelle). Heqet later became identified as a goddess of childbirth while Anukis and Satis remained with Khnum and presided over the sacred pool on Elephantine island from which the annual inundation was believed to flow. He should be petitioned for creative energy.

Prayer or Invocation

May nought stand up to oppose me at my judgement;
May there be no opposition to me in the presence of the
  sovereign princes;
May there be no parting of thee from me in the presence of
  him
that keepeth the Balance.
Thou art my ka, the dweller in my body;
The god Khnum who knitted and strengthened my limbs.
May thou come forth into the place of happiness whither we
  go.
[Book of the Dead – Papyrus of Ani. BM]

Day 10 – 27th August: Feast of Atum. *Proceeding the Majesty of Bastet ... the Majesty of Re... to pay tribute to the August tree* [The holy tree in Heliopolis on the leaves of which the gods' names were inscribed – symbolically the sycamore]. *Favourable is to do everything.* Prayer or divinatory time: throughout the day.

Day 11 – 28th August: Feast of Dwmutef [one of the four sons of Horus responsible for the protection of the stomach after embalming. Shown in the form of a jackal]. *Everything is good on this day.* Prayer or divinatory time: in the afternoon.

Day 12 – 29th August: Feast of Kebeh [daughter of Anubis]. Prayer or divinatory time: throughout the day.

Day 13 – 30th August: Feast of Imstey [one of the four sons of Horus responsible for the protection of the liver after embalming. Shown in human form]. *Favourable to everything on this day.* Prayer or divinatory time: throughout the day.

Day 14 – 31st August: Feast of Hapy [one of the four sons of

Horus responsible for the protection of the lungs after embalming. Shown in the form of a baboon; also the name of the god of the Inundation. Note that the fourth son of Horus, the hawk-headed Qebehsenuef, responsible for the intestines after embalming, is not allocated a feast day]. *Offer to your local gods, and pacify the spirits.* Prayer or divination time: dawn.

Day 15 – 1st September: Feast of Isis. *Do not go out of your house at eventide. The Going Forth of the Majesty of Re at nightfall with his followers.* Prayer or divinatory time: throughout the day.

Isis: 3st

Originally a modest deity associated with the Delta and protective goddess of Perehbet (north of Busiris) where she always retained a special temple. Very early in Egyptian history she was identified with Osiris (the god of a neighbouring city), and Horus to form the Osirian Triad – but in later days she became so popular that she finally absorbed the qualities of all the other goddesses. She plays a prominent part in the mythical struggle between Osiris, Horus and Set, but according to one source, meddled so much in their affairs that Horus cut off her head in a fit of exasperation.

The cult of Isis spread into Greek and Roman society throughout the Mediterranean and into Northern Europe. Although her rites were often the subject of mockery, the popularity of the imported Isian mystery cult was so strong that she surpassed Osiris in terms of importance. In the ancient world her sanctuaries could be found on the Acropolis at Athens and at Pompeii. Early Christianity found it easier to incorporate the mother and child image into its own canon rather than attempt to suppress it. She is patron of women and marriage.

> **Prayer or Invocation:**
> *The goddess Isis is with thee and she never leaveth thee;*
> *May the blood of Isis, and the powers of Isis,*
> *and the enchantments of Isis be powers to protect thee.*
> [Book of the Dead]

Day 16 – 2nd September: Feast of Osiris-Onnophris. Feast of the Eye of Horus. *The gods who are in his retinue are in great festivity. If you see anything on this day, it will be good.* Prayer or divinatory time: do not observe – not a suitable day.

Day 17 – 3rd September: *Give up beer and bread* [i.e. fast]. *Burn incense to Re and the invocation-offering to the spirits. It is important so that your words may be listened to by your local gods. On this good day ... favourable in everything.* Prayer or divinatory time: do not observe – not a suitable day.

Day 18 – 4th September: *Do not do anything on this day.* Prayer or divinatory time: at dawn and in the afternoon.

Day 19 – 5th September: Feast of Ptah, lord of the workshop. *Do everything on this day.* Prayer or divinatory time: dawn.

Day 20 – 6th September: Feast of Horus and Set. *Do everything on this day.* Prayer or divinatory time: dawn.

Day 21 – 7th September: *It is the day of the Going Forth of Neith in the presence of the Majesty of Atum Re-Harakhti – may he live and be prosperous.* Prayer or divinatory time: in the afternoon.

Day 22 – 8th September: *Do not bathe on this day.* Prayer or divinatory time: in the afternoon.

Day 23 – 9th September: [Damaged] Prayer or divinatory time: dawn

Day 24 – 10th September: *Do not go out of your house, or in any wind until Re sets.* Prayer or divinatory time: dawn.

Day 25 – 11th September: *Do not go out on this day on any road.* Prayer or divinatory time: do not observe – not a suitable day.

Day 26 – 12th September: *Do not order any work. Do not do any work on this day. It is the day of opening and sealing the windows of the place of Busiris* [Old Kingdom temple complex at Abusir]. Prayer or divinatory time: in the afternoon.

Day 27 – 13th September: *Do not go out. Do not give your back to any work until the sun sets.* Prayer or divinatory time: throughout the day.

Day 28 – 14th September: *If you see anything, it will be good on this day.* Prayer or divinatory time: throughout the day.

Day 29 – 15th September: *Anyone born on this day will die as an honourable man among his people.* Prayer or divinatory time: throughout the day.

Day 30 – 16th September: *The land is in festivity on this day.* **House of Re, House of Osiris, House of Horus.** Prayer or divinatory time: in the afternoon.

Third month: Athyr

Day 1—17th September: *Feast of Hathor, the Mistress of Heaven.* Prayer or divinatory time: dawn.

Hathor: *Hwt-hr*

One of the most popular and fun-loving of all the deities. The goddess of women and the family, she loves music and dancing. She is shown as either a cow-headed woman, or a woman wearing cow's horns with the solar disc between; her emblem is the sistrum – a musical instrument similar to a rattle with tiny cymbals. Hathor is one of the oldest and most complex of deities, although in later times many of her attributes were conferred upon Isis. She should be petitioned for any women's matters.

> **Prayer or Invocation:**
> *Hathor, Lady of the West, She of the West;*
> *Lady of the Sacred Land.*
> *Eye of Re which is on his forehead.*
> *Kindly of countenance in the Barque of a Million Years;*
> *A resting place for him who has done right*
> *Within the boat of the blessed;*
> *Who built the Great Barque of Osiris*
> *In order to cross the water of truth.*
> [Book of the Dead – Spell 186]

Day 2 – 18th September: *Return of Wedjet from Dep.* [Dep is the pre-Dynastic name for Buto, of which Wedjet was the patron goddess.] Prayer or divinatory time: noon.

Day 3 – 19th September: *If you see anything it will be good on this day.* Prayer or divinatory time: do not observe – not a suitable day.

Day 4 – 20th September: *The trembling of the earth under Nun* [the god who personified the original formless ocean of Chaos]. Prayer or divinatory time: dawn.

Day 5 – 21st September: *Do not keep fire burning in the house on this day.* The turning of the year with the Autumn (Spring in Egypt) Equinox. In Egypt traditionally the time for planting – in the Northern hemisphere, harvest and the end of summer. Prayer or divinatory time: dawn.

Day 6 – 22nd September: *The encouragement of the gods of the Two Lands* [Set and Horus]. Prayer or divinatory time: do not observe – not a suitable day.

Day 7 – 23rd September: *If you see anything it will be good on this day.* Prayer or divinatory time: noon.

Day 8 – 24th September: *Isis goes forth unto her son, Horus.* Sun rises in Libra. Prayer or divinatory time: throughout the day.

Day 9 – 25th September: *Do not go outside on any road from your house* *on this day. Do not let light fall on your face until Re is set in his horizon. It is the day of blaming the great ones ... who were in his presence.* Prayer or divinatory time: do not observe – not a suitable day.

Day 10 – 26th September: *Great rejoicing in heaven; the crew of Re are in peace, his Ennead is cheerful* [lit. 'shout loudly']. *Those in the fields are working. It is the day of judgement between Horus and Set.* Prayer or divinatory time: throughout the day.

Day 11 – 27th September: *If you see anything it will be good on this day.* Prayer or divinatory time: in the afternoon.

Day 12 – 28th September: *Do not go to your antagonist but go to answer the neighbours* [Obviously a time of strife in ancient Egypt]. Prayer or divinatory time: throughout the day.

Day 13 – 29th September: *This is the day of cutting into pieces ...This **neshmet**-boat of Osiris is sailing up-stream to Abydos to the great town of Onnophris. Set entered the embalming booth ... to announce the god's limbs. Then they became fresh* [Opening of the Mouth Ceremony]. Prayer or divinatory time: throughout the day.

Day 14 – 30th September: *Do not do anything on this day.* Prayer or divinatory time: dawn.

Day 15 – 1st October: *Let a man sleep with his wife on this day.* Prayer or divinatory time: throughout the day.

Day 16 – 2nd October: *The appearance of the Great Ones of the Ogduad* [The Hermopolitan group of eight deities connected to the Creation myth]. *A happy day of infinity and eternity. Do not go out of your house on this day. Let not a man sleep with his wife.* Prayer or divinatory time: do not observe – not a suitable day.

Day 17 – 3rd October: *Landing of the Great Ones, the Upper and Lower Ones at Abydos; loud weeping and wailing by Isis and Nephthys, her sister, over Onnophris* [Osiris] *in Sais. The weeping and crying is heard in Abydos.* Prayer or divinatory time: do not observe – not a suitable day.

Day 18 – 4th October: *It is the day of strife by the children of Geb ... do not approach any road for making a journey on it.* Prayer or

49

divinatory time: at dawn and in the afternoon.

Geb: *Gb*

The earth god and brother-consort of the sky-goddess Nut, on whom he fathered the deities of the Osirian myth. Geb features widely in the Pyramid era where he is referred to as the 'eldest of Shu' and depicted with a green skin (which he shares with his son, Osiris). He is usually represented lying on the earth. Raised on one elbow, with one knee bent, he symbolises the undulations of the earth's surface. He was the third divine Pharaoh and all subsequent human Pharaohs claimed to be descended from him – the royal throne was referred to in the Pyramid Texts as 'the throne of Geb'. As a chthonic deity, he also has a 'dark' side and was believed to imprison the dead within the earth, preventing them free access to the Otherworld. He was called upon in spells to treat scorpion stings and snake bites.

Prayer or Invocation:
Re openeth for thee the doors of heaven,
And Geb unbolteth for thee the earth.
The god Geb hath opened for thee thy two eyes which were
blind,
And hath given thee the power to stretch out thy legs in
walking.
[Book of the Dead]

Day 19 – 5th October: *Beware the children of the storm … Let a man eat bread in his house. Do not go outside on the road on this day.* Prayer or divinatory time: dawn.

Day 20 – 6th October: *The Going Forth of Bastet. Offer to the gods on this day.* Prayer or divinatory time: dawn.

Day 21 – 7th October: *The Feast of Shu, son of Re.* Prayer or divinatory time: in the afternoon.

Shu: *Sw*

The god of air and sunlight whose name has been translated as 'he who rises up'. With his sister-wife, Tefnut, goddess of moisture, they were the first two gods created by Atum according to the Creation myth of Heliopolis. Although one of the oldest gods, his cult did not come into prominence until the New Kingdom when the 'force of life' became an important element in the religion. He was usually depicted in human form wearing a plumed headdress – the hieroglyph for his name. In *The Cairo Calendar*, Shu is hailed as the champion of Re having seized back the Eye of Horus during a power struggle, and for sedating Apophis, the snake-god of the Underworld. Repelling Apophis from the barque of Re is a theme dealt with in the funerary texts and traditionally the role of Set is the slayer of Apophis and protector of Re – Apophis is the original creature of Chaos, not Set. An invocation to Shu would probably involve a request for protection or for the bringing together of those who have been separated for legitimate or unavoidable reasons.

Prayer or Invocation:

I will fulfil at every season of the heavens when Shu cometh forth,

In such a wise that none of the evil things which can reach a person

Who is in the condition, in which [Name] is,

Shall reach [him/her] at any season of the heavens when Shu cometh forth

---

> *From the waters with his weapons and when day beginneth in the sky.*
> [Book of the Dead]

Day 22 – 8th October: *The raising of Ma'at in order to see Re, when she is summoned by the gods in the presence of Re.* Prayer or divinatory time: in the afternoon.

Day 23 – 9th October: [Damaged] Prayer or divinatory time: dawn.

Day 24 – 10th October: *Isis goes forth, her heart being happy and Nephthys being also in jubilation when they see Onnophris [Osiris]. He had given his throne to his son, Horus, in front of Re.* Prayer or divinatory time: dawn.

Day 25 – 11th October: *If you see anything, it will be good on this day. Do not offer to the gods on this day.* Prayer or divinatory time: do not observe – not a suitable day.

Day 26 – 12th October: *Establishing the Djed ... of Atum in the heaven and land of Heliopolis reconciliation of the Two Lords and causing the land to be in peace. The whole of Egypt is given to Horus, and all the desert land to Set. Going forth of Thoth in order to judge in the presence of Re. Do not offer to the gods.* Prayer or divinatory time: in the afternoon.

Day 27 – 13th October: *Judging of Horus and Set; stopping the fighting.* Prayer or divinatory time: throughout the day.

Day 28 – 14th October: *The gods are in jubilation and in joy ... The land is in festivity and the gods are pleased. If you see anything, it will be good.* Prayer or divinatory time: throughout the day.

Day 29 – 15th October: *The going forth of the three noble ladies in the presence of Ptah, beautiful of face, while giving praise to Re, him who belongs to the throne of truth of the temples of the goddesses. Giving the White Crown to Horus, and the Red Crown to Set.* [Usually Horus represents Lower Egypt and Set Upper Egypt, so the ascription of the Crowns may seem puzzling. But as 'all the desert land' is assigned to Set, perhaps the association of the same word, now applies to the Red Crown, and explains the previous statement.] *Do not dispute with your antagonist on this day.* Prayer or divinatory time: throughout the day.

Day 30 – 16th October: *If you see anything, it will be good on this day. Do not offer to the male gods. Do not offer to the goddesses on this day.* **House of Re, House of Osiris, House of Horus.** Prayer or divinatory time: in the afternoon.

Fourth Month: Khoiak

Day 1 – 17th October: *The Great and the Small Ennead is in festivity and all those who came into being in the primordial age, their form is in every body of thine* [Re]. Prayer or divinatory time: dawn.

Day 2 – 18th October: *Gods and goddesses are in festivity; the heaven and the land are in joy. If you see anything, it will be good on this day.* Prayer or divinatory time: at noon.

Day 3 – 19th October: *Do not do anything on this day.* Prayer or divinatory time: do not observe – not a suitable day.

Day 4 – 20th October: *One should perform the rituals in the Temple of Sokar and in thy house on this day, with all provisions in the necropolis.* [Sokar was primarily a funerary god who was later associated with both Osiris and Ptah – perhaps a day for remembering the Ancestors.] Prayer or divinatory time: dawn.

Sokar: Zkr

Originally the hawk-god of the Memphite necropolis, by the Old Kingdom he was amalgamated with Ptah as Ptah-Sokar; by the Middle Kingdom prayers were being address to Ptah-Sokar-Osiris. In the Pyramid Age, Sokar was referred to as the manufacturer of royal bones and in the *Book of the Dead*, he fashions grave goods. The festival of

---

Sokar was celebrated on a grand scale in Western Thebes where there is evidence that it almost rivalled the annual festival of Opet. At Karnak is the Festival Temple of Tuthmosis III which contains a 'chamber of the ancestors' and suites of rooms dedicated to Sokar. He should be called upon as a Guardian of the Ancestors.

Prayer or Invocation
Homage to thee, O happy one
Divine lord who art endowed with
the sight of the Utchat. [Wedjet Eye]
Ptah-Sokar hath bound thee up.
...The god Ptah-Sokar hath given unto thee
The ornaments of the divine house.
[Papyrus of Nefer-uben]

Day 5 – 21st October: *The Going Forth of Khentet-'abet* [a goddess whose horns are prominent, i.e. Hathor, probably as the mother of Horus the Elder] *in the presence of the Great Ones.* Prayer or divinatory time: dawn.

Day 6 – 22nd October: *Do not go out on this day.* Prayer or divinatory time: do not observe – not a suitable day.

Day 7 – 23rd October: *Do not eat or taste fish on this day.* Prayer or divinatory time: at noon.

Day 8 – 24th October: *If you see anything it will be good on this day.* Sun rises in Scorpio. Prayer or divinatory time: throughout the day.

Day 9 – 25th October: *It is the day of the action performed by Thoth. Thereupon the gods, together with Thoth caused the enemy of Set to kill himself* [Apophis]. Prayer or divinatory time: do not observe – not a suitable day.

Day 10 – 26th October: *As to anyone born on this day, he will die of* *old age.* Prayer or divinatory time: throughout the day.

Day 11 – 27th October: *Feast of Osiris in Abydos. The dead are in jubilation.* Prayer or divinatory time: in the afternoon.

Day 12 – 28th October: *Do not go out on this day on any road in the wind. It is the day of the Transformation of the Benu. Offer to the Benu in your house on this day.* Prayer or divinatory time: throughout the day.

The Transformation of the Benu refers to the phoenix, which personifies the everlasting sun god. The benu bird is thought to be the phoenix – the heron. Two days later the '*Hedj-hotpe and the Tayet* [both goddesses of weaving] *come forth from the Temple of Benben on this day. They handed things* [gifts] *to Neith on this day.*' It is possible that this second festival coincides with the receding of the flood waters that symbolise the re-emergence of the land with its newly enriched soil. The goddesses of weaving also suggest that the second date is a women's festival attached to the Temple of Benben – the holy stone that symbolised the primeval Mound and closely associated with the benu-bird.

Day 13 – 29th October: *The Going Forth of the White One* (or 'the Majesty of Heaven'- an attribute of Hathor]. *The Great Ennead is in festivity. Make a holiday in your house on this day.* Prayer or divinatory time: throughout the day.

Day 14 – 30th October: [The goddesses of weaving] *come forth from the Temple of Benben on this day. They hand things to Neith on this day. Their hearts are happy.* [Obviously an ancient festival and one dedicated to domestic affairs rather than commerce or business. Weaving goddesses are also associated with fate and destiny, and the intertwining of lives. Explore the strands of this special weaving, especially at a time when the festival coincides with the end of the old year in the Northern hemisphere.] Prayer or divinatory time: dawn.

Neith: *Nt*

A hunter goddess of great antiquity whose cult centre was at Sais in the Delta. She is usually depicted wearing the distinctive red crown of Lower Egypt or bearing her most ancient emblem – a shield and crossed arrows. Her name appears as early as Dynasty I and two of the most important royal women of that time had names incorporating her name in their own – Her-neith and Neithhotep. Later her attribute became a weaver's shuttle, the hieroglyph of her name, which she sometimes wears on her head as a distinguishing emblem; she was the great weaver who wove the world with her shuttle. Neith has a double role in Egyptian religion: as a warrior-hunter goddess and as a woman skilled in the domestic arts. This is why she was identified with the Greek Athene. By the Pyramid Age she was assigned as the consort of Set and the mother of Sobek, the crocodile god.

Prayer or Invocation

I am all that has been, that is, and that will be.
No mortal has yet been able to lift the veil which covers me.
[Temple inscription to Neith at Sais. Plutarch]

Day 15 – 31st October: *Do nothing on this day.* Prayer or divinatory time: throughout the day.

Day 16 – 1st November: Feast of Sekhmet and Bast. Prayer or divinatory time: do not observe – not a suitable day.

Day 17 – 2nd November: Feast of Horus the Elder. *Do not go out at midday on this day.* Prayer or divinatory time: do not observe – not a suitable day.

Day 18 – 3rd November: [Damaged entry] Prayer or divinatory time: at dawn and in the afternoon.

Day 19 – 4th November: *Do not taste beer and bread on this day. Drink water (i.e. juice) of the grapes until Re sets.* A day of fasting. Prayer or divinatory time: dawn.

Day 20 – 5th November: *Do not go out on any road on this day. Do not anoint thyself with ointment on this day. Do not go out of your house at midday.* Prayer or divinatory time: dawn.

Day 21 – 6th November: *It is the day of the going forth of the mysterious Great Ones to look for the Akhet-eye. Do not go out of your house in the day time.* Prayer or divinatory time: in the afternoon.

Day 22 – 7th November: *If you see anything, it will be good on this day.* A time for beginning the formula for the making of the spirit of Osiris (i.e. resurrection). To be repeated for the next four days. Prayer or divinatory time: in the afternoon.

Day 23 – 8th November: *Do not go out during night-time.* Prayer or divinatory time: dawn.

Day 24 – 9th November: Prayer or divinatory time: dawn.

Day 25 – 10th: November: Prayer or divinatory time: do not observe – not a suitable day.

Day 26 – 11th November: The end of the formula for the making of the spirit of Osiris. Prayer or divinatory time: in the afternoon.

Day 27 – 12th November: Feast of Thoth. Prayer or divinatory time: throughout the day.

Thoth: *Dhwty*

The most popular and enduring of all the gods, Thoth has been responsible for keeping Egyptian magic in the forefront of learning since the collapse of the empire. Although in the later Dynastic period he was merely labelled the 'scribe of the gods', Thoth was endowed with complete knowledge and wisdom. He invented all the arts and sciences, astronomy, soothsaying, magic, medicine,

---

surgery and most important of all – writing. As inventor of hieroglyphics he was titled 'Lord of the Holy Words'; he was the first of magicians and compiled books of magic that contained formulae that commanded all the forces of nature and subdued the very gods themselves. When he was referred to as the 'Thrice Great Thoth' in the temple at Isna, this served as his epitaph when his wisdom was preserved for posterity in the Hermetic writings.

Prayer or Invocation
Such was all-knowing Tahuti [Thoth], who saw all things,
and seeing understood,
and understanding has the power to disclose
and to give explanation.
For what he knew, he graved on stone;
Yet though he graved them onto stone he hid them mostly ...
The sacred symbols of the cosmic elements
he hid away hard by the secrets of Osiris
... keeping sure silence,
that every younger age of cosmic time might seek for them.
[Kore Kosmu – G S R Meade translation]

Day 28 – 13th November: *If you see anything, it will be good. Do not go out at night-time on this day.* Prayer or divinatory time: throughout the day

Day 29 – 14th November: *Do not eat fish on this day. Do not offer it to the gods on this day.* Prayer or divinatory time: throughout the day.

Day 30 – 15th November: *If you see anything, it will be pleasing to the heart of the gods and goddesses on this day. Offer to the gods and the assistants of the Ennead. Make an invocation to the spirits, and give food in accordance with their lust. It is the day of the pleasure of the*

Great Ennead. **House of Re, House of Osiris, House of Horus.** Prayer or divinatory time: in the afternoon.

Proyet-Season (Emergence)
First Month: Tybi

Day 1 – 16th November: *Double the offerings and present the gifts of* **nhb-kaw** [for the sprouting of the new crops] *to the gods in the presence of Ptah in the shrines of the gods and goddesses, saviours of Re and his own followers ... and of Ptah-Sokar and Sekhmet the great, Nerfertem, Horus-Hekenu, Bastet, the great fire ... propitiating the Wedjet eye* [the cobra goddess]. *It will be good ... offering before ... in nourishment.* [The traditional first day of planting, i.e. spring for the ancient Egyptians.] Prayer or divinatory time: dawn.

Bast: *B3stt*

Along with Hathor, Bast (or Bastet) is one of the most popular of Egyptian deities. Her earliest image was that of the lion and it was not until around 1000BC that the representation of Bast as a cat became common. Her most important cult centre was at Bubastis (*per*-Bastet = house of Bastet). That she was also a daughter of Atum suggests that she may have embodied the gentler or healing aspect of Sekhmet. Bast would be invoked for domestic purposes and is often thought of as a women's deity.

Prayer or Invocation

I am she who is called Divine among women.
For me was built the city of Bubastis.
I brought together woman and man.
I burdened woman with the new-born babe in the tenth month.
I ordained that parents should be beloved by their children.

> *I inflict retribution on those that feel no love for their parents.*
> *I compelled women to be loved by men.*
> *I found out marriage contracts for women.*
> [Greek translation]

Day 2 – 17th November: *Make a holiday in your house.* Prayer or divinatory time: at noon.

Day 3 – 18th November: *Do not burn fire* [i.e. incense] *in the presence of Re.* Prayer or divinatory time: do not observe – not a suitable day.

Day 4 – 19th November: *If you see anything it will be good. Anyone born on this day will die old among his people. He will spend a long life, and be well received by his father.* Prayer or divinatory time: dawn.

Day 5 – 20th November: *It is the day of placing the flame in front of the great ones by Sekhmet who presides in the Lower Egyptian sanctuary when she was violent in her manifestations because of her detention by Ma'at, Ptah, Thoth, Heh* [the personification of infinity] *and Sia* [the personification of the perceptive mind] *and the gods on this day.* Prayer or divinatory time: dawn.

Day 6 – 21st November: *Repeat the offerings of the victuals of him who dwells in **wrt*** [a holy place], *and return the victuals of the noble Khenti-irty* [the earliest form of Osiris which shows him as a hawk with a flail] *and offerings to the gods were doubled by everyone on this day.* Prayer or divinatory time: do not observe – not a suitable day.

Day 7 – 22nd November: *Do not copulate with any woman, or any person in front of the great flame* [i.e. the sun – during the day] *which is in your house on this day.* Prayer or divinatory time: at noon.

Day 8 – 23rd November: *If you see anything, it will be good on this day.* Sun rises in Sagittarius. Prayer or divinatory time: throughout the day.

Day 9 – 24th November: *The gods are joyful with the offerings of*

Sekhmet [on this] day. Repeat the offerings. It will be pleasant to the heart of the gods and the spirits. Prayer or divinatory time: do not observe – not a suitable day.

Day 10 – 25th November: *Do not burn any **wbd**-papyrus on this day. It is the day of the Coming Forth of the flame (together with Horus from the marshes) on this day.* Prayer or divinatory time: throughout the day.

Day 11 – 26th November: *Do not approach the flame on this day.* Prayer or divinatory time: in the afternoon.

Day 12 – 27th November: *If you see any dog on this day, do not approach him on the day of answering every speech of Sekhmet on this day.* [Possibly referring to a superstition of the time.] Prayer or divinatory time: throughout the day.

Day 13 – 28th November: *Prolonging life-time and making beneficent the goddess of truth [Ma'at] in the temple.* Prayer or divinatory time: throughout the day.

Day 14 – 29th November: *Weeping of Isis and Nephthys. It is the day when they mourned Osiris in Busiris in remembrance of that which he had seen. Do not listen to singing and chanting on this day.* Prayer or divinatory time: dawn.

Nephthys: *Nbt-hwt*

Although part of the Great Ennead, there is very little in Egyptian writing to give Nephthys much of an identity. The transcription of the name *nbt-hwt* = lady of the house, offers no information and so she remains an evasive shadowy creature. It has been suggested that she was a creation of later 'dualistic Egyptian thought' when the need arose to give Set a companion. She later evolved into a funerary goddess and is largely featured performing the lamentations for Osiris, in the company of Isis. Magically she is associated with illusion and her emblem is a basket.

Prayer or Invocation

Nephthys said: 'I go round about behind thee. I have come that

I may protect thee, and my strength which protecteth shall be behind thee for ever and ever.'

[Papyrus of Mut-hetep BM 10010.5]

Day 15 – 30th November: *If you see anything it will be good on this day. It is the day of the Going forth of Nun through the cave to the place (where the gods are) ... (in) darkness ...* [Coming into the light.] Prayer or divinatory time: throughout the day.

Day 16 – 1st December: *The Going Forth of Shu.* Prayer or divinatory time: do not observe – not a suitable day.

Day 17 – 2nd December: *Do not wash yourself with water on this day. It is the day of the Going Forth of Nun to the place where the gods are. Those who are above and below come into existence; the land being still in darkness.* Prayer or divinatory time: do not observe – not a suitable day.

Nun: Nw

Personification of the primeval waters from which the Creation derived; the references in the text to darkness involves the state before Creation. Often the texts refer to him as the 'father of the gods' and 'Infinity, Nothingness, Nowhere and Darkness' but throughout Egyptian history he remained a purely intellectual concept, having neither temple nor worshippers. It was believed that if the correct precatory observances were not carried out, then the waters of Nun would re-envelop the world and everything would plunge back into Chaos. As the waters of Nun receded, the hill that emerged was an important concept in religious thought and imagery. The emergence of the Mound was symbolised every year with the Inundation. As the waters receded, leaving rich fertile soil in its wake, so the Mound was held to have risen out of the primeval waters to provide the birth-place for the gods. Although there were several different creation myths the overall 'original hill' legend continued to influence the design and layout in temples and tombs until the end of the empire.

Prayer or Invocation

O god of the Celestial Waters. I have come forth from the god of creation. I am Nun coming forth from his might. He hath lighted for thee the lamp, he hath performed the ceremony of transferring the fluid of life upon thee.
[Pyramid Texts]

Day 18 – 3rd December: *The Going Forth of the gods to Abydos.* Prayer or divinatory time: at dawn and in the afternoon.

Day 19 – 4th December: *The great gods are in heaven on this day and* (lit. *mixed with*) *the pestilence of the year.* Prayer or divinatory time: dawn.

Day 20 – 5th December: *Do not do anything on this day. It is the day of the Going Forth of Bastet who protects the Two Lands and cares for him who comes in darkness. Beware of passing on land until Re sets.* Prayer or divinatory time: dawn.

Day 21 – 6th December: *Guidance of the Two Lands by Bastet and making 'abt-offering to the followers of Re on this day.* Prayer or divinatory time: in the afternoon.

Day 22 – 7th December: *If you see anything it will be good on this day.* Prayer or divinatory time: in the afternoon.

Day 23 – 8th December: *Anyone born on this day will die in great* *old age and rich in every good thing.* Prayer or divinatory time: dawn.

Day 24 – 9th December: *Happiness is in heaven and earth on this day.* Prayer or divinatory time: dawn.

Day 25 – 10th December: *Do not eat milk on this day. Drink and eat honey on this day.* [The prohibition of drinking milk probably means it was exclusively offered to the cow-goddess – Hathor or Nut. Purification by means of milk is also referred to in other texts.] Prayer or divinatory time: do not observe – not a suitable day.

Day 26 – 11th December: *Do not go out in it* [the day] *until Re sets when offerings are diminished in Busiris.* [The subject of diminishing offerings is frequently mentioned in the *Book of the Dead.*] Prayer or divinatory time: in the afternoon.

Day 27 – 12th December: *Great festivity on this day.* Prayer or divinatory time: throughout the day.

Day 28 – 13th December: *Taking a solemn oath by Thoth in Ashmunein, and the Going Forth of the noble one.* [The most solemn oath one can take and refers to that pledged by Horus the Elder and Set.] *The land is in festivity on this day. Make a holiday in your house.* Prayer or divinatory time: throughout the day.

Day 29 – 14th December: *Appearance in the sight of Hu* [personification of the authority of a word of command.] *Thoth will send his command southwards to guide the Two Lands by Bastet together with the sole mistress as Sekhmet the great, the gods being happy. If you see anything it will be good on this day.* Prayer or divinatory time: throughout the day.

Day 30 – 15th December: *Crossing over in the presence of Nun from the Temple of Hapi, the father of the gods and the Ennead. Do not neglect them while incense is on the fire according to their lists on this day.* **House of Re, House of Osiris, House of Horus.** Prayer or divinatory time: in the afternoon.

Second Month: Mekhir

Day 1 – 16th December: *The god and goddesses are in festivity on this day (namely), in the feast of* [lifting] *the heaven of Re by Ptah, with his hands (he who has no equal).* [The notion of the sky being lifted by Ptah rather than Shu is found in a hymn to this god, which is now in Berlin.] *A holiday in the entire land.* Prayer or divinatory time: dawn.

Day 2 – 17th December: *The day of receiving Re by the gods. The heart of the Two Lands is in festivity.* Prayer or divinatory time: at noon.

Atum-Re: '*Itm*

Re signifies the 'Creator' and is the name of the sun and sovereign lord of the sky. Like Atum, his principle sanctuary was at Heliopolis and from a very early time the priesthood identified the two gods as one. Re was the rising sun that manifested on the primeval Mound, while Atum personified the setting sun. This dual deity emerged in the morning from behind the mountain of sunrise and began his journey across the sky in what was called the *manjet*-boat, or 'barque of millions of years', accompanied by a number of gods who act as the boat's crew. At dusk, for his 12 hours of darkness, Re sailed in the *meseket*-boat or night-barque with a different crew. Just as the images of the gods were carried in ritual procession in ceremonial barques, so Atum-Re was believed to travel through the Otherworld in a solar-barque. There were two distinct types of barque (see above) and it is possible that those examples excavated in the pyramid complex of Khufu at Giza (one of which has been reconstructed and displayed *in situ*) were intended to carry the deceased Pharaoh on his final journey through Amenti.

> **Prayer or Invocation**
> *Hail to you Re, at your rising,*
> *and to you Atum, at your setting.*
> *You rise every day, you shine brightly every day,*
> *while you appear in glory, king of the gods.*
> *You are Lord of the sky and Lord of the earth,*
> *who has created the creatures above and those below.*
> [Book of the Dead – Ch. 15]

Day 3 – 18th December: *Do not go out of your house on any road on this day. It is the day of the Going Forth of Set with his confederates to the eastern horizon, and the navigation of Ma'at to the place (where the gods are).* Prayer or divinatory time: do not observe – not a suitable day.

Day 4 – 19th December: *Apply your heart to your local gods; propitiate your spirits.* Prayer or divinatory time: dawn.

Day 5 – 20th December: *If you see anything, it will be good on this day.* Prayer or divinatory time: dawn.

Day 6 – 21st December: *It is the day of putting up the **djet** by the Majesty of Osiris. The gods are sad with their faces turned downwards when they remember the Majesty of this god.* [Refers to the resurrection of Osiris represented by the *djet*-pillar. For ritual purposes it is highly appropriate that this day coincides with Winter Solstice in the northern hemisphere.] Prayer or divinatory time: do not observe – not a suitable day.

Day 7 – 22nd December: *Make invocation and offering to the spirits in your house. Make offerings to the gods, and they will be accepted on this day.* Sun rises in Capricorn. Prayer or divinatory time: at noon.

Day 8 – 23rd December: *The gods and goddesses are in festivity on this day.* Prayer or divinatory time: throughout the day.

Day 9 – 24th December: *If you see anything, it will be good on this* *day*. Prayer or divinatory time: do not observe – not a suitable day.

Day 10 – 25th December: *The Going Forth of the Wedjet-eye. The raising up of the female Majesty of the sanctuary by Mnevis. Re raised up Ma'at again and again to Atum.* Prayer or divinatory time: throughout the day.

Ma'at: *M3't*

In ancient Egypt the concept of Chaos was not an abstract idea. The gods would remain happy as long as the country functioned properly; as long as the people continued to work for the benefit of the Pharaoh; as long as Pharaoh continued to work for the benefit of the gods. This state of correct being was known as *ma'at* and may be understood in terms of stability or balance (which also incorporated justice and truth). In later times Ma'at, as a daughter of Re, was depicted as a beautiful young woman, wearing an ostrich feature on her head. In the Judgement Hall of Osiris, the heart of the deceased was placed on one pan of the balance-scale of Anubis, the jackal-headed god of the dead, with a feather of Ma'at in the other, while Thoth recorded the result. If the heart weighed no more than the feather and was not burdened with guilt, the soul went to Amenti, the Egyptian afterlife. If the heart was heavier than the feather, the guilty one was devoured by the monster, Ammet.

Prayer or Invocation
May Ma'at grant ...
And there shall be made unto them
an offering of a libation of one vase upon the earth.
[BM Papyrus 10,478, sheet 2-7]

Day 11 – 26th December: Feast of Neith. *The Going Forth of Sobek to guide her Majesty. Thou wilt see good at her hands.* Prayer or divinatory time: in the afternoon.

Day 12 – 27th December: *If you see anything, it will be good on this day.* Prayer or divinatory time: throughout the day.

Day 13 – 28th December: *Do not go out of your house on any road on this day. It is the day of the preceding of Sekhmet to Letopolis on this day.* Prayer or divinatory time: throughout the day.

Day 14 – 29th December: *Do not go out on this day at the beginning* (lit. *in the face*) *of dawn. The day of the slaying of Apophis by Set.* Prayer or divinatory time: dawn.

Day 15 – 30th December: *The gods go forth for him in heaven.* Prayer or divinatory time: throughout the day.

Day 16 – 31st December: *Awakening of Isis by the Majesty of Re … when the son Horus saved his father. He has beaten Set and his confederates.* Prayer or divinatory time: do not observe – not a suitable day.

Day 17 – 1st January: *A day of keeping those things (of Osiris) which have been placed in the hands of Anubis (for safe keeping).* A day for remembering 'absent friends'. Prayer or divinatory time: do not observe – not a suitable day.

Day 18 – 2nd January: This is the day when a search was made to retrieve the eye of Horus that had been torn out during his battle with Set. It symbolises the eternal renewal of royal divinity and Egyptian faith in the continual reintegration of universal harmony. Prayer or divinatory time: at dawn and in the afternoon.

Day 19 – 3rd January: *Decide not to go out during day-time. It is a day of (mourning the god).* [Refers to the slaying of Osiris by Set, which interrupts the harmonious cosmic flow and endangers the whole social order.] Prayer or divinatory time: dawn.

Day 20 – 4th January: *The proceeding of the (female) Majesty of Heaven southward to the road …* [Referring to a ritual procession of a statue of Hathor.] Prayer or divinatory time: dawn.

Day 21 – 5th January: Prayer or divinatory time: in the afternoon.

Day 22 – 6th January: *If you see anything, it will be good on this day.*

Prayer or divinatory time: in the afternoon.

Day 23 – 7th January: *If you see anything, it will be good on this day.* Prayer or divinatory time: dawn.

Day 24 – 8th January: Prayer or divinatory time: dawn.

Day 25 – 9th January: *If you see anything, it will be good on this day.* Prayer or divinatory time: do not observe – not a suitable day.

Day 26 – 10th January: *The Going Forth of Min from Coptos on this day.* Prayer or divinatory time: in the afternoon.

Min: *Mwn*

An indigenous deity of great antiquity whose totem, a thunderbolt, appeared at the top of prehistoric standards. He was worshipped at Coptos as a god of roads and protector of travellers in the desert; he was also a god of fertility and vegetation, and protector of crops. His image is invariably shown with an enormous erect phallus and as the harvest god, the first sheaf to be cut was offered in his name. Offerings could also be made in the form of lettuce since the milky fluid of the sap resembled semen and was therefore said to have aphrodisiac properties. Oracular decrees worn as amulets of Min were obtainable from the temples. A decree from Min 'the great in love' and Isis promises the wearer that she will conceive healthy male and female children, and that she will have an easy and joyful delivery.

Prayer or Invocation

For a spell to relieve impotence, on a goose egg write the following and bury the egg under the threshold of the afflicted person.

I am bound, thou shall unbind me
And the god Min shall protect me
[*The Search for Omm Seti*]

Day 27 – 11th January: The Feast of Sokar. Prayer or divinatory time: throughout the day.

Day 28 – 12th January: *The spirits are joyful, the dead are also in festivity.* [A day for honouring the Ancestors and 'speaking the name of the dead in order to make them live again'.] Prayer or divinatory time: throughout the day.

Day 29 – 13th January: *Do not do anything on this day.* [An unlucky day, marking the start of the fighting between the children of Nut and Geb. Often referred to as the 'children of disorder' because of their incessant quarrelling and the disturbances they provoked.] Prayer or divinatory time: throughout the day.

Day 30 – 14th January: *Do not talk with anybody (in a loud voice) on this day.* **House of Re, House of Osiris, House of Horus.** Prayer or divinatory time: in the afternoon.

Third Month: Phamenoth

Day 1 – 15th January: *It is the day (of jubilation) in heaven and earth and everybody likewise. Feast of entering into heaven and the two banks. Horus is jubilating.* Feast of Horus the Elder. Prayer or divinatory time: dawn.

Horus: *Hrw*

Horus the Elder and Set, although normally considered as opponents, are combined into a single deity: brothers who are at the same time enemies and inseparable. The cult of Horus the Elder flourished and divided – on one hand he was reduced to the son of Isis and Osiris; on the other he retained his solar image and was identified in the living image of Pharaoh. During the early period of Egyptian history, the King was given the title of 'son of Hathor' and identified with the sky-god; Hathor's name means 'house of Horus'. This mother-son-consort concept was later

---

absorbed into the myth of Isis and Horus and, as a result, the identities of the two goddesses later merged into one. The original myth survived, realigning the image of Hathor as the wife of the sky-god, Horus of Edfu, during the building of the Ptolemaic temple on a much earlier site.

Prayer or Invocation

Enter in peace, leave in peace, go in happiness. For life is in His hand, peace is in His grasp, all good things are with Him. There is food for him who remains at His table, and nourishment for him who partakes of His offerings. No misfortune or evil will befall the one who serves Him for His care reaches to heaven and His security to earth and His protection is greater than that of all the gods.

[Inscription – Temple of Edfu]

Day 2 – 16th January: *If you see anything, it will be good on this day.* Prayer or divinatory time: at noon.

Day 3 – 17th January: [Damaged entry] Prayer or divinatory time: do not observe – not a suitable day.

Day 4 – 18th January: A Feast of Propitiation for Set. *Announcement of fighting; call in Heliopolis by Set, his voice being in heaven* [thunder], *his voice being on earth, through great fury* [storm]. Prayer or divinatory time: dawn.

Set: *Sts*

The oldest and most complex of all the Egyptian deities since his name and reputation underwent some drastic character assassination during the march of history. He is rarely dealt with in depth in popular renditions of

Egyptian mythology, often being merely given as the evil murderer of his brother Osiris. His distinctive image, however, first appeared among the standards on King Scorpion's mace-head from pre-dynastic times. The conflict of Horus (the Elder) and Set is the older version of what has become better known as the feud between Set and Osiris – with Horus (the Younger) being given a secondary role. The pre-Osirian Horus and Set were sky and stellar gods, with Set representing the oldest beliefs in early Egypt.

Prayer or Invocation

Brother, as long as you burn
You belong to life.
You say you want Me with you in the Beyond?
Forget the Beyond! When you bring your flesh to rest
And thus reach the Beyond, in that stillness
Shall I alight upon you;
Then united we shall form the Abode.
For Above is exalted by Below
As is written in the Scriptures.
[Berlin Papyrus 3024]

Day 5 – 19th January: *Neith goes forth from Sais when they see (her) beauty in the night for four and a half (hours).* [Possibly referral to an eclipse] Feast of Neith. Prayer or divinatory time: dawn.

Day 6 – 20th January: *Jubilation of Osiris is Bursiris … Going Forth of Anubis, (his adorers) following him … he has received everybody in the hall. Mayest thou make the ritual.* Prayer or divinatory time: do not observe – not a suitable day.

Day 7 – 21st January: *Do not go out of your house until Re sets. It is the day when the eye of Re called the followers, and they reached him* *(in) the evening. Beware of it.* [Marking the day when Sekhmet punished mankind for rebelling against Re.] Sun rises in Aquarius. Prayer or divinatory time: at noon.

Day 8 – 22nd January: *If you see anything, it will be good on this day. It is the day of making way for the gods. Khnum who presides over those who remove themselves from him.* The Feast Day of Khumn, the creator-god, who fashions human beings on his potter's wheel. Prayer or divinatory time: throughout the day.

Day 9 – 23rd January: *Judgement in Heliopolis.* The anniversary of the judgement of the gods between Set and Horus. Sun rises in Aquarius. Prayer or divinatory time: do not observe – not a suitable day.

Day 10 – 24th January: *It is the day of the coming of Thoth. They guided the very great Flame into her house of the desert of eternity (along) the way which she found among them.* The celebration of Thoth bringing Sekhmet, the lion-goddess, back from her self-imposed exile. Prayer or divinatory time: throughout the day.

Day 11 – 25th January: *As to the dead who go about in the necropolis on this day, the dead are going about in order to repel the anger of the enemy who is in the said land.* A Feast of Osiris in Amenti. A day for honouring the Ancestors in the Otherworld. Prayer or divinatory time: in the afternoon.

Day 12 – 26th January: *Wsr [the Nile] comes from Nun on this day.* Traditionally a celebration of the first appearance of the life-giving waters at the Creation. The Feast of the Nile. Prayer or divinatory time: throughout the day.

Day 13 – 27th January: *The coming of Thoth (with his spirits) on this day.* A Feast of Thoth. Prayer or divinatory time: throughout the day.

Day 14 – 28th January: *Do not go out of your house (on any road) on this day.* Prayer or divinatory time: dawn.

Day 15 – 29th January: *Rebellion in the shrine(?). Do not do any work on this day.* Prayer or divinatory time: throughout the day.

Day 16 – 30th January: *Opening of the windows and opening of the court, and looking into the doorways of Karnak, where his place is. Do not look into the darkness on this day.* Reference to the cleaning of the temple. [There is a dark, inner sanctuary of Sekhmet in the Temple of Ptah at Karnak.] Prayer or divinatory time: do not observe – not a suitable day.

Day 17 – 31st January: *Do not pronounce the name of Set on this day. As to him who pronounces his name without his knowledge, he will not stop from fighting in his house eternally.* Set was the god of Chaos who was always at odds with his siblings. Prayer or divinatory time: do not observe – not a suitable day.

Day 18 – 1st February: *Feast of Nut who counts the days. Make a holiday in your house.* Prayer or divinatory time: at dawn and in the afternoon.

Nut: *Nwt*

The pre-dynastic Nut was the personification of 'Our Lady of the Starry Heavens' and, in primeval belief, the destination of the Pharaoh's soul – the Imperishable Stars. By day or night, Nut was the space that hinted at all that was concealed from view since her body only represented the limits of the domain Re travelled through every day. She did not represent the whole of existing space. As the Egyptian pantheon developed she became identified with the Great Ennead and as the mother of Osiris, Horus, Set, Isis and Nephthys.

Prayer or Invocation:
Thou are raised up, thou art established,
Yea established in the body of Nut,
Who united herself unto thee,
and who cometh forth with thee.

> *Thy heart is established in thy breast,*
> *Thy breath is firmly fixed with life and power,*
> *Thou livest, and thou art renewed,*
> *And thou makest thyself young like Re each and every day.*
> [Papyrus of Met-hetep BM No. 10,010, sheet 4]

Day 19 – 2nd February: *Birth of Nut anew … Do not go out of your house; do not see the light (sw).* Prayer or divinatory time: dawn.

Day 20 – 3rd February: *Do not go out of your house on any road. Do not see the light.* Prayer or divinatory time: dawn.

Day 21 – 4th February: [Damaged entry] Prayer or divinatory time: in the afternoon.

Day 22 – 5th February: *Birth of the mysterious one (Apophis). Do not get the thought of pronouncing the names of the snakes.* [Obscure meaning but some snakes were unlucky and Apophis is the serpent-god of the netherworld.] Prayer or divinatory time: in the afternoon.

Day 23 – 6th February: *Feast of Horus on this day of his years in his very beautiful images.* Prayer or divinatory time: dawn.

Day 24 – 7th February: *Do not go out of your house on any road on this day.* Prayer or divinatory time: dawn.

Day 25 – 8th February: *Do not do anything on this day.* Prayer or divinatory time: do not observe – not a suitable day.

Day 26 – 9th February: [Obscure meaning] Prayer or divinatory time: in the afternoon.

Day 27 – 10th February: *Do not do anything on this day.* Prayer or divinatory time: throughout the day.

Day 28 – 11th February: *Feast of Osiris in Abydos.* Prayer or divinatory time: throughout the day.

Day 29 – 12th February: *If you see anything it will be good.* Prayer or divinatory time: throughout the day.

Day 30 – 13th February: *Feast in Busiris. The names of the doorways*

come into existence. **House of Re, House of Osiris, House of Horus.**
Prayer or divinatory time: in the afternoon.

Fourth Month: Pharmuthi

Day 1 – 14th February: *Great feasting in heaven.* Prayer or divinatory time: dawn.

Day 2 – 15th February: *The Majesty of Geb proceeds to the throne of Busiris to see Anubis, who commands the council on the requirements of the day.* Prayer or divinatory time: at noon.

Anubis: *'Inpw*

The most distinctive of all the Egyptian gods and best known for the imposing life-size image found in the tomb of Tutankhamen. This was the canine god of the dead who was the overseer of embalming and mummification, usually depicted as a seated black dog, or a man with a dog's head. Although he is often referred to as jackal-headed, it is open to debate whether Anubis is a dog or a jackal. His black coat symbolises the colour of putrefying corpses and the fertile black soil of the Nile Valley. From the earliest times, however, Anubis was the companion or guide of the deceased Pharaoh on his journey to Otherworld and is often found seated beside the scales weighing the heart in the Hall of Two Truths.

Prayer or Invocation:

The earth speaks: The doors of the earth-god are opened for you, the doors of Geb are thrown open for you, you come forth at the voice of Anubis, he makes a spirit of you like Thoth, you judge the gods, you set bounds to the celestial expanses between the Two Wands in this your spiritualised state which Anubis commanded. [Pyramid Texts 796-798]

Day 3 – 16th February: *Do not do anything on this day.* Prayer or divinatory time: do not observe – not a suitable day.

Day 4 – 17th February: *If you see anything it will be good on this day. The gods and goddesses are satisfied when they see the children of Geb sitting in their places* (i.e. at peace). Prayer or divinatory time: dawn.

Day 5 – 18th February: *Feast of Horus.* Prayer or divinatory time: dawn.

Day 6 – 19th February: *Going Forth of the stars.* Prayer or divinatory time: do not observe – not a suitable day.

Day 7 – 20th February: *The Going Forth of Min in festivity. The gods are jubilating. Pay attention to the incense on the fire smelling of sweet myrrh.* Sun rises in Pisces. Prayer or divinatory time: at noon.

Day 8 – 21st February: *The Ennead is in adoration when they see this eye of Horus (the Elder) in its place. A feast day for Horus whose magnificence stretches into infinity.* Prayer or divinatory time: throughout the day.

Day 9 – 22nd February: *Do not go out at the time of darkness when Re goes into the West. If you see anything, it will be good on this day.* Prayer or divinatory time: do not observe – not a suitable day.

Day 10 – 23rd February: *Do not go out of your house on any road on this day.* Prayer or divinatory time: throughout the day.

Day 11 – 24th February: *The gods are in the shrines of the temples.* Prayer or divinatory time: in the afternoon.

Day 12 – 25th February: *Feast of Montu.* Prayer or divinatory time: throughout the day.

Montu: *Mntw*

Apart from Neith, who was identified as a hunter/warrior goddess, the only other war god was Montu. He first puts in an appearance in Thebes around 2000BC, being depicted as a falcon-headed man, crowned with a solar

---

disc. Several kings of Dynasty XI were given the 'birth name' of Mentuhotep ('Montu is content') and he became the embodiment of the 'conquering vitality of the Pharaoh and the more aggressive aspects of kingship'. He eventually became fused with the sun god as Montu-Re.

Prayer or Invocation:
When Montu is high, I will be high with him;
When Montu runs, I will run with him.
[Pyramid Texts, 1081]

Day 13 – 26th February: *It is the day of conducting Osiris on his ship to Abydos on this day.* Prayer or divinatory time: throughout the day.

Day 14 – 27th February: *Do not be courageous on this day.* Prayer or divinatory time: dawn.

Day 15 – 28th February: *A great happy day in the Eastern Horizon of heaven when instructions were given to the followers of the gods in their temples in the presence of the Great Ones in the Two Horizons.* Prayer or divinatory time: throughout the day.

[The ancient calendar made no allowance for Leap Year.]

Day 16 – 1st March: *The Going Forth of Khepri. Every town is in joy.* Prayer or divinatory time: do not observe – not a suitable day.

Khepri: *Hprr*

The Creator-god whose emblem, the scarab, is one of the most familiar images in Egyptian art. The scarab is a dung-beetle in which the Egyptians saw the symbol of the self-generative aspect of the sun-god. Khepri represented the rising sun, which, like the scarab, emerges from its own substance and is reborn of itself. He was the god of the transformations which life, forever renewing itself, manifests. In choosing this insect to convey one of the forms of the sun-god, is a typical example of the way the Egyptian mind attempted to understand the universe and creation.

Prayer or Invocation:

O Temu-Khepra when thou hadst raised thyself on your standard, and hadst shone as the 'Great One in the place of shining', you didst send forth the water in the form of Shu, and didst spit in the form of Tefnut, and thou didst place thy hands behind them, and verily thy ka existeth in them.

[Inscription from the Pyramid of Pepi II]

Day 17 – 2nd March: *The Going Forth of Set, son of Nut, to disturb the Great Ones.* Prayer or divinatory time: do not observe – not a suitable day.

Day 18 – 3rd March: *Do not approach when the Majesty of Re goes forth. Do not wash yourself with water on this day.* Prayer or divinatory time: at dawn and in the afternoon.

Day 19 – 4th March: *The Majesty of Re goes forth in his barque of heaven. If you see anything, it will be good on this day.* Prayer or divinatory time: dawn.

Day 20 – 5th March: *Do not do any work on this day.* Prayer or divinatory time: dawn.

Day 21 – 6th March: *Do not go out on any road on this day.* Prayer or divinatory time: in the afternoon.

Day 22 – 7th March: *An unlucky day.* Prayer or divinatory time: in the afternoon.

Day 23 – 8th March: *It is the day of offering victuals … invocation offering to the spirits.* Prayer or divinatory time: dawn.

Day 24 – 9th March: *Do not mention the name of Set in a loud voice on this day. As to anyone who mentions his name forgetfully, fighting is made in his house forever.* Prayer or divinatory time: dawn.

Day 25 – 10th March: *Do not eat anything which comes from or on water on this day.* Prayer or divinatory time: do not observe – not a suitable day.

Day 26 – 11th March: [Damaged entry.] Prayer or divinatory time: in the afternoon.

Day 27 – 12th March: *Do not go out of your house until Re sets because the Majesty of the goddess Sekhmet is angry.* Prayer or divinatory time: throughout the day.

Day 28 – 13th March: *If you see anything it will be good on this day.* Prayer or divinatory time: throughout the day.

Day 29 – 14th March: *The gods are satisfied when they give adoration to Onnophris (Osiris), incense being on the fire; offer to your local gods myrrh which is pleasant on this day.* Prayer or divinatory time: throughout the day.

Day 30 – 15th March: *Offer to Ptah-Sokar-Osiris ... Atum, Lord of the Two Lands... to all the gods ... on this day.* **House of Re, House of Osiris, House of Horus.** Prayer or divinatory time: in the afternoon.

Shomu-Season (Harvest)
First Month: Pakhons

Day 1 – 16th March: *Feast of Horus, son of Isis and his followers on this day.* Prayer or divinatory time: dawn.

Day 2 – 17th March: *Do not sail in any wind on this day.* Prayer or divinatory time: at noon.

Day 3 – 18th March: *If you see anything it will be good on this day.* Prayer or divinatory time: do not observe – not a suitable day.

Day 4 – 19th March: *Do not go out of your house on any road on this day. Follow Horus on this day.* Prayer or divinatory time: dawn.

Day 5 – 20th March: *Feast of Ba-neb-dedet on this day.* [Ba-neb-dedet was the ram-god of Djet wrongly translated by Greek historians as 'the Goat of Mendes'.] Prayer or divinatory time: dawn.

Day 6 – 21st March: *Coming of the Great Ones from the House of Re, rejoicing on this day when they receive the Wedjet-eye, together with their followers. If you see anything, it will be good on this day.* Spring Equinox (Autumn in Egypt). Sun rises in Aries. Prayer or divinatory time: do not observe – not a suitable day.

Wedjet: W3dt

The royal cobra-goddess whose name means 'the green one' – she was particularly associated with the Lower Egyptian town of Buto, which dates back to the pre-dynastic period. Usually portrayed as a rearing cobra, she is an integral part of the *uraeus*, the archetypal Egyptian serpent-image of kingship that protruded just above the forehead in most royal crowns and headdresses throughout the country's history. According to the Pyramid Texts, Geb awarded the cobra to Pharaoh as the legitimate holder of the throne and her emblem rises up to spit flames in defence of the monarch. Snakes or serpents play a conflicting and confusing part in Egyptian imagery. Although a symbol of kingship, this was also the form of the god Apophis who threatened Re during his journey in Otherworld. Snakes were also linked with creation and look upon as primeval chthonic creatures as well as the *ouroboros*, the serpent whose body coiled around the universe until it devoured its own tail – representing the powers of resurrection and renewal.

Prayer or Invocation:
O papyrus-plant which issued from Wedjet,
you have gone forth in the King,

> *and the King has gone forth in you,*
> *the King is powerful through your strength.*
> [Pyramid Texts, 1875]

Day 7 – 22nd March: *The crew follow Horus in the foreign land ...*
Every land is happy, and their heart is glad ... Prayer or divinatory
time: at noon.

Day 8 – 23rd March: *If you see anything, it will be good on this day.*
Prayer or divinatory time: throughout the day.

Day 9 – 24th March: *If you see anything, it will be good on this day.*
Prayer or divinatory time: do not observe – not a suitable day.

Day 10 – 25th March: *The proceeding of the White One of Heaven*
[Feast day of Osiris]. Prayer or divinatory time: throughout the
day.

Day 11 – 26th March: [Damaged entry.] Prayer or divinatory
time: in the afternoon.

Day 12 – 27th March: [Damaged entry.] Prayer or divinatory
time: throughout the day.

Day 13 – 28th March: [Damaged entry.] Prayer or divinatory
time: throughout the day.

Day 14 – 29th March: [Damaged entry.] Prayer or divinatory
time: dawn.

Day 15 – 30th March: *Do not go out of your house until Re sets in the*
horizon. Prayer or divinatory time: throughout the day.

Day 16 – 31st March: [Damaged entry.] Prayer or divinatory time:
do not observe –not a suitable day.

Day 17 – 1st April: *If you see anything, it will be good on this day.*
Prayer or divinatory time: do not observe – not a suitable day.

Day 18 – 2nd April: *If you see anything it will be good on this day.*
Prayer or divinatory time: at dawn and in the afternoon.

Day 19 – 3rd April: *A feast day of Thoth and Ma'at. All the gods are*
in great festivity. Prayer or divinatory time: dawn.

Day 20 – 4th April: *Ma'at judges in front of the gods who became angry. The Majesty of Horus revised (over-ruled) it.* Prayer or divinatory time: dawn.

Day 21 – 5th April: [Obscure text.] Prayer or divinatory time: in the afternoon.

Nekhbet: *Nhbt*

Together with Wedjet, the vulture-goddess Nekhbet was the dual protector of Pharaoh and usually shown with wings spread, grasping the symbols of eternity in her claws. Nekhbet was favoured by the rulers of the South (Upper Egypt); with one wing outstretched she presides over royal and ritual scenes as a protective deity. She is sometimes portrayed as a woman wearing the white crown of Egypt, or on a headdress shaped like a vulture. The vulture and cobra together became the symbol of the unification of Lower and Upper Egypt: known as 'the two ladies', the epithet that indicated the two protectresses.

Prayer or Invocation:
I live by the grace of my father Atum;
protect me O Nekhbet
[Pyramid Texts, 1451]

Day 22 – 6th April: *Anyone born on this day will die of old age.* Prayer or divinatory time: in the afternoon.

Day 23 – 7th April: *If you see anything, it will be good on this day.* Prayer or divinatory time: dawn.

Day 24 – 8th April: [Damaged entry.] Prayer or divinatory time: dawn.

Day 25 – 9th April: [Damaged entry.] Prayer or divinatory time: do not observe – not a suitable day.

Day 26 – 10th April: *If you see anything, it will be good on this day.* Prayer or divinatory time: in the afternoon.

Day 27 – 11th April: [Damaged entry.] Prayer or divinatory time: throughout the day.

Day 28 – 12th April: [Damaged entry.] Prayer or divinatory time: throughout the day.

Day 29 – 13th April: *If you see anything, it will be good on this day.* Prayer or divinatory time: throughout the day.

Day 30 – 14th April: *Feast of … happiness.* **House of Re, House of Osiris, House of Horus.** Prayer or divinatory time: in the afternoon.

Second Month: Payni

Day 1 – 15th April: [Damaged entry.] Prayer or divinatory time: dawn. The lack of celebration and public feast days in the calendar continues to reflect the preoccupation with working on the land. The harvest season meant that every available pair of hands were required to gather in the crops.

Day 2 – 16th April: *O heart of the gods, listen well … The crew of Re is in festivity.* [Refers to the crew of the solar barque.] Prayer or divinatory time: at noon.

Day 3 – 17th April: *The month of the followers of Re. A day is fixed in heaven and on earth as a feast.* [A time of public celebration.] Prayer or divinatory time: do not observe – not a suitable day.

Day 4 – 18th April: A feast day for Geb and Nut – possibly a celebration of fruitfulness. Prayer or divinatory time: dawn.

Tefnut: *Tfnt*

The goddess of moisture who, with her brother-consort Shu, were the first gods created by Atum. When Atum merged with Re, Tefnut and Shu became the 'eyes of Re' although the 'eye' was later identified with a number of

---

other goddesses – Hathor, Sekhmet and Wedjet. Goddess of the dew and the rain, she was worshipped in the form of a lioness, or as a woman with the head of a lioness; she was also the mother of Geb and Nut.

Prayer or Invocation:
My hunger is from the hand of Shu,
My thirst is from the hand of Tefnut,
But I live on the morning-bread
which comes in due season.
I live on that whereon Shu lives,
I eat of that whereof Tefnut eats.
[Pyramid Texts, Utterance 339]

Day 5 – 19th April: *If you see anything, it will be good on this day.* Prayer or divinatory time: dawn.

Day 6 – 20th April: *A feast day for Horus who is celebrated in his guise as protector of his father Onnophris (Osiris) on this day.* Prayer or divinatory time: do not observe – not a suitable day.

Day 7 – 21st April: *Do not go out of your house during waking time … Re is in the horizon. It is the day of the executioners of Sekhmet counting by names.* [An anniversary of the slaughtering of the human race.] Sun rises in Taurus. Prayer or divinatory time: at noon.

Day 8 – 22nd April: *Make a holiday for Re and his followers – make a good day on this day.* Prayer or divinatory time: throughout the day.

Day 9 – 23rd April: *Make incense of sweet herbs for his (Re) followers while pleasing him on this day.* Prayer or divinatory time: do not observe – not a suitable day.

Day 10 – 24th April: *Anyone born on this day will be noble.* Prayer or divinatory time: throughout the day.

Day 11 – 25th April: *Do not sail in a boat on the river. It is the day* *of catching birds and fish by the followers of Re.* [Obviously a warning not to incur the wrath of the gods.] Prayer or divinatory time: in the afternoon.

Day 12 – 26th April: *If you see anything, it will be good on this day.* Prayer or divinatory time: throughout the day.

Day 13 – 27th April: *Feast of Wedjet in Dep and her followers are also in festivity when singing and chanting take place on the day of offering the incense and all kinds of sweet herbs.* Prayer or divinatory time: throughout the day.

Day 14 – 28th April: [Obscure entry.] Prayer or divinatory time: dawn.

Day 15 – 29th April: *Do not judge yourself on this day.* Prayer or divinatory time: throughout the day.

Day 16 – 30th April: *Anyone born on this day will die a great man amongst his people.* Prayer or divinatory time: do not observe – not a suitable day.

Tauret: *'Ipy*

This was a popular goddess of childbirth. Symbolising maternity and suckling, she was represented as a pregnant hippopotamus standing upright on her back legs and holding the hieroglyphic sign of protection, *ka*, a plait of rolled papyrus. Her head and back was partly crocodile and she had lion's feet. She was especially worshipped in Thebes where, during the New Kingdom, she enjoyed great popularity among the people of the middle and working classes, who often gave her name to their children and decorated their houses with her image. As well as her role of protectress, Tauret sometimes appeared as an avenging deity brandishing a dagger.

> **Prayer or Invocation:**
> *O my mother Ipy* [Tauret]*, give me this breast of yours,*
> *That I may apply it to my mouth and suck this your white,*
> *gleaming, sweet milk. As for yonder land in which I walk,*
> *I will neither thirst not hunger in it for ever.*
> [Pyramid Texts, 381-382]

Day 17 – 1st May: *Do not go out on it. Do not do anything, or any work on this day.* Prayer or divinatory time: do not observe – not a suitable day.

Day 18 – 2nd May: *Do not eat meat on this day. It is the day of the Going Forth of Khenti (Osiris) of the god's house when he goes out to the august mountain (West).* A day of fasting and prayer. Prayer or divinatory time: at dawn and in the afternoon.

Day 19 – 3rd May: *The Ennead sails, they are much in the entire land. It is the judging of the Great Ones on this day.* Prayer or divinatory time: dawn.

Day 20 – 4th May: *Do not go out in any wind on this day.* Prayer or divinatory time: dawn.

Day 21 – 5th May: *It is the day of the living-w'rty, the children of Nut. Do not go out until daybreak.* Prayer or divinatory time: in the afternoon.

Day 22 – 6th May: *Disturbance below and uproar of the gods of the kri-shrines on this day when Shu was complaining to Re about the Great Ones of infinity. Do not go out in it.* Prayer or divinatory time: in the afternoon.

Day 23 – 7th May: *The crew rest when they see the enemy (Apophis) of their master (Re).* [Set protected Re from the attack by Apophis in order to prevent the return to Chaos.] Prayer or divinatory time: dawn.

Day 24 – 8th May: *If you see anything, it will be good on this day.* Prayer or divinatory time: dawn.

Day 25 – 9th May: *Everything and everybody is pacified. It is pleasant to the gods and Re.* Prayer or divinatory time: do not observe – not a suitable day.

Day 26 – 10th May: *The Going Forth of Neith. She treads this day in the flood in order to look for things of Sobek (her son).* Prayer or divinatory time: in the afternoon.

Sobek: *Sbk*

The crocodile-god who was especially venerated in the Fayum where the whole province came under his protection. Mentioned in the Pyramid Texts as the son of Neith, Sobek later appears in the Osirian myth where he always seems to be getting himself into trouble. Despite this, his cult came to prominence during Dynasty XII and XIII when several Pharaohs were given his name. He is depicted as a crocodile with a crown of plumes or as a man with a crocodile's head. He should be called upon for protection.

Prayer or Invocation

Now the Mountain of Bakhau (the mountains of the sunrise) whereupon this heaven supports itself, is situated in the eastern part of heaven; Sebek, the lord of Bakhau dwelleth to the east of the Mountain, and his temple is on the earth there.
[Papyrus of Nu. BM No. 10,477, sheet 8]

Day 27 – 11th May: *Do not do any work on this day.* Prayer or divinatory time: throughout the day.

Day 28 – 12th May: *Purifying things and offerings in Busiris. The gods spend the day in festivity. Act in accordance with that which happens on this day.* Prayer or divinatory time: throughout the day.

Day 29 – 13th May: *If you see anything it will be good on this day.*

Prayer or divinatory time: throughout the day.

Day 30 – 14th May: *The Going Forth of Shu with the intention of bringing back the Wedjet-eye, and appeasing Thoth on this day.* **House of Re, House of Osiris, House of Horus.** Prayer or divinatory time: in the afternoon.

Third Month: Ipt-hmt

Day 1 – 15th May: *A great feast in the southern Heaven. Every land and everybody starts jubilating. The Mistress of Heaven (Hathor) and every land are in festivity on this day.* Prayer or divinatory time: dawn.

Day 2 – 16th May: *Every god and every goddess spends the day in festivity in the sacred temple.* Prayer or divinatory time: at noon.

Day 3 – 17th May: *Anger of the divine Majesty. Do not do anything on this day.* Prayer or divinatory time: do not observe – not a suitable day.

Day 4 – 18th May: *If you see anything it will be good on this day.* Prayer or divinatory time: dawn.

Day 5 – 19th May: *Do not go out of your house. Do not proceed on a boat. Do not do any work on this day. It is the day of the departure of the goddess to the place from whence she came. The heart of the gods is sad.* Prayer or divinatory time: dawn.

Day 6 – 20th May: *Do not fight or make uproar in your house while every temple of the goddess is in like manner* [mourning]. Prayer or divinatory time: do not observe – not a suitable day.

Day 7 – 21st May: *Sailing of the gods after the Majesty of the goddess … a flame which takes place in front of everybody on this day.* [All the gods depart and a consecrated flame should be allowed to burn to guide their passage.] Prayer or divinatory time: at noon.

Day 8 – 22nd May: *Do not beat anybody. Do not strike anybody. It is the day of the massacre of the followers of the Majesty of the goddess (Sekhmet).* Sun rises in Gemini. Prayer or divinatory time: throughout the day.

Day 9 – 23rd May: *The gods are content* (i.e. have returned to their respective temples) *and they are happy because Re is at peace with the Akhet-eye. Every god is in festivity on this day.* Prayer or divinatory time: do not observe – not a suitable day.

Bes: *Bs*

A rather demonic looking creature to be identified with childbirth, children, marriage and the 'toilet of women', appearing as a grotesque dwarf with a big head, huge eyes and prominent cheeks. His chin is hairy and an enormous tongue lolls from a wide-open mouth. In carvings and paintings he is frequently shown full-face, contrary to the familiar profile of Egyptian art. Despite appearances, Bes was jovial and belligerent, fond of dancing and fighting. He originally appears to have been a local deity of the common people, but during the New Kingdom he was adopted by the middle classes who kept his statue in their houses and named their children after him. His image is often found on toilet articles and cosmetic containers. A talisman with Bes's image should be given to anyone who wishes to conceive a child (Bes was present when Isis conceived Horus – Temple of Denderah) or to keep women safe during childbirth.

Prayer or invocation:
To obtain a vision from Bes, make a drawing of the god on your left hand and before the setting sun say: *'Send the truthful seer out of the holy shrine, I beseech thee. Now, now, quickly, quickly. Come this very night.'* Envelop your hand in a strip of black cloth and lie down to sleep without speaking a word.
[BM Papyrus 122]

Day 10 – 24th May: *The gods who are in the shrine, their hearts are sad* (at having to return). Prayer or divinatory time: throughout the day.

Day 11 – 25th May: *Do not perform any ritual on this day.* Prayer or divinatory time: in the afternoon.

Day 12 – 26th May: *Holiday … reception of Re. His followers are in festivity, and everybody is in festivity.* Prayer or divinatory time: throughout the day.

Day 13 – 27th May: *The Majesty of this god proceeds sailing westwards to see the beauty of Onnophris (Osiris) on this day.* Prayer or divinatory time: throughout the day.

Day 14 – 28th May: *Do not burn anything in your house in the way of flame with any of its glow on that day of the anger of the eye of Horus the Elder.* [Traditionally all fires in the house should be extinguished for a day of fasting until sunset.] Prayer or divinatory time: dawn.

Day 15 – 29th May: *If you see anything, it will be good on this day. Horus hears your words in the presence of every god and every goddess on this day. You will see every good thing in your house.* Prayer or divinatory time: throughout the day.

Day 16 – 30th May: *It is the day of the transmitting of Ma'at to the shrine by the Majesty of Re. The gods learnt that she was much blamed for this.* [Justice is sometimes seen as blind even though it follows due process of the law.] Prayer or divinatory time: do not observe – not a suitable day.

Day 17 – 31st May: [Obscure entry.] Prayer or divinatory time: do not observe – not a suitable day.

Day 18 – 1st June: *Do not go out of your house on any road on this day. The Going Forth of Ma'at and Re in secret on this day.* Prayer or divinatory time: at dawn and in the afternoon.

Day 19 – 2nd June: *Do not do any work on this day.* Prayer or divinatory time: dawn.

Day 20 – 3rd June: *Do not go out of your house on any road on this day.* Prayer or divinatory time: dawn.

Day 21 – 4th June: *If you see anything, it will be good on this day.* Prayer or divinatory time: in the afternoon.

Day 22 – 5th June: *It is the day of Sepa in Tura coming from Heliopolis.* [Sepa was a centipede-god who was invoked in charms and spells against dangerous creatures. Carry a talisman with this image for protection.] Prayer or divinatory time: in the afternoon.

Day 23 – 6th June: *It is a day of quarrelling and reproaching.* Prayer or divinatory time: dawn.

Day 24 – 7th June: [Obscure entry.] Prayer or divinatory time: dawn.

Day 25 – 8th June: *Do not go out at mid-day, the great enemy* [Apophis] *is in the temple of Sekhmet.* Prayer or divinatory time: do not observe – not a suitable day.

Apophis: *Apep*

The chief of Re's enemies was Apophis, a huge serpent-god who lived in the waters of Nun, or in the depths of the celestial Nile, and who each day attempted to obstruct the passage of the solar barque. Eternal and persistently hostile, Apophis represents the primeval forces of Chaos. This was a serious challenge to Re and it was Set (himself a chaotic deity) who stands in the prow and vanquishes all the enemies of Re, casting them back into the Abyss. When there was a solar eclipse the Egyptians believed that Apophis had swallowed the solar barque.

Prayer or Invocation

I have driven back for him the serpent fiend Apep; I have made my road and I have passed in among you. I am, he who dwelleth among the gods, come let me pass onwards in the boat, the boat of the lord Sa. Behold, there is a flame, but the

> *fire hath been extinguished ... For I am the mighty one, the lord of divine strength, and I am the spiritual body of the lord of divine right and truth made by the goddess* [Wedjet?]. [Papyrus of Nu. BM No 10,477, sheet 16]

Day 26 – 9th June: *If you see anything, it will be good on this day.* Prayer or divinatory time: in the afternoon.

Day 27 – 10th June: *Do not go out of your house on this day.* Prayer or divinatory time: throughout the day.

Day 28 – 11th June: *Creating misery, and bringing terror into existence in conformity with the custom of what is in the year.* [At this time of the year the Nile was at its lowest and this entry deals with the misery of the land when disease and pestilence were at their most dangerous.] Prayer or divinatory time: throughout the day.

Day 29 – 12th June: *The Feast of Mut in Shera* (a lake at Karnak) *on this day. It is the day of feeding the gods and her followers.* Prayer or divinatory time: throughout the day.

Mut: Mwt

Although identified as the consort of Amun-Re, Mut still remains a vague and rather ill-defined deity, whose name merely signified 'Mother'. She is usually represented as a woman wearing a headdress in the form of a vulture – the hieroglyph for her name. As Thebes became the centre of government, Mut replaced the original consort of Amun and, with the adoption of the boy moon-god, Khonsu, she featured as the female aspect of the Theban sacred triad. She was also, at times, identified with Sekhmet and Bast and should be called upon to watch over domestic matters.

> **Prayer or Invocation**
> *Homage to thee, O Sekhmet-Bast-Re, thou mistress of the gods, thou bearer of wings, queen of the crowns of the South and of the North, only One, sovereign of her father, superior to whom the gods cannot be, thou mighty one of enchantments in the Barque*
> *of Millions of Years*
> [From Lepsius, *Todtenbuch*, Bl.78]

Day 30 – 13th June: *If you see anything, it will be good on this day.* **House of Re, House of Osiris, House of Horus.** Prayer or divinatory time: in the afternoon.

Fourth Month: Wp-rnpt

Day 1 – 14th June: *Transmitting offerings to those who are in heaven. Every god and goddess spend the day in the Feast of Onnophris (Osiris) on this day.* Prayer or divinatory time: dawn.

Day 2 – 15th June: *Truth … and all gods perform the rites as one who is in heaven (i.e. Onnophris).* A feast day dedicated to Osiris as god of the dead. Prayer or divinatory time: at noon.

Day 3 – 16th June: *Proceeding of the Majesty of this goddess to Heliopolis of Re. A feast was made on this day. Do not go out in order to do anything on this day.* [Continuing the Osirian feast days; this one is celebrated by the followers of Isis as a private affair.] Prayer or divinatory time: do not observe – not a suitable day.

Day 4 – 17th June: *It is the day of the precession of Sopdu* [ancient god of the 20th *nome* of Lower Egypt] *together with his followers, being in a state of youth and remaining so in the course of the day.* Suggests a festival of youth. Prayer or divinatory time: dawn.

Day 5 – 18th June: *Min being in Akhmin* [a sanctuary at Letopolis]. *If you see anything, it will be good on this day.* Prayer or divinatory time: dawn.

Day 6 – 19th June: *Transmitting the rejuvenated one (Onnophris/Osiris) and the hiding of the conspirators on this day. Do not do anything on this day.* Prayer or divinatory time: do not observe – not a suitable day.

Day 7 – 20th June: *The dead one goes about in the necropolis and comes on earth.* [A continuance of the Osirian mysteries.] Prayer or divinatory time: at noon.

Selket: *Sekt*

The old scorpion-goddess who was shown wearing a scorpion on her head, its tail raised to strike. The first reference to her can be dated to a stelae at Saqqara dating from Dynasty I; by the Pyramid Age she had been assigned a protective role around the throne of Pharaoh and was the patron of 'magician-medics' dealing with poisonous bites. From the New Kingdom, Selket played an important part in the ceremony of embalming and in the company of Neith, Isis and Nephthys presided over the canopic jars containing the viscera of the deceased. Like the other goddesses she also protected the dead by extending her winged arms across the inner walls of sarcophagi.

Prayer or Invocation

O my father Atum in darkness! Fetch me to your side, so that I may kindle a light for you and that I may protect you, even as Nu protected these four goddesses on the day when they protected the throne, namely Isis, Nephthys, Neith and Selket-hetu.

[Pyramid Texts. 605-606]

Day 8 – 21st June. *If you see anything, it will be good on this day.*

Summer Solstice – the ancient New Year and the rising of Sirius. Prayer or divinatory time: throughout the day.

Day 9 – 22nd June: *Anyone born on this day will have noble honour.* Prayer or divinatory time: do not observe – not a suitable day.

Day 10 – 23rd June: *It is the day of the entering of the eye of Re unto his horizon when he sees his beauty.* Sun rises in Cancer. Prayer or divinatory time: throughout the day.

Day 11 – 24th June: *Causing disturbance in the presence of the followers of Re, and repelling the confederates of Set into the eastern country.* [A continuance of the Osirian mysteries.] Prayer or divinatory time: in the afternoon.

Day 12 – 25th June: *Jubilation throughout the entire land on this day. The heart of those who are in the shrine are happy.* Prayer or divinatory time: throughout the day.

Day 13 – 26th June: *A holiday because of the defending of the son of Osiris ... back of the portal by Set.* Prayer or divinatory time: throughout the day.

Day 14 – 27th June: *Establishing her (Isis) seat and hail ...on the first occasion on this day.* Prayer or divinatory time: dawn.

Day 15 – 28th June: *Do not do anything. Do not go out on any road on this day ... Going Forth of Re on it* (i.e. this day) *to propitiate Nun* [Re's father] *... in his cavern in front of his followers and the Ennead of the mesektet-barque on this day.* Prayer or divinatory time: throughout the day.

Day 16 – 29th June: *Give water to those who are in the Underworld ... Ennead of the West. It is pleasant to your father and mother who are in the necropolis* (refers to all male and female predecessors). A day for honouring the Ancestors. Prayer or divinatory time: do not observe – not a suitable day.

Wepwawet: *Wp-w3wt*

A wolf-headed or jackal-headed god often confused with Anubis. Wepwawet is 'he who opens the way' and in pre-dynastic representations he is shown as the wolf-god being 'borne high upon his standard' and leading the warriors of his tribe into enemy territory. A former warrior-god, he was also worshipped as a god of the dead and at Abydos he was known as the Lord of the Necropolis = 'he who rules the West'. Both his name and function were usurped by the Osirian priesthood, and he was relegated to the position of a follower of Osiris. A powerful protective deity.

Prayer or Invocation:

You shall ascend to the sky, you shall become Wapwawet, your son Horus will lead you on the celestial ways; the sky is given to you, the earth is given to you, the Field of rushes is given to you in company with the two great gods who come out of On.

[Pyramid Texts]

Day 17 – 30th June: *If you see anything, it will be good on this day.* Prayer or divinatory time: do not observe – not a suitable day.

Day 18 – 1st July: *Do not go out at the time of the morning (dawn).* Prayer or divinatory time: at dawn and in the afternoon.

Day 19 – 2nd July: *Celebrate your feast of your god.* Prayer or divinatory time: dawn.

Day 20 – 3rd July: *Do not kill a 'nkyt-reptile on this day. It is the day of the cleaning and revision of the noble ones. There is silence because of it on earth in order to propitiate the Wedjet-eye on this day.* The beginning of the 'dog days' – noted from ancient times as the hottest period in the year and one of the three New Year festivals.

The day is sacred to Wedjet. Prayer or divinatory time: dawn.

Day 21 – 4th July: *If you see anything, it will be good on this day.* Prayer or divinatory time: in the afternoon.

Day 22 – 5th July: *The feast of Anubis who is on his mountain on this day. The children of Geb and Nut spend the day in festivity, which is a holiday after the good bath of the gods on this day.* Prayer or divinatory time: in the afternoon.

Day 23 – 6th July: *Do not taste bread or beer on this day. A day of fasting.* Prayer or divinatory time: dawn.

Day 24 – 7th July: *Make abt-offerings to the gods in the presence of Re. Make a holiday in your house.* Prayer or divinatory time: dawn.

Day 25 – 8th July: *The god is established in front of the crew of Re who is happy. The sun-god is currently at his highest and most powerful (i.e. dangerous).* Prayer or divinatory time: do not observe – not a suitable day.

Day 26 – 9th July: *Do not go out at midday. The gods sail with the winds … Do not go out of your house.* Prayer or divinatory time: in the afternoon.

Day 27 – 10th July: *Do not do anything on this day.* Prayer or divinatory time: throughout the day.

Day 28 – 11th July: *Feast of Min. If you see anything, it will be good on this day.* Prayer or divinatory time: throughout the day.

Day 29 – 12th July: *Holiday in the temple of Sokar, in the estate of Ptah, and those who are in this estate are in great festivity, being healthy.* Prayer or divinatory time: throughout the day.

Ptah: *Pth*

The principal god of Memphis who was protector of artisans and artists, and the inventor of the arts. Usually represented as a mummified figure, his skull encased in a tight headband, Ptah was worshipped from the earliest times, but did not come to national prominence until Dynasty XIX. By the end of the Ramesside era, he was the third most prominent god of Egypt (after Amon and Re) in terms of importance and wealth. According to his own priests, however, he was the Universal Demiurge who with his own hands fashioned the universe: the other gods being mere personifications of the different aspects of Ptah. He was frequently invoked under the names as Ptah-Tetenen, Ptah-Sokar, and even Ptah-Sokar-Osiris.

Imhotep was a vizier at the court of Djoser (Dynasty III) and the architect of Pharaoh's great funerary complex with its Step Pyramid. His talent and fame was such that he was reported to be the son of Ptah, although statues show him as an ordinary man with a scroll of papyrus laid across his knees. He became the patron of scribes and the protector of all who were occupied with the sciences and occult arts. He also became the patron of doctors and when the ordinary people began to celebrate his miraculous cures he was proclaimed 'the demi-god of medicine'.

Prayer or Invocation
Thine enemies have fallen and the god Ptah hath thrown down headlong thy foes; thou hast triumphed over them and thou hast gained great power over them.
[Papyrus of Nebseni. BM No. 9900, sheets 32-33]

Day 30 – 13th July: *Anything which comes forth on it* [i.e. this day] *in the estate of Ptah will be good. As for anything (or offering), any rite, or anybody on this day, it is good throughout the year. Sing and offer much.* Prayer or divinatory time: in the afternoon.

The Five Epagomenal or Unlucky Days
The Great Ones (wrw) are born. As for the great ones ('aw) whose forms are not mysterious, beware of them. Their occasion (or deed)

will not come ...They have proceeded ... the birth of Osiris, birth of Haeoeris [Horus the Elder], *birth of Set, birth of Isis, birth of Nephthys. As to anyone who knows the name of the five epagomenal days, he does not hunger, he does not thirst* [both conditions were feared in the underworld], *Bastet* [other translations mention Sekhmet] *does not overpower him. He will not enter into the great law court, he will not die through an enemy of the king and will not die (or, depart) through the pestilence of the year. But he will last every day (till) death arrives, whereas no illness ill take possession of him. As to him who knows them, he will be prosperous within him, his speech is important to listen to in the presence of Re.*

N.B. This point of high summer was the time of widespread disease, illness and pestilence, which was attributed to the 'arrows of Sekhmet' and so the people would wear amulets of her image for protection. These five days that divided the old year from the new, were considered unlucky since they were the birth days of the Children of Nut, who were continuously quarrelling and attempting to murder each other. The prayers were to be spoken in an attempt to pacify the divine wrath.

*Make for thyself an amulet as protection about the neck for the five epagomenal days in the name of the gods on the day and know the words to be recited over a figure of Osiris, of Horus, a figure of Set, and the female figure of Isis, the female figure of Nephthys, drawn on choice **pakt**-linen and placed around a man's neck ... As for him who knows the names of the five epagomenal days, he will not fall on any bad or evil things; he shall not hunger; he shall not thirst. Bastete shall not overpower him, fighting shall not overpower the birth of Osiris ... of this earth, the beneficent one who is lamented in the entire land in Egypt.*

Turn back, O that enemy, death and so on when descending in the five epagomenal days. If you depart, you will not come to me for you will find Osiris, the Ruler of the West, and Thoth. Behold, that is the enemy of this land, that enemy death, and so on. May their bones be smitten. May their corpses be annihilated in the five epagomenal days. May they save me from all bad things or evil things.

First Day: The Birth of Osiris – 14th July:

Words to be said on it: *'O Osiris, bull in his cavern whose name is hidden, offspring of his mother. Hail to thee, hail to thee. I am thy son … O father Osiris.'* The Name of the Day: The Pure One.

Second Day: The Birth of Horus – 15th July:

Words to be said on it: *'O Horus the Elder, might of strength, lord of fear. Will you save me from any bad and evil things, from any slaughter.'* The Name of the Day: Strong of Heart.

Third Day: The Birth of Set – 16th July:

Words to be said on it: *'O Set, son of Nut, great of strength … protection is at thy hands of thy holiness. May you save me from any bad and evil thing, from any slaughter of this year.'* The Name of the Day: Powerful of Heart.

Fourth Day: The Birth of Isis – 17th July:

Words to be said on it: *'O Isis, daughter of Nut the eldest, mistress of magic, provider of the book, mistress who appeases the Two Lands, her face is glorious. Save me from any bad and evil things.'* The Name of the Day: Making Preparation.

Fifth Day: Birth of Nephthys – 18th July:

Words to be said on it: *'O, Nephthys, daughter of Nut, sister of Set. Save me from any bad thing of this year, from any slaughter of this year, just as you have made my protection. Protect me again in the name of this year.'* The Name of the Day: The Protected Child

On the night of the fifth day:

*Black colour anointed with first class oil and fumigate with incense on a burner. They [the amulets] should be purified, loosened, and thrown into water for the father Nun and for the mother Nut after the birth of Re. Behold, make for thyself a big offering of bread, beer, oxen, fowl, carob beans, incense, **ty-sps**-wood and all kinds of dates and vegetables – being clean in front of Re-Harakhti, when he shines in the eastern horizon of heaven and when he sets in the western horizon. Behold, thou bathest in the fresh water ... of the beginning of Inundation. Paint thine eyes with green paint; take a drink of wine and anoint thyself ... this day and night in this first day of the Coming Year.*

Words to be said after dark when the Epagomenal Days are completed on the fifth day:

Hail to you! O great ones according to their names, children of a goddess who have come forth from the sacred womb, lords because of their father, goddesses because of their mother, without knowing the necropolis. Behold, may you protect me and save me. May you make me prosperous, may you make protection, may you repeat and may you protect me. I am the one who is on their list.

Throughout this predominantly Dynasty XIX version of the *Book of Days* there remain scattered references to the old stellar cult, which had still not been entirely suppressed by later religious developments. Nut, 'Lady of the Starry Heavens' still protected the ancestral dead, her star-spangled body painted on the ceilings of tombs, inside coffins and depicted in sacred writings. Set, in his own inimitable way, was still causing mayhem; while the heroic Horus (the Elder) continued to hold sway in a more subtle, earth-bound capacity.

Perhaps, however, we should bring things more up to date by using as analogy a quote from that old Hollywood classic, *Now Voyager*, with Bette Davis's concluding lines to her married lover:

'Don't let's ask for the moon. We have the stars.' An innocuous enough little romantic phrase that appears in countless books of cinematic quotations, but what does it *really* mean? On one hand (and that which probably came into the mind of the scriptwriter), why strive for the unattainable when you can settle for a reasonably acceptable alternative. On the other (and the thought which would immediately occur to the mystic) – why go for the familiar and safe when you can reach out to infinity.

And even with celebrity astrophysicist Professor Brian Cox explaining the wonders of the universe in layman's terms on television, it is still perfectly reasonable to feel that the stars are still too far away and too remote for us to contemplate for practical purposes. More often than not, our view of the heavens is obscured by cloud or, in urban areas, light pollution. The stars do not offer up their energies for examination on a regular basis like the moon (monthly) or the sun (quarterly) because this is an annual cycle – a gigantic cosmic carousel that endlessly circles Polaris, the Pole Star. The stars are pretty enough – occasionally spectacular – but they offer very little by the way of magical or devotional focus in our modern world.

Or do they?

It depends how you like your magical energies served. If you like plain, wholesome fare with few surprises; if you prefer a satisfying but unchanging recipe in your ritual, or if adventure plays no part in your quest, then the stellar path certainly isn't for you. The pursuit of stellar wisdom is, literally, as old as Time. It has its roots in all the ancient Creation myths – the primordial, indigenous forces, later classed as 'demonic' by conquerors and invaders, and those great social innovators, the incoming priest-hoods.

Stellar power reaches from the inner chthonic planes of the Earth to the outer limits of Space. The ancient Egyptians knew this – and it isn't one of those screw-ball theories, which conveniently align known facts to fit the hypothesis. In *The Magic*

Furnace, cosmologist Marcus Chown explains how *every* particle that makes up this world of ours originated in a 'magic furnace' somewhere in outer space, and is still playing out its part in a cosmic drama that began some 15 billion years ago.

> *The iron in our blood, the calcium in our bones, the oxygen in our very breath – all were forged in blistering furnaces deep inside stars, and blown into space when those stars exploded and died.*
>
> *We are connected directly to the most dramatic and awe-inspiring of cosmic events – everyone of us is stardust made flesh.*

So ... armed with a template for earthly observance, let's walk for a while in the footsteps of that early astronomer-priesthood from the Nile Valley and see where our own 'Voyager' takes us ...

Part Three

The Divine Funeral Pyre

Every man and every woman is a star.
[Liber AL Vel Legis pt 1 v.3]

And then there was only the silence of the stars, and space, and blackness and a void which was and is, and is to come, for in the end is also the beginning, and this void, being Nothing, could not be created, and this void, being Nothing could not be destroyed, and this void being Nothing, is and was and will be, and this void, being Nothing, is not, was not and will not be. It exists and does not exist forever, has existed and has not existed forever, will exist and will not exist forever; no words can describe that Nothing which is perceived and yet not perceived We are separate from that Nothing, and we judge time as a series of events. Were we One with that Nothing, there could be no Time.
[The Devil's Maze, Gerald Suster]

And what the ancient Egyptians feared most – the return to Chaos – *will* eventually come to pass. Because this planet of ours is doomed, even if the Earth doesn't suffer a cataclysmic collision with an asteroid – or our own pollution doesn't get us first. Not during the next century, nor even by the next millennium, but sometime within the far distant future, our Sun – their Sun-God – will die.

In astronomical terms, this 'yellow dwarf' star is barely middle-aged and located some 25,000 light years from the centre of the galaxy. It is held together by gravity, which is constantly trying to pull everything down into its centre: if that gravitational pull was unopposed, it would crush the sun to a mere speck in less than an hour, turning it into a black hole. The fact that such a catastrophic event has not taken place is due to another, equally powerful force within the solar interior, which counteracts gravity.

This state of cosmic equilibrium, however, will not last forever. At some stage the supply of the Sun's natural resources will run out; the core will shrink and the heat will increase; the outer layers will expand and cool – the Sun will become a 'red giant' star, 100 times brighter that it is today. Its heat will be so intense that the Earth, along with the Moon, Mercury, Venus and Mars, will be incinerated and probably totally destroyed. The outer planets Jupiter, Saturn, Uranus, Neptune and Pluto *may* survive, but only Saturn's moon, Titan, seems to have the right ingredients to sustain life despite its cold and rather noxious atmosphere.

The Egyptians, of course, had no way of knowing that this solar funeral pyre will only last for a relatively short time before the core collapses and the Sun dwindles to a very small, feeble star known as a white dwarf. Gradually it will fade to become a cold, dead globe – a black dwarf ... attended by the ghosts of its surviving family. And this is not some science fiction fantasy, it is *scientific reality* based on the observations of eminent physicists, cosmologists and astronomers, such as Fred Hoyle, Stephen Hawking, Patrick Moore and Brian Cox. Regardless of the fact that these events lie so far in the future that we need not concern ourselves with them, it does raise one very important question for us to ponder.

Where, we *must* ask ourselves, does 'God' – of the past, present or future – come into all this? Because there is no power in the Universe, either spiritual or temporal that can prevent this *natural* phenomenon from taking place. Faced with the inevitable destruction of our solar system, it is enough to force even the most blinkered of believers to question the existence and omnipotence of any Supreme Being. At first glance it would seem that astro-science has indeed finally put the last nail in God's coffin – so why would we want to revive an ancient belief in a 'Dying God'?

As Andrew Norman Wilson observed in *God's Funeral*, '*Even a fervent religious believer must, if honest, confront problems in relation to faith which were not necessarily present for those of earlier generations.*' The truth can't be resisted, of course, but the religious establishments have made martyrs out of those who challenged those early beliefs: '*Reacting furiously to the notion that the earth was not the centre of the universe, nor man the most important being on earth*'.

Nevertheless, however much we might like to deny it, evidence of God or more correctly – the 'Creator' – or what is left of Him/Her/It, *is* out there. This may not be the benevolent, divine presence of the religious textbooks, but current space exploration produces a more reasonable argument for the continuing existence of god-power from the *scientist's* point of view, rather than from the theologian's. By facing up to the inevitable destruction of our planet by natural forces, rather than confirming the *non-existence* of God, science actually proclaims long and loud that there is proof of the everlasting, regenerating life force of the ancient Egyptian 'Bornless One'. Eliphas Levi wrote:

> *Without faith, science leads to doubt; without science, faith leads to superstition Uniting them brings certainty, but in so doing they must never be confused with each other. The science of the Qabalah makes doubt, as regards religion, impossible, for it alone reconciles reason with faith by showing that universal dogma, at bottom is always and everywhere the same, though formulated differently in certain times and places, is the purest expression of the aspirations of the human mind, enlightened by a necessary faith ...*

Levi formulated much of what we recognise in today's esoteric teachings and enables us to see that in every religious symbol from the collective unconscious, the occult sciences of the Qabalah, ritual and ceremonial magic, and the *Hermetica* of Hermes Trismegistus (the 'Thrice Great Thoth'), brings out the true and the false, separating the realities and the counterfeit to provide us with a religion for the future.

> *The Qabalah can be seen as the mathematics of human thought; the algebra of faith as it were; solving all problems of the soul as equations, by isolating the unknowns. Magic is the science of the magi, utilising the knowledge of secret and particular laws of nature that produce and conceal hidden forces. Hermetica is the science of nature hidden in the hieroglyphics and symbols of the ancient world ...*

Exercise: Creating an Altar/Shrine

Trying to meditate, follow psychic exercises, or conduct magical workings requires privacy and, where possible, no interference from extraneous noises. Most traditions teach how to create our own special areas wherever we happen to be, so we do not need a specific place to site an altar or shrine. It is, however, more convenient if we are able to set aside somewhere in our home to keep magical/mystical objects, or to use a sacred space for reflection and ritual.

- Wherever you choose, remember that the Egyptian Mystery Tradition, unlike many northern European traditions, does not demand that you cut yourself off completely from the sunlight. Even at midday, the rays from the desert sun would never reach the inner sanctum of the temple, despite the clever use of architectural apertures to shed diffused light into the building.
- In many traditions, the north is known as the 'place of power'. For the Egyptians, the source of solar

power/strength/rebirth was directed towards the east (air); the north represents elemental earth and the south elemental fire. The west (water) represents the door to Otherworld/astral. Try to establish your altar/shrine centrally so that you can face the direction from which you wish to draw energy.

- The altar/shrine itself can consist of anything that provides a flat surface for holding an assortment of objects. What *is* essential, is that our shrine has an altar-image of the deity with whom we identify. For the Egyptians, who relied strongly on sympathetic magic, the shrine or temple statue *was* the god, and so the priest was either dealing with the deity direct, or became the god himself.

The most common objects found in any sacred area are the sacred lamps. There are small lotus-design opaque glass candle-holders available, which take night-lights and give the appearance of alabaster – which can also be used to mark the quarters. Another essential piece of equipment is a special altar lamp, since this will often be the focal point of your devotion/meditation.

In the Beginning

And as we have seen, from the earliest development of human myth, the stars have been symbolic of the Old Gods of that ancient world. We are talking, of course, about those powerful Creation deities, the majority of whom were later made redundant by incoming priesthoods. Apart from recording the annual changes in the position of the stars, however, early man would have quickly realised that those distant pinpoints of light, had no dramatic or immediate effect on his life on Earth, in the same way as the Sun or Moon. Nevertheless, the remote stars were universally viewed as being the dwelling place of the Mighty Dead, or even a form of manifestation of individual deities.

From the historical and religious perspective, variations on the theme of the Creation of the World, its Destruction, and the subsequent origins of mankind, generally fall into two easily identifiable categories: those concerned with the origin of things, and those connected to periodic ceremonies which were performed to ensure the continuity and wellbeing of the people. The earliest recorded cosmogonies were an amalgam of thought and imagery that reflected the religious needs of emerging civilisation, and the continuing influence of the primitive folklore of its ancestral beliefs.

We know that the earliest examples of Creation myths are those of Mesopotamia and Egypt, which chronicle the world emerging from the chaotic waters to bring in what is often described as a 'Golden Age' at the dawn of time. The Egyptians viewed this as *zep tepi*, the 'First Time', starting with Atum emerging from the waters of Nun and beginning the work of Creation on the primeval hill, known as the Mound. These myths are cosmogonies in the literal sense, since they refer to the beginning of the *cosmos* (i.e. the known world of the time) and the diverse relationships of the gods, but contain little reference to the creation of mankind itself. Although Khnum fashioned humans from clay on his potter's wheel, the Egyptians, with their early beliefs reflecting a return to the stars after death, were obviously less pre-occupied with earthly human creativity than the neighbouring Mesopotamians and Hebrews.

By contrast, the Mesopotamians focused more on the beginning of civilisation and mankind, than on the origins of the cosmos, with one legend describing Enki creating humans out of clay to act as servants of the gods. The most famous of the Creation myths, however, is the Babylonian *Enuma elish* that reflected the Egyptian concept of exalting the gods. Much later Hebrew Creation myths, detailed in the first three chapters of the *Book of Genesis*, exercised a profound influence upon later

Western thought and culture. This priestly tradition plagiarised the idea of primordial waters from earlier cosmogonies but did not have the world being created out of Nothing, as later theologians maintained: a watery chaos existed *before* the Hebrew god's act of Creation. Early Yahwist tradition concentrated on the creation of mankind (drawing on earlier Egyptian and Mesopotamian myths), whereby the later Hebrew god created the first man (Adam) out of the earth, and woman (Lilith) from the primordial slime.

Parallel concepts of identifying the gods with the stars and the observation of the constellations can also be traced to the Babylonian Creation myth, the *Enuma elish*, where Marduk *'created stations for the great gods, fixing their astral likeness as constellations. He determined the year by designing the zones* [zodiac]: *he set up three constellations for the 12 months'* [*Man, Myth & Magic*]. Mesopotamians regarded the movement of the stars and planets as the 'writing of heaven' and from it evolved the development of astrology as a means of divination. The casting of horoscopes fuelled the idea that human destiny was controlled by the stars; an idea that much later spread rapidly throughout the Graeco-Roman world.

For the Egyptians, however, those stars 'which grow not weary' have *always* had immense significance in their culture. The circumpolar stars that never set in the west, were identified as 'the Imperishable Ones' and, according to the Pyramid Texts, the kings were raised up to heaven to join their company on death, to be free from change or decay. As we have seen from previous chapters, this association of the stars with the revered dead has a longstanding tradition in Egypt, which is revealed on the ceilings of the many tombs that were painted with stars, or the image of the arched sky-goddess depicted on the lids of the coffins and sarcophagi.

The hieroglyph of the five-pointed star represented the celestial 'world beyond the tomb' while the five-pointed star in a circle [an image so familiar in modern paganism] was the symbol for the place in the sky where the sun and the stars re-appeared after having been invisible, according to the Pyramid Texts. In later times it came to represent Otherworld – celestial or subterranean, i.e. the *dwat* and Amenti.

The ancients also identified their gods and goddesses with specific stars and planets. To the Egyptians, the constellation Ursa Major suggested a ritual object used ceremonially in 'the Opening of the Mouth' as part of the Osirian funerary rites. It also represented the thigh of a sacrificial animal and therefore connected to Set; while some sources have linked the constellation of Draco with the 'Mother of Set', Nut. The distinctive constellation of Orion was first attributed to Sah, and later as 'the glorious soul of Osiris', holding a deep significance in Egyptian belief because of their continuing traditional connection between the stars and the dead.

Sothis (or Sirius), the 'Dog Star' was originally identified with Sopdet, and later Isis, but more importantly, it was associated the annual flooding of the Nile. The calendar, having been based on the date of the heliacal rising of Sothis near the sun at the Summer Solstice, coincided with the commencement of the Inundation. Ancient texts also assign other planets to the various gods – Jupiter with Horus 'who limits the two lands'; Mars with Horus of the Horizon; Mercury with Sebegu (a god associated with Set); Saturn with Horus 'bull of the sky'; and Venus ('the one who crosses' or 'god of the morning') with Re or Osiris.

Although the Egyptians had both civic and astronomical calendars, it is almost impossible to fix precise dates in the chronology of the history of the Nile Valley. That said, as Raymond A. Wells points out in *Astronomy Before the Telescope*, more than six millennia ago, man's primal gleanings from the night sky crystallised into a variety of myths that formed the basis of Egyptian religion. *'Since its principal deities were heavenly bodies, the priesthood mastered the ability to predict the time and place of their gods' appearances ...* **Many of these achievements were already in place before the unification of Upper (Nile Valley) and Lower (Delta) Egypt.'** [Author's emphasis. MD]

During the Old Kingdom, the belief that mortals were reborn among the circumpolar stars led to the continued depiction of stars on the ceiling of the tombs as an important part of the funerary art of the day. As Wells also makes a point of explaining: *'The mythology of the sky goddess Nut giving birth to Re, catalysed both time-keeping and calendar development, endowed the concept of divine royalty, and instituted the matrilineal inheritance of the throne.'* One of the utterances from the Pyramid Texts exhorts the sky goddess, Nut, to spread her protective body over the deceased so that he might ascend to join those already placed among the Imperishable Stars. The funerary rites with their attendant deities were regarded as microcosms of the universe itself, and just as Nut spread her star-spangled body over the earth, so she stretched herself over the dead. Even when the stellar beliefs of early Egypt were merged into the later solar and lunar cults of Atum-Re and Osiris, the practice of stellar decoration continued throughout the rest of the empire's history.

The Greeks accredited the Egyptians with recognising the existence of the movement of the stars, and the earliest detailed records are the 'diagonal calendars' or star-clocks, also painted on the wooden coffin lids of the early Middle Kingdom. These calendars consisted of 36 columns, listing 36 groups of stars referred to as 'decans' into which the night sky was divided. Each decan rose above the horizon at dawn for a period of ten days every year. This system, however, was also flawed, since it did not take into account the fact that the Egyptian year was always around six hours short, adding up to a difference of 10 days every 40 years. Because of this 'slippage' it is doubtful whether these Middle Kingdom star-clocks were ever considered to be a practical measure of time, nevertheless this was another integral ingredient of tomb decoration, if only paying symbolic lip-service to the Old Ways.

The astronomical knowledge of the early priests and architects is further confirmed by examples of the ceremony of *pedj shes* ('stretching the cord'), first recorded on a granite block during the reign of the Dynasty II ruler, Khasekhemwy (c2686BC). This method was reliant on the sighting of Ursa Major and Orion, using 'an instrument of knowing' (*merkhet*), which functioned on the same principle as the astrolabe, and a sighting tool (*bay*) constructed from a central rib of a palm leaf. Although many later texts described the *pedj shes*, it has been suggested that this, like all the old stellar religion's symbolism, had become mere ceremony and that in practice the temples were simply aligned in relation to the river, the *British Museum Dictionary of Ancient Egypt* tells us.

Exercise: Keep it Secret, Keep it Safe

It may not be possible to leave magical/mystical objects on view for fear of interference that will lessen or even destroy their psychic potency. There are, however, ways of getting around this problem. Remember the old adage of 'hide in plain sight'? If there is no convenient opportunity to make a permanent shrine in your home, do not despair, occultists have always made the best of their situations, and many only set up a sacred area when they are about to perform a ritual.

- Use a lockable display cabinet or cupboard to which only you have the key; when you need to meditate, etc., all you need to do is open the doors – although it might not be a good idea to light incense or candles *inside* the cupboard.
- Use a large box or chest, which can remain locked when not in use, to house magical equipment. A large workman's tool chest from a DIY store can be used for this purpose.
- Someone who was forced to keep her magical interests *very* secret used a large-leafed scrapbook in which she created

evocative scenes using collages of pictures cut from magazines. Result – instant focus at the turn of a page.

- An unobtrusive object by the bed also acts as a protector while we sleep.

Finally, and this is an excellent exercise to try if you are unable to set up a physical shrine or altar: create such an area within your imagination. This will function perfectly well on a magical level since all spells require your imagination in order to work. This is where a simple image, piece of jewellery, or amulet comes in handy, or if you need to carry out an impromptu working on the physical level.

The Pyramid Age

As recent popular histories have revealed, the Great Pyramid was almost certainly aligned with the stars and, along with the Sphinx, are literally 'oriented' (that is, they faced due east, the direction of sunrise at the equinoxes. The shafts in the King's and Queen's Chambers in the Great Pyramid demonstrate the stellar alignments of all four shafts in the epoch of 2500BC. The northern shaft in the Queen's Chamber is angled at 39 degrees and was aimed at Kochab (Beta Ursa Minor) in the constellation of Ursa Minor. The southern shaft angled at 39 degrees 30, was directed at Sirius in the constellation of Alpha Canis Major.

In the King's Chamber, the northern shaft, angled at 32 degrees 28, was directed at the ancient Pole Star, Thuban (Alpha Draconis) in the constellation of Draco. The southern shaft, angled at 45 degrees 14, focused on Al Nitak (Zeta Orionis), the brightest and lowest of the three stars in Orion's Belt. In their book, *The Orion Mystery*, Bauval and Hancock also demonstrate that the three stars in Orion's Belt might possibly correspond to the faulty diagonal line of the Great Pyramid (of Cheops) and the second Pyramid (of Chephren), with the third Pyramid (of Mycerinus) being off-set slightly to the east. *'The first two stars*

(Al Nitak and Al Nilam) *are in direct alignment, like the first and second Pyramids, and the third star* (Mintaka) *lies off-set somewhat to the east of the axis formed by the other two.'*

The Egyptian word for pyramid (*mer*) means 'place of ascent' or more correctly 'what goes [straight] up from the *us*' (a word of uncertain meaning), the suggested ascending being done by the dead Pharaoh as he was transported into the sky to spend eternity among the Imperishable Ones. The development of the pyramids, of which there are some 80 (although many are now reduced to piles of rubble), began after 3000BC and culminated in the colossal structures known as the Giza Group that were built between 2600-2500BC. After that, pyramid building went into decline, with ever-smaller structures being built.

Some of the later (and grossly inferior) pyramids are nevertheless significant in that they contain fine examples of the Pyramid Texts: the set of magic spells dating from prehistoric times, giving a safe passage to the Pharaoh into the sky. Many of the texts describe the journey of the king to the Otherworld, situated in the sky beyond the eastern horizon, and his activities upon arrival. Judging from the formation of the texts, it is significant that the king could not rely on any divine assistance from the gods during his journey but, armed with the magical power of the texts, he might overcome the hazards of his final trials before joining the Sun-god in his daily travels across the sky.

According to Professor I E S Edwards (*The Pyramids of Egypt*) for most part, the Pyramid Texts were certainly *not* inventions of Dynasties V and VI, but had originated in much earlier times. *'It is hardly surprising, therefore, that they sometimes contain allusions to conditions which no longer prevailed at the time of Unas and his successors.'* A relic of an even more ancient culture is contained in a passage (Spells 273-4) that describes the dead king as a hunter who catches and devours the gods so that he may appropriate their qualities unto himself. When compiling the texts during Dynasty V, the priesthood used older religious and funerary spells, supplementing them with incantations of a later date to meet contemporary needs.

In his academic paper, 'The King and the Star-Religion in the Pyramid Texts', R O Faulkner, acknowledged expert on ancient Egyptian writing, pointed out that the funerary art forms from the Middle Kingdom onwards were contemporary interpretations of *'a very ancient stratum of stellar religion, in which the stars were regarded as gods, or as the souls of the blessed dead'*. Here we learn that there was a distinction between the sky (*pt*) as a natural element of daily life, and the 'Starry Sky' (*shdw*) where the King goes on death, as in *'May you* [the King] *go to those northern gods the circumpolar stars ...'*

In his conclusion, Faulkner's analysis of the Pyramid Texts shows two distinct strata. One, being concerned with the circumpolar stars and the northern sky, which appears as the abode of the gods and the illustrious royal dead, to which the King ascends on his journey from this world. The other is connected with the constellation of Orion and Sothis, the Morning Star and the Lone Star, with only three mentions of the moon.

It is noticeable that these two strata overlap very little and, while one deals with the ultimate abode of the dead King in the northern sky, the other, the Lone Star apart, appears to be concerned with those celestial bodies which mark the passage of time in the course of the year ... Orion is either a companion of the King, and is joined by him, making with Sothis a celestial trio; the King may thus be thought of as sharing in the responsibility for regulating times and seasons.

The association of the Morning Star with the dead King and the entourage of Re often displays conflicting details, but without doubt it refers to Phosphorus-Venus as seen at dawn. The Lone Star is the King himself, and Faulkner suggests this is Hesperus-Venus as seen just after sunset, since the Lone Star is spoken of as 'ascending from the eastern sky' and as a 'hawk seen in the evening traversing the sky'. As fragmented as these details are, it shows that the power of this archaic stellar-cult was still making itself felt, well into the Pyramid Age and beyond.

But why, we may ask ourselves, did the Egyptians choose those pyramidal shaped structures in the first place, and why the continuous references to the stars when everyone knows that the chief Egyptian god was the solar deity Atum-Re?

In *Rogue Asteroids and Doomsday Comets*, research astronomer at the Anglo-Australian Observatory, Duncan Steel, offered some further points to ponder which may alter the way we view the astronomer-priesthood of the Nile Valley. Apparently our Earth moves through a permanent cloud called *zodiacal dust*. This name gets its name because it gives rise to the *zodiacal light*, a diffuse glow in a huge triangular shape that follows the path of the sun across the sky. This natural phenomenon is best seen an hour or two after sunset or before dawn, in near-tropical latitudes.

Few people are fortunate enough to observe zodiacal light today because it is necessary to be well away from any light pollution to be able to distinguish it, but it was known to the ancient people of the Middle East as the 'false dawn' because it stretched far above the horizon, more than half way to the zenith. From an especially dark viewing site, it may even be possible to perceive a dim band reaching right across the sky along the ecliptic. *'This zodiacal band is due to dust that is exterior to the terrestrial orbit, while the zodiacal light proper (the pyramid in the sky) is due pre-dominantly to sunlight scattered from dust interior to our orbit.'*

Steel goes on to explain that when a large comet breaks up, an enormous amount of zodiacal dust will occur, making the zodiacal cloud and band much brighter than they appear today. *'In fact,'* he writes, *'they would look like the river that Re navigates his boat along each day, followed also at night by the newly bright comets in low-inclination orbits. At each end of the 'river' lies the triangular profile of the main zodiacal light, a pyramidal shape.'* Could this be the 'ladder' the dead King needed to ascend in order to climb his stairway to heaven?

Early written accounts of the sky speak of a phenomenon that historians *'primed by astronomers who assumed in error that what was seen then was the same as what we see now, have interpreted as being the Milky Way'*. The same records state that this 'Milky Way' was the path formerly taken by the Sun (that is, ecliptic) and that it was produced by comets. *'This is obviously* not *the Milky Way that we see now: what was being described was a super-intense zodiacal light and band.'*

Another important point is how the zodiacal light and band would appear as sunrise approached. According to Steel, the zodiacal band would come closer to being perpendicular to the horizon as the middle of the night passes and, as the pyramid of light begins to peek above the horizon hours before daybreak, it is still tilted far over. As time progresses, it straightens more and more, never quite reaching the perpendicular position. Then the whole sky would begin to brighten and redden in the northeast, until eventually the Sun would rise from the middle of the zodiacal cloud. This would have created a very strong impression on the Egyptian people, especially if that zodiacal light was much brighter 5,000 years ago than it is now.

Before *'inviting anthropologists and antiquarians to have their paroxysms and apoplectic attacks'*, Steel presses home his theory that the ancient Egyptians would also have seen a much more pronounced 'brightness enhancement' due to the huge amount of dust released at that period into the Taurid stream. *'Is there anything to link the ancient Egyptians with such calamitous events occurring in the sky?'* he asks. *'Well, one example, is from the Egyptian hieroglyphics; the symbols for thunder and meteorite are the same, and contain a star. It seems that the Egyptians associated meteors and meteorites with explosions above their heads, which is certainly indicative of a tumult taking place in the sky of a type different to our experiences today.'*

Finally, as even more food for thought, and one that will probably also upset the Atlanteans, he supports this theory by asking where else in the world were pyramids built? Those that immediately spring to our minds are Mexico (the Mayan pyramids are known to have had astronomical/calendrical motivations), East Asia, and the Babylonian and Assyrian ziggurats. And what these all have in common is their *latitude* – all near the Tropic of Cancer. *'From tropical latitudes the zodiacal light is most impressive and therefore we might anticipate finding buildings there that mimic its shape.'*

Nevertheless, although the stars played an integral part in Egyptian religion, we know that they did not adopt the astrological belief that the stars controlled human destiny until the Hellenistic period (330-30BC). Absorbing these later influences from Mesopotamian astral beliefs and Chaldean astrologers they quickly made up for lost time and immersed themselves in this new 'science'. According to S G F Brandon (in *Man, Myth & Magic*) these 'new age' Egyptians adopted the idea with enthusiasm and developed a form of astral religion or mystical philosophy that became widely influential in the world of Graeco-Roman culture. *'Star charts were elaborated, comprising 56 deities who presided over the various time units of the year ... the importance of horoscopes became so great that they were inscribed on the roofs of* [later] *tombs.'*

Despite the contemporary popularity of astrology, for thousands of years the human race lived without these illusions simply because it was inconceivable that the stars could have even the remotest link with *everyday* existence. Those sparkling beads of light were too remote from the familiar world of direct experience: they were the home of the gods. Divination, however, always played an important role in ancient times and those 'new age' astrologers often held prominent places within the higher echelons of society. As with all cultures, however, it was superstition that continued to keep the common people in check under the watchful eye of the priesthood.

The first known book of astrological lore with its pseudo-scientific overtones, *Tetrabiblos*, was written by Ptolemy around the 2nd century AD, in which he attributes all manner of influences to the planets in much the same way that modern astrology is consulted today. This star-lore was elaborated even further into the complex doctrine known as the *Corpus Hermetucum* (which also still exists), being attributed to Hermes Trismegistus, the Egyptian god Thoth/Tahuti himself, although it is now accepted that they were compiled by an unknown Christian scholar.

By the first century AD, the Babylonion zodiac at Dendera had been adopted and accepted as the 'Egyptian zodiac'. With the onset of Christianity, we can see why the myth was swiftly created that Jesus had delivered mankind from the domination of the stars ... and there is a great deal of reference to this in the writings of St Paul. Nevertheless, astrology survived through the Middle Ages and beyond to re-emerge as one of the more profitable aspects of the new New Ageism.

Exercise: Lucid Dreaming

For this exercise you will need to acquire a small pyramid to act as a focus for meditation. This can be anything from a small silver charm, or a miniature reconstituted stone paperweight ... it can be any size as long as it is free-standing, and can be held in the palm of the hand.

- Lucid dreaming is a half-waking, half-dream state where the practitioner is fully conscious and aware of his/her surroundings, but still able to receive images or impressions from the astral. The astral image is often superimposed over the immediate surroundings like the double-exposure on a photograph.

- This technique is highly useful when looking for the

answer to a problem, and is best performed in the daytime, preferably on a sunny day. Sit in a comfortable chair, or on the floor in a patch of sunlight where it comes through a window. Place your pyramid next to a lighted candle, or hold it cradled loosely in the left hand.

- Place the candle in the sunlit area and stare into the flame, which will become almost invisible in the sunshine. Think of the problem that needs resolving and as you stare at the flame, you will feel yourself slipping into a light semi-hypnotic state. At the same time you will be fully conscious of what's going on around you; the pyramid acting as an 'earthing' device.

In this psychic 'slip-stream, it would be very surprising if the appropriate messages don't come filtering through. Contemplate the results in a relaxed frame of mind with a hot drink and a sweet biscuit to remove any psychic dross from hanging about.

Written in the Stars

But let's turn the clock back to the beginning ... to those archetypal figures known as the 'Imperishable Ones' who personified the ever-visible circumpolar stars in the north of the sky. As we have discovered, archaeological evidence shows that for the predynastic Egyptians (5500-3200BC), the religion of the time was stellar-based. It was from this point in history that the observations made by those early people of the Nile Valley noted the northern-most and southern-most turning points of the Sun at the solstices from which almost all of Egyptian astronomy and religion were ultimately derived.

In other words, even from the earliest period of history, the beliefs of the Egyptians *were* based on scientific observation, not primitive superstition, and as such, we can still identify with them today. *All* esoteric language is shot through with allegory and metaphor, sigils and correspondences, hieroglyphics and symbolism – and the Egyptian Mysteries are no exception – but we should not allow ourselves to forget that this astronomer-priesthood were at the scientific cutting-edge of their time. In fact, if we refer back to the quote from Carl Jung in Part One relating to the collective unconscious ...

In a pristine society such as Egypt's it should be possible to see it at work in a way quite different from the experience of later cultures. The collective unconscious is the fountain from which the archetypes flow. The collective unconscious in Egypt would, in this view, be especially powerful and as pristine a phenomenon as the society itself.

... we see how the thread of scientific observation, influencing the magical symbology of religious and ritual magic archetypes, has endured for something like 6,000 years!

Here we have Nut, the celestial mother, portrayed as a naked female stretched across the sky with the sun shown entering her mouth, passing through her star-speckled body, and emerging from her birth canal. The faint outer arm of the Milky Way was perceived as the goddess, whose legs are formed by a bifurcation at the cross-shape of the constellation Cygnus with its principal star Deneb marking the birth canal exit; while the face is situated in the 'swirling star clouds' in the vicinity of Gemini. About 45 minutes after sunset at the Vernal Equinox, the head of Nut can be seen passing below the horizon face upwards with her mouth open at (or very close to) the position where the sun had set. Farfetched ideas? Not at all ...

Ronald Wells, contributor to the academic paper 'Astronomy in Egypt' (*Astronomy Before the Telescope*) describes the final act of the drama as occurring 272 days later on the morning of the Winter Solstice, when the lower half the goddess is visible above the horizon for only a few hours. As the rosy-hued dawn spreads across the sky, Deneb intersects the horizon at exactly the spot where the sun rises ... a phenomena only valid at the Winter Solstice, since the point of sunrise is further north on other dates. In other words, Re enters Nut at sunset on the Spring Equinox (at which time the goddess presumably conceives) and nine months later, she gives birth to him on the Winter Solstice. *'Perhaps the most remarkable aspect of these events, a convincing tie to actual astronomical observations, is that the number of days between the spring equinox and the winter solstice is the period of human gestation!'* he concludes. *'The implied method of conception is oral, but that is not an unusual belief in a primitive society.'*

By the Old Kingdom (2686-2181BC) this stellar belief was confirmed by texts outlining the ruler's role in the Afterlife; here Pharaoh, represented by the Lone Star, devolves into the guide for the wise Imperishable Ones (the *ikhemu-sek*, literally 'the ones not knowing destruction') by the order of Atum. From those Old Kingdom texts we find one of the keys to the ancient stellar Mysteries. Here, it is revealed that the divinity of Pharaoh is not diminished by physical death; it is also recorded that Egypt will descend back into the chaotic waters of Nun should he be prevented from becoming one with the star-gods in the Afterlife. As if to emphasise this continuing or ancestral divinity, the deceased Pharaoh is referred to by the title 'god older than the oldest' – in true Mystery Tradition meaning that he becomes One with the Creator until the Divine King is reborn in his successor.

In historical terms, this can be seen as an attempt to amalgamate firmly entrenched stellar beliefs with the now dominant solar theology, and throughout remaining Egyptian history the Sun-god travels across the celestial ocean with the Imperishable Ones (including Pharaoh) in his barque. By the New Kingdom (1567-1085BC) the Imperishable Ones are merely 12 oar-carrying gods who are described as coming out of the primeval waters with Re. The rapid growth of the Osirian death-cult, however, saw them relegated to being merely referred to 'the followers of Osiris'.

The subsequent Hellenisation of Egyptian culture introduced a much more elaborate conceptualisation of the night sky as it developed and expanded the concept of the 'decans' – the 36 star-gods (constellations) moving by barque across the firmament in 10-day cycles. Tomb paintings depicting the star-gods travelling across the ceiling reveal the images of the constellations, but present-day archaeologists and astronomers remain uncertain about identifying the Egyptian star groupings by any equivalent 'modern' names. The only major constellations that can be identified with any certainty are Orion with Sothis (Sirius), and Ursa Major (The Great Bear, or Plough) known as 'the four spirits of the north' who comprise the 'foreleg of Set'. Had we retained the Egyptian symbols for the constellations, we would today have a crocodile and the hippopotamus amongst the signs of the zodiac. Virginia Lee Davis writing in *Archaeoastronomy* admits that the identification of ancient Egyptian constellations is a tantalising field of study.

> *On the one hand there is the almost embarrassing abundance of constellation pictures produced in the course of more than two millennia and beautifully preserved right down to the present day. On the other hand there is an almost complete dearth of reliable data on which to base attempts at identifying the pictured constellations. Presumably the Egyptians felt no lack, each one having learned the constellations from the cradle up by the simple expedient of having them pointed out to him.*

As an archaeologist, Davis is willing to trawl through the vast quantities of religious and mythological material in the hope of finding a few vague clues, but is no doubt hampered by an academic reluctance that prevents the cross-pollination of ideas between the applications of science, history, theology, philosophy and magic. The old Egyptian stellar-cult continued to form the basis of the ancient Mysteries, but just as every

Egyptian child could have identified the stars themselves, only the higher astronomer-priesthood would have known the religio-magical significance of each of the constellations. Neither child nor priest, however, would have required them to be written in stone on the walls of the funerary monuments in order to understand their symbolism, but even committed Egyptologists seem to demonstrate a marked reluctance to credit these people with even a fundamental grasp of astrophysics.

Davis also cites the occasional reference in the Pyramid Texts of 'two skies', with frequent mention of a 'northern sky' and a 'southern sky' – but, she says, there is no mention of an eastern or western sky. *'There is also mention of 'two horizons' and frequent mention of 'eastern horizon' and 'western horizon'* (meaning the places of sunrise and sunset) *but no mention of northern horizon or southern horizon.'* When dealing with mystical, religious and philosophical matters it is unwise to take the written word literally, since esoteric texts were never intended for the eyes or understanding of the layman.

We know that the Egyptians built the pyramids and aligned them with the stars ... they were obviously descended from generations of star-gazers, so why shouldn't they be aware of the movement of certain stars between the northern and southern hemispheres, just as modern astronomers are today. They may not have been able to explain the phenomena, but that does not mean they weren't aware of it, just as they were aware of the shifting position of the Milky Way in the heavens throughout the changing months of the year. The dual-headed god, Aker, was the guardian of the entrance and exit of the underworld; with one head facing east and the other west: and only places of mystical/magical significance would have been included in the Pyramid Texts. Sir Norman Lockyer, one of the great Victorian astronomers, recorded his observations of this ancient science in *The Dawn of Astronomy*, first published in 1894.

The various apparent movements of the heavenly bodies which are produced by the rotation and the revolution of the earth, and the effects of precession, were familiar to the ancient Egyptians, however ignorant they may have been of their causes; they carefully studied what they saw, and attempted to put their knowledge together in the most convenient fashion, associating it with their strange imaginings and their system of worship.

And if you remember, in her Introduction to Christian Jacq's earlier edition of *Egyptian Magic*, Rosalie David stated that for the Egyptians, *magic was regarded as an exact science in its highest form*, its secrets revealed only to the highest orders of priesthood. This area of magic was used as a system of defence, and played an important role in the service of the State, protecting the country and its king. In reality, however, by the end of the Old Kingdom, Egypt's 'Golden Age' was over as the land was plunged into anarchy and chaos as revolution overturned the old established order.

From pre-dynastic times, right up until the collapse of the Old Kingdom, the king, was considered personally responsible for the wellbeing and stability of the Land and its people. He was the intermediary between gods and men, and his role in life was to ensure this equilibrium was maintained via the channels of daily prayers and offerings at the temple. If the king did not fulfil his daily obligations to the gods on behalf of his people, then there *was* the danger of plunging everything back into Chaos and darkness from which it had originally sprung. We also know from historical evidence that around the end of the Old Kingdom, this system did, in fact, break down.

Archaeologists argue over whether the cause for such social catastrophe was due to several long years of famine, or civil unrest against the established system of a failing monarchy, but recent excavations suggest that it could have been a combination of both. During work at the temple site of Mendes, in Lower

Egypt, during 1999-2000, Professor Donald B Redford's team discovered under the Dynasty XVIII foundations, human remains dating to the second half of Dynasty VI.

> *Found sprawled where they had fallen … were the remains, in whole or in part, of 20 human individuals of all ages and sexes. Some lay in piles: an old woman over an old man who in turn lay over a child; others lay singly: two adult males beside a slain pig. A young teen had fallen … clutching a rodent of all things! Not a few had been dismembered as they lay. Following the slaughter (for such it surely was) came the destruction: parts of the mud-brick structure, which can only be the temple itself, had been demolished, and the debris allowed to fall on the bodies. Then someone had set fire to some combustibles and a conflagration had ensured, sending more fired and reddened brick cascading over the area …'*
>
> [*The Akhenaten Temple Project Newsletter*, ed. Susan Redford]

The excavation revealed that a number of people had perished in the destruction – the team having recovered the remains of 20 – with many sprawled in groups, attempting to flee the temple, and in the aftermath no one returned to retrieve the corpses for burial. At other sites dating from the same period (Dynasty VI), excavations have uncovered mass graves, which indicate that people died, or were killed in large enough numbers that traditional burial was impossible. Whatever happened at the end of Dynasty VI, the Old Order that had lasted for so long was finally shattered by social revolution. This affected the whole governing system as the different classes threw off their burden of obligation and resorted to violence, bringing about a revolutionary upheaval that destroyed the ancient customs and traditional religious practice forever. Archaeological evidence indicates that the fury of the mob spared neither temples nor royal monuments; even the archives of government buildings, and tombs were not respected.

From the cemeteries of the great, blocks of stone were removed and used for the tombs of little men. As a result a whole world was rent asunder ... For more than a century, social and religious values declined until the country reverted to a primitive state not seen in the Nile Valley since pre-dynastic times. Those remnants of the old traditions, which remained after the radical upheaval, were combined and modified to form a new mode of social existence in the new order, but the soul of ancient Egypt never recovered completely from the shock of this decisive change.
[*Egypt*, K Lange and M Hirmer]

This social upheaval, which destroyed the elitism of the Old Kingdom, needed to be brought back under control, and religion for the masses has always proved to have a uniting or calming effect on civic unrest. While the Sun-god remained the deity of the ruling family, the Theban priesthood had cornered the market with their own particular brand of evangelism; the propaganda machine geared into action, introducing the Cult of Osiris, which subsequent Greek historians faithfully recorded for posterity as if nothing else had ever existed.

What history *doesn't* tell us is what happened to the priesthood of the old stellar-cult following this revolutionary uprising? *If* the discoveries at the Temple of the Divine Cult of *Ba-neb-djed* ('Ram-Lord of Djedet') at Mendes are anything to go by, it is possible that many of the stellar-priesthood were butchered within the confines of their own temples. *If* the people believed the gods had deserted them, then someone would need to be held to account – and who more appropriate that the priests who had failed to serve them. *If* such massacres took place, then some of the priests (along with their families) would have been forced to flee the country, taking their vast stores of magico-religious knowledge with them.

Logic and historical precedence tells us that isolated pockets of Egyptian 'Magi' would have survived, both inside and outside

Egypt since it is impossible, either by legislation or genocide, to wipe a faith out of existence. There are subtle hints that the Mysteries still played an important part in Egyptian royal worship right up until Dynasty XIX, but this would have been a private affair, hidden from the scrutiny of the public and the lower echelons of the priesthood. Nevertheless, oral traditions can be incredibly tenacious, especially those that have been subjected to local variations and, in this manner, quite a considerable amount of stellar wisdom would have spread around the Mediterranean as the exiles moved further away from their native land – just as much later material would survive in the form of *Hermetic* texts.

To summarise: from a very early stage in their long history, the Egyptians were familiar with certain identifiable astronomical phenomena. As Christian Jacq observes in *Egyptian Magic: 'We find ourselves faced with a sacred science which needs specialists trained for many years to grasp the most secret forces of the Universe ...'*

Consider for a moment:

- They had calculated that the calendar consisted of 365 days [although did not take the necessity of the leap-year into account].
- They understood that precession forced the calendar out of alignment, resulting in the civil and astronomical calendars only coinciding every 1,460 years.
- There are a number of artefacts dating from the Old Kingdom that appear to have come from naturally occurring meteoric iron.
- From at least as early as the Middle Kingdom, they recognised five of the planets in our solar system.
- They used an early form of astrolabe to align the foundation of the pyramids and sun-temples with the

cardinal points and constellations, with an error of less than half a degree.

- The early Greek credited them with formulating the zodiac despite the fact that the idea of astrology didn't reach Egypt until the Ptolemaic age and the famous 'Egyptian zodiac' at Dendera is of Babylonian origin.
- They plotted and charted the movement of stars and constellations.
- They believed we come from the stars and return to the stars when we die.
- They also believed that all elements of life, both animate and inanimate, were animated by a force or energy and that the spiritual and material were woven from the same substance.

But even if this 'sacred science' was of little interest (or use) to the usurping Osirian, or great Theban priesthoods, the ancient stellar-wisdom continued to flow along like a stream of unconscious thought throughout the remaining march of Egyptian history. And Osirian funerary rites still followed the tradition of painting the ceilings of tombs with stars and the image of the archaic star-goddess. In *Daily Life of the Egyptian Gods*, however, the authors offer a more tantalising glimpse of Egypt's concept of the heavens.

The sky, both the portion that men could see and the portion that remained hidden from them, was incarnated by the body of a woman who took her place on high in the final stages of creation. This body, that of the goddess Nut, represented the limits of the domain Re travelled through every day. It made it possible to put the entire mechanism of the universe into place and established the framework of the organised world, of which it was an integral, concrete part. But Nut's body and the area delimited by it did not constitute the whole of existing space. Beyond it were regions the sun never *reached. Unknown to the other gods, or even to the dead, **this** **peripheral zone was shrouded in eternal darkness: the sun** **never rose there. It would one day serve as the creator's** **ultimate refuge: he would return to it when the world came to** **an end …***

By day or by night, Nut offered a space for men to observe. Yet *what they saw only hinted at all that was concealed from them. The* *heavenly bodies – no matter which ones were involved and no matter* *when one observed them – **were but the luminous images of a*** ***vaster whole one could only guess at. The more intense the*** ***light – and the sun's is intense – the more it hid, and the more*** ***effectively it prevented people from looking at it …** men* *received all manner of things from the day sky; from the night sky,* *they had all manner of things to learn. The Sun had knowledge of all* *the space he travelled through; but he delegated the nocturnal space* *of knowledge to the god of the moon, Thoth.*

[Author uses **bold** for added emphasis. MD]

Exercise: The Personal Calendar

From the calendar given in Part Two – *The Book of Days* – create your own listing of special days and record them in your personal day-to-day diary. These will immediately show when an important observance or feast day is about to occur, alongside normal family events. Begin by selecting 'days' that have some special personal significance, such as:

- The feast-days of the deity with whom you have an affinity
- Feast-days of your Ancestors
- Your own birthday
- Important family days
- The solstices and equinoxes
- Any other days that seem appropriate

By slowly integrating the Egyptian calendar into your own

modern calendar, you will quickly become accustomed to thinking in 'Egyptian mode', even if your family do not share your enthusiasm or interest.

The Atlantis Syndrome

Before the dawning of the science of Egyptology and the deciphering of the hieroglyphs, much of what passed for early authority on the subject of history and the religious beliefs of Egypt was taken from the Greek historian, Herodotus (480-425BC). Exiled from his homeland as a young man, he travelled widely in Egypt and in other parts of the Greek world, and relied much on what he was told by foreigners when writing Book 2 of his *History*. As a result, the historical errors arose from the untrustworthiness of his sources, i.e. the contemporary Egyptian priesthood, who would no doubt have delighted in telling a visiting historian tall-tales about Egypt's great past.

By the time Herodotus visited Egypt, it was during what is referred to chronologically as Dynasty XXVII, the First Persian Period, and had been under Persian rule for almost a hundred years. His writings also reflect the later 'Greek propaganda' that was to colour views of the Persian dynasty, at a time when the 'Old Religion' of stellar worship was all but forgotten outside the realms of folklore and funerary customs. By then, most of the Egyptian deities had been assimilated with the Greek pantheon, and it is from Herodotus that many of the Graeco-Egyptian names of the gods, as we know them today, passed into the history books.

By reading Herodotus, we can see that nothing remained of the old religious beliefs of archaic Egypt and yet ... there must have been some 'magical truths' hidden in those tall stories that had filtered down to the Graeco-Roman world. Perhaps there is room here for a *personal* theory that Plato's concept of 'Atlantis' partly had its roots in the collapse of Egypt's Old Order: an age that had lasted for so long but was finally shattered, destroying established customs and traditional magico-religious practice in its wake.

When Plato (427-348BC) wrote about Atlantis in his *Timaeus* and the incomplete *Critias*, he was in old age and was also living through 'disillusioning times'. Taking the explanation for Plato's work from *The Atlantis Syndrome*, Paul Jordan writes that is was *'a basically rationalistic attempt to arrive at a system of absolute validity not only in scientific terms but also in the realms of politics, law, ethics and theology'*. In short, Plato was trying to come up with a universal philosophy for 'an ideal state in a far from perfect world', but first he had to grab the contemporary world's attention, and force it back from the brink of the chaos into which it was about to descend, by using shock tactics.

The basis for *Timaeus*, is an imaginary conversation between Socrates and his friends, which took place in 421BC, during an annual Athenian festival, in which Socrates advocates an ideal, self-sufficient state where everyone knows their place, and no one engages in trade, or piles up unnecessary wealth. A classic demonstration of good old-fashioned Athenian intellectual snobbery! Nevertheless, Plato realised that the Athenian establishment would not take kindly to being publicly denounced as being a corrupt, godless bunch, since it was only in 399BC that Socrates himself had been executed for 'introducing new deities and corrupting youth' following his public comments on the weaknesses of democratic governments.

Plato did what any good fiction writer of today would do, and that was to draw on familiar historical happenings of his world as a setting for the 'plot'. The great famine and social uprising during Egypt's Old Kingdom was probably still part of Mediterranean folklore and the principal character, *Critias*, tells of the origins of the Atlantis legend as coming from the priesthood of Egypt *'who opened his eyes to the long-forgotten history ...'* and no doubt to the fount of all wisdom and knowledge as well. Modern archaeology has revealed evidence of the destruction of a particular Minoan community on Santorini (the Greek name was Thera), when the volcano erupted and the whole island disappeared beneath the waves. The additional collapse of Cretan culture, at much the same time, no doubt also played its part in the creation of the Atlantis myth and the 'detailed' plan of Atlantis with its inner and outer cities and harbour, bears more than a passing resemblance to a passage in the *Odyssey* ... and Plato would have known his Homer.

The story tells of divine wrath against the luckless Atlanteans for their *'greedy pursuit of wealth and power for its own sake, and to the loss of their own virtue'* and a whole range of ancient authors regarded Atlantis as a pure form of allegory **... which is what Plato had intended.** Paul Jordan sums it up as follows:

> *Atlantis started with Plato and in his hands it was never a super-civilisation of the sort conjectured by later authors; perhaps in strictly Greek* [philosophical] *terms it was no civilisation at all but rather a fatally luxurious elaboration of an essentially barbarian way of life, for all its inception by a god. At all events, it was no seminal civilisation: it wasn't the* fons et origo *of all later civilisations in the world, indeed Athens was its independent contemporary. Both Atlantis and old Athens were, for Plato, but episodes in the ever-ongoing cycle of catastrophes and renewals that he saw as the most rational and scientific interpretation to which the field of human experience could be subjected. For him, science and religion were quite bound up together, so that the natural catastrophes were at the same time eras in which the divine light was withdrawn from the world and the equally natural renewals were times when it returned ...*

But what of the legendary 'wisdom' that survivors from Atlantis were supposed to have carried with them to the far flung corners of the earth? The author merely puts forward the suggestion that this *was* the old pre-dynastic stellar-wisdom, carried into exile by the surviving priesthood and their families of the Egyptian Old Kingdom, fleeing from banishment and massacre. Nevertheless ...

- It would explain why there are familiar refrains underlying the Inner Mysteries of the various Western Traditions.
- It would explain why historians and archaeologists periodically discover some dubious 'Egyptian' influence among early European artefacts.
- It would explain why some people are inexplicably drawn to the anthropomorphic deities of proto-dynastic Egypt, when in Western culture these images would normally be viewed as demonic.
- It would explain why the early Church was so keen to stamp out 'the domination of the stars', and why St Paul wrote condemning the practice of astrology at some length.

But people in the ancient world would often hark back to 'that which is never fully remembered, and yet never fully forgotten'. Lucretius, the great Roman philosophical poet lived at a time when the old Roman religion had lost its hold on the educated classes *and a general scepticism prevailed; but the gloom and uncertainty of the times no doubt rendered people superstition and nervous.* In his *De Rerum Natura* (*On The Nature of Things*), we find echoes of the classical Egyptian view of the cosmos, its dangers, and the fact that life itself emanated from deep space and subsequently returns to it, which was also prevalent among other earlier Greek philosophers such as Leucippus, Epicurus and Democritus.

Democritus (c460BC), hailed as the greatest of the Greek physical philosophers, had himself travelled extensively in Egypt and Asia in pursuit of learning, and lived to a great age. He settled in Egypt for seven years, during which time he studied the mathematical and physical systems of the ancient schools, although according to the entry in the *Encyclopaedia Britannica*, the extent to which he was influenced by the magi and the eastern astrologers is a matter for pure conjecture. He adopted and developed the earlier atomistic doctrine of Leucippus, believing that the atoms of which the universe is composed were similar in quality but differing in volume and form, moved about in space – and were variously grouped into bodies: but whereas the latter decay and perish, the atoms themselves are eternal. (*Nothing can arise out of nothing; nothing can be reduced to nothing*).

Despite access to the Egyptian Creation myths, Democritus rejected the notion of a deity being instrumental in the creation of the universe, but acknowledged the existence of a class of 'beings', of the same form as men, but grander and composed of even more subtle atoms: less liable to dissolution, but still mortal, that dwelled in the upper regions of air. According to Plutarch, Democritus recognised the One God in the form of a fiery sphere – the soul of the world – *the anima mundi* – and he attributed the popular belief in 'gods' to offer an explanation for extraordinary phenomena (thunder, lightning, earthquakes) as reference to superhuman agency.

Lucretius (99BC-55AD) believed that: *'After an invocation of Venus, the great creative force of nature, sets forth the atomic theory of Epicurus, which satisfactorily explains, and alone explains, the phenomena of the world. The atoms, infinite in number and eternal, endlessly falling through space by their own nature, colliding when they swerve a little from their path, form into masses, from which the universe by chance arrangement is built up.'* [*The Oxford Companion to Classical Literature*] Lucretius, however, held that: *'this universe and all that is in it act according to law, and there is no room in it for the gods and their interference. Popular religion and the terrors introduced by it have no foundation ... The soul, material in its nature, though composed of extremely rarefied elements, is mortal and dies with the body.'*

Two philosophers, one Greek and one Roman writing almost

400 years apart, and expounding similar theories to those pre-dynastic beliefs that existed in Egypt some 2,500 years earlier – that all life came from and returns to the stars. Alexandria housed the greatest library of the ancient world and contained texts from all over the known world, plus thousands of manuscripts from Egypt itself. Was it from this source that the ancient wisdom passed into the writings of later scholars? And was this the reason for the library's destruction?

An Introduction to the *Hermetica* also suggests that Plato (or rather his teacher Socrates) also learnt much of what he put down in the *Timaeus* from Egyptian sources, and that both Plato and the later Christian writer who compiled the *Hermetica* drew on a common source – supposedly the secret teachings handed down by Egyptian Initiates. Did Democritus find evidence to support his atomistic theory in the Great Library, and what other great stellar secrets were destroyed by Roman arsonists?

The classic atomistic theory offered that: *'the endless variety of substances known to man can be explained if matter is assumed to be composed of small indivisible and indestructible particles – or atoms.'* In all its various forms, however, the atomism of the ancient Greeks (and later of the Romans) was a philosophic rather than a scientific doctrine, and although as a philosopher, Lucretius might not pay homage to the old gods, his *De Rerum Natura* left no doubts as to what he believed would someday happen to the planet: and it was not divine retribution:

And so some day,
The mighty ramparts of the mighty universe
Ringed round with hostile force,
Will yield and face decay and come crumbling to ruin.

In fact, a belief in some form of Armageddon is deep-rooted in most religions and cultures (both ancient and modern) just the same as most cultures have similar flood myths, often involving

some object arriving from the sky with catastrophic consequences. In 1694, Sir Edmond Halley (he of comet fame)
presented a lecture to the Royal Society of London, in which he
expressed the view that the story of the biblical flood may have
been a result of cometary impact. This suggestion was too much
for the Church of the time, because his explanation of the flood
threatened the concept of divine intervention, and so his ideas
were quickly suppressed!

Exercise: Protective Pouch

In addition to your pyramid, try to acquire a selection of
Egyptian symbols you can handle. It doesn't matter how small
they are, but you must be able to take them with you, wherever
you go. This is the start of your own protective pouch – and for
the moment you'll need just one of the archetypal symbols and a
fabric pouch to keep the amulets safe from negative influences.

- Amulets were popular with the ancient Egyptians, which
  were called *meket* (to protect) or *wedja* (well-being) with
  thousands of examples housed in various museums.
  Egyptian Magic by Sir A E Wallis Budge discusses the
  symbolism and usage of a great number of amulets and
  talismans.
- Amulets frequently depicted sacred objects or animals,
  such as an *ankh*, scarab, buckle of Isis, cobra, hawk, ibis,
  baboon, the Horus-eye, or the Osirian *djed*, and were made
  from materials selected for their magical properties, or the
  'correspondences' relating to a particular deity. They were
  carried to protect the bearer from danger and avert the
  crisis of everyday life – see *The Book of Days*.
- Preparation for each item should be carried out first by
  running the object under cold running water. Light an
  appropriate blend of incense (or joss stick) and holding the
  object in the smoke say: *'By the Name of ... (deity) ... imbue*

this amulet with the power to keep me from harm.'

- Add as many symbols as you like to the pouch, including the single cowrie shell, if that was your choice from Part One. Each item should be washed and passed through the smoke before being added to your pouch.

By using the appropriate symbol for meditational purposes, it will automatically begin to attract magical propensities generated by your own magical working. Carry the pouch containing the amulets with you always, bearing in mind that anyone touching it will contaminate the contents.

The Setian

With all these cosmic goings-on, it is little wonder that the ancients spoke of wondrous visions in the sky, moving across the heavens and causing widespread panic and consternation. With no light pollution to obscure the view, much more would have been seen of this inter-stellar activity. Comet Halley has re-appeared every 76 years for more than two millennia, periodically manifesting brighter than the planets with its highly distinctive tail and its comparatively swift motion when approaching the Earth. For the Egyptians, there was only one god responsible for all this highly volatile aerial activity: Set.

Posterity has attributed a demonic role to 'this most unloved of all the ancient Egyptian gods' but as we know, recorded history is always the province of the victor. As Alan Richardson wrote in his Introduction to *The Setian*:

The venom that came to be directed toward Set became so intense that any fair-minded researcher eventually pauses to ask whether any deity could be that bad – or whether in fact, something else was going on behind the scenes. Any serious study of archaic Egypt inevitably unearths fragments of worship from times when Set was the deity of choice for the common folk, long before the usurper

Osiris came on the scene. They worshipped him, not because they feared his power, but perhaps because they understood the qualities of Night and Darkness better than we do today.

As we discussed earlier, the 'body' of the goddess Nut did not constitute the whole of existing space. *Beyond* her starry form were regions that only hinted at all that was concealed from the early astronomer-priesthood. The distant heavenly bodies of deep space were merely the luminous images of a vaster whole, about which they could only speculate. This then, was the realm attributed to Set: the realm of spirit to where the dead returned after the correct funerary rites had been performed, and the soul of the king made its final journey in the company of the mighty psychopomp, the 'Son of Nut'.

Set's original role in the ancient Mysteries was (in the company of Horus the Elder) to escort the deceased king to take his place among his ancestors and, as we have seen from the Pyramid Texts, there *is* evidence of these earliest beliefs, which held that the soul returned to the stars after the death of the body. This belief harks back to an even remoter time when the indigenous Egyptians worshipped a stellar-goddess who, in dynastic times, became known as Nut; the origins of Setian belief can also be traced back to the Egyptian stellar or cosmic religion at the dawn of their civilisation. Again we remind ourselves that the *Berlin Papyrus 3024* expresses these Setian sentiments in referring to the Mysteries:

Brother, As long as you burn you belong to life.
You say you want ME with you in the Beyond!
Forget the Beyond!
When you bring your flesh to rest
And thus reach the Beyond,
In that stillness shall I alight on you;
Thus united we shall form the Abode.

For above is exalted by below
As is written in the Scriptures.

Just as the emerging Christian Church made a point of stamping out 'the domination of the stars', it was merely following the attempts of the Osirian priesthood who tried (and failed) to eliminate the Setian-stellar religion over 2,000 years earlier. Even after the collapse of the Old Ways at the end of the Pyramid Age, there was still nothing the Egyptians feared more than the descent into Chaos, that negative state and the opposite of Ma'at – the order of all things. Set was the god of Chaos, pure primordial energy that fuelled the Will of the individual as opposed to a society that held Ma'at (order and harmony) as sacrosanct. By demonising Set, the Osirian priesthood created their own 'imbalance', albeit a benign one: but good intentions were not enough if the disorder (which has been the ultimate fate of every subsequent civilisation), was to be avoided.

Despite all the 'bad press', however, Egyptologists are now beginning to look behind the myth and recognise that throughout the empire, Set remained a royal god and patron of the King. Hilary Wilson in *People of the Pharaohs* explains: *'The patronage of Horus and Set was an essential aspect of the overall duality of Egypt itself. The Pyramid Texts include references to the role of the Two Lords, as in the hymn for 'awakening' the dead King: '...Cause the Two Lands to bow to this King even as they bow to Horus; cause the Two Lands to dread this King even as they dread Set.'... Set continued to be shown as a tutor of the King, especially in the arts of war.'*

Exercise: Psychic Cleansing

There are actually two stages involved in the psychic cleansing of an object, person or place: the first stage is the thorough preparation impressed both on our conscious and subconscious mind that we are about to undertake a very special operation. The objects we will make use of are in themselves very special, and not a part of the normal everyday experience.

- In the case of many magical or ritual objects, and *especially* skrying objects such as glass or crystal spheres because impressions can be picked up simply by someone looking at, or into them. The object does not even have been physically touched.
- If you intend using existing magical tools or implements for Egyptian path workings these will need to be thoroughly cleansed to remove any conflicting energies. In an ideal world, it would be better to start with 'new' tools, but if you are attached to a particular ritual object then pay special attention to the cleansing. Accept that you will be washing away *all* the psychic energy previously associated with the item and that it will become 'virgin' until the new build-up of psychic energy develops during magical working.
- The first stage of any psychic cleansing is always its physical aspect. The room you are going to make use of should be thoroughly cleaned, and this could well mean cleaning the walls, ceilings and fittings, as well as vacuuming the floor or carpet. Your magical tools must be cleaned and polished in appropriate ways, too.

Before becoming too fanatical about ritual cleansing, however, bear in mind that there will obviously be times in your magical life when you will be unable to be as thorough as you would like because impromptu magical workings will not always allow for personal cleansing. Providing your magical tools remain undefiled, impromptu workings such as healing, divining, etc., can be undertaken without personal cleansing. Desperate situations require immediate action and under these circumstances the gods will overlook a spiritual 'cat-lick'.

To quote the narrator from the film version of *The Lord of the Rings*: *'The world is changed. Much that once was, is lost, for none now live who remember it. History became legend, legend became myth and some things that should not have been forgotten were lost ...'*

But, like the Ring in that fabulous fictional quest, some things can lie dormant for many centuries before bursting into life again, if only we know *how* to look. The widely travelled Strabo, writing in his 17-volume *Geographica*, says: *'All discussion respecting the gods requires an examination of ancient opinions, and of fables, since the ancients expressed enigmatically their physical notions concerning the nature of things, and always intermixed fable with their discoveries.'*

In other words, even from classical times we were being warned against taking things literally when it comes to the interpretation of ancient texts. The Egyptians themselves, held that *'God is hidden, and no man knoweth his form'*, so why should we expect to pick up a collection of ancient esoteric writings and be handed the secrets of the Universe on a platter, without bothering to seek for the answers. For 15 years, scholar George St Clair (*Creation Records*, 1898) conducted a systematic study of Egyptian mythology and among the results he concluded that:

- The myths of Egypt were all related to one another, and were neither separate fables nor idle fantasies.
- They revealed an astro-religious system and told a true story of astronomical progress, calendar correction, and theological changes, from before the time of written histories.
- An era not far removed from the traditional Creation was an important era in history, but not the Beginning.
- They had a good deal of knowledge of astronomy; they discovered that the Earth was a globe; and they were acquainted with the precession of the equinoxes, though

they did not know its cause.

- The magnificence of their temples bears witness to the seriousness of their piety, and the after-history of the world shows how deep were the impressions made so early by those priesthoods.

St Clair realised that:

> *this Wisdom is so ancient that it passed out of knowledge 2,000 years ago* [sic]; *the language was dead, the clue to the allegory was lost, and Plutarch protests against those who would seek to rationalise it ... The discovery of the key does not mean that all the doors can be unlocked at once by an unpractised hand.* [The] *task has been like that of rebuilding an overthrown structure, and showing that what seemed to be only a chance melody of stones was the ruin of a majestic temple. The proof is in the manifest design, when the parts are put together again ...*

We must also remember that in Egypt those early priests *were* astronomers, and that there were probably no astronomers who were not members of the priesthood. The study of the stars was unequivocally a priestly business and shows why it is impossible to disconnect Egyptian belief from astronomy. According to St Clair, we also have to accept that nearly everything in its early religious symbology appears to be mythical or mysterious, and embraces certain astronomical 'facts', in order to reproduce a harmony between terrestrial and celestial phenomena. Although George St Clair's identification of the deities is often incorrect, or out of chronological sequence (his writing and knowledge were products of his time), his *Creation Records* offer us a template by which to pursue our quest of this ancient stellar wisdom.

Two things are required in order to unravel the Egyptian system of mythology, the first being a knowledge of the astronomical clues, and the second an acquaintance with the natural language of symbols ...

The facts and ideas of the Egyptian astro-religious system are set forth by emblems or symbols [hieroglyphics], as for example when the returning year is indicated by a migratory bird, an annual visitant (i.e. the swallow); and the repetition of the cycles of time is represented as the renewal of the life of the phoenix (i.e. the blue heron). When the astronomical facts and phenomena are numerous and run into narrative, the symbolical relation extends itself into allegory. The mythology of Egypt is chiefly an allegory of the heavens and the calendar. The language of this allegory has long been lost, but it is recoverable ...

For those well-versed in the language [i.e. correspondences] of magic, it is easy to grasp how natural this language of symbols is, and how easy and obvious (in some instances) is the interpretation. George St Clair goes on:

When we find the god Amun ram-headed, we may suspect that he is connected with the ram-constellation, and that what is stated concerning Amun will be found true of Aries, if we know how to interpret it ... Among the sacred animals of the Egyptians was the scarabæus, a beetle common in the country. But the Egyptians did not worship the beetle itself, they only reverenced it as a symbol of the sun, or as being in some other way an emblem of time ...

By now, the seeker will have realised that the language of the old stellar Mysteries (like all Higher Magic) has always been made up of allegory, symbol and metaphor. Mystical truths that are concealed behind symbolic narrative; emblems that traditionally represent something else; and figures of speech by which a thing is spoken of as being that which it only resembles. By confining his (or her) studies to book-learning, the seeker cannot even begin to grasp the immense store of energy that is generated in this uncharted sphere of the cosmos.

What we also need to contemplate, is that *if* the old stellar priesthood of Egypt was forced to flee and live in exile, then the remnants of the Mysteries they took with them to foreign lands may been partially absorbed into the cultures that welcomed them, thereby preserving the 'key' that has been waiting for thousands of years to be rediscovered. And *if* we really wish to rediscover these ancient powers, then we must turn our attention to the stars.

Question:

But what exactly is this stellar wisdom? And what could a revivalist star-worship offer us in an age of computer technology, when a space probe is capable of examining Saturn's rings at close quarters? Why should we need to resurrect primitive beliefs, reminiscent of the worst kind of superstition and astrological mumbo-jumbo?

Answer:

To finally understand and embrace the true meaning of everlasting Life; a concept that drove the Egyptians to build the pyramids and seek to preserve their dead for eternity. The old stellar religion might have gone into the Shadows after the civil uprising at the end of the Pyramid Age, but modern science can help the modern seeker to subscribe to this knowledge where successive generations of the Egyptian priesthood failed.

Part Four

The Company of Heaven

Your holy place shall be untouched throughout the centuries.
[Liber AL Vel Legis pt 3v.34]

For all the other dead whose memory spread over the sky like the smear of stars up in the cold black night.
[*Summer People*, Marge Piercy]

Nevertheless, so far all we have is a potted history of early astronomy and astrology, combining history, ancient beliefs and superstition with 16th century occultism and New Age mysticism – none of which can be regarded as having the least connection with science or astro-physics, and a relevance of ancient Egyptian beliefs in the 21st century!

Or can they?

Back in the late 1960s there were mixed feelings about the first lunar landing because it ostensibly debunked the mysterious influence the moon had held over mankind for thousands of years thereby *'reducing the goddess Diana to a lump of sterile clay'*. Sceptic Owen S Rachleff in the *The Secrets of Superstitions*, wrote scathingly about those he termed as 'stargazers':

> *True, the Aquarian Age implies wonder and adventure and far-reaching exploration, but not the type of exploration that will destroy their myths and dreams. Don't tell them astrology is unscientific and out of step with astronomy … Aquarius is a giver of dreams, a sustainer of illusions, not someone who strips away the veil of mystery and leaves them naked in the ice-cold climate of space.*

Agreed the lunar landing did strip away the 'dream-veil' but in doing so, science gave an even more tantalising view of the cosmos and to be frank, *serious* occultists are made of sterner stuff. Rather than destroying the illusion of mystery, science offered a much more enthralling view of the stars than the ancient astronomer-priesthoods could ever have imagined. Those more discerning occultists who were also students of their own cultural history swiftly drew parallels between the ancient stellar wisdom and new astronomical discoveries. Rather than disproving the fragmented, esoteric teachings that had filtered down through the ages, it *confirmed* that the ancients had indeed, had their fingers on the cosmic pulse.

What the Egyptians didn't know, of course, was that the Universe began in a colossal explosion, in which energy, space, time and matter were created. With the aid of modern science, however, we can now trace the history of the Universe to within a minute fraction of a second after the Big Bang. We can also see the way the Universe expanded from its primeval origins, and how the material that emerged from this cosmic explosion, served to determine its ultimate future. The fact is inescapable: the beginning and the end of the Universe are inextricably inter-twined ... **as the ancient Egyptians instinctively understood.**

Similarly, although a supernova spells death to the star, the explosion – like all natural cycles – *does* have a creative aspect to it: *nothing can arise out of nothing; nothing can be reduced to nothing.* Heavy elements beyond iron – such as gold, lead and uranium – are forged in that final and most intense of stellar furnaces. The enormous release of energy blasts these elements out into space to mingle with the detritus of countless other supernovas and, over the ensuing æons, these elements are scooped up into new generations of stars and planets. Without the manufacture and dissemination of these elements, there could be no planets like the Earth. Life-giving carbon and oxygen, the gold in our banks, the lead sheeting on our roofs, the uranium fuel rods of our nuclear reactors – the iron in our blood, all owe their terrestrial presence to the death throes of stars that vanished well *before* our Sun existed. It is a humbling thought that the very stuff of our own bodies, here on Earth, is composed of the nuclear ash of long-dead stars … **as the ancient Egyptians instinctively understood.**

Marcus Chown describes this quite poetically but with plenty of good scientific data to back it up.

Every breath you take contains atoms forged in the blistering furnaces deep inside stars. Every flower you pick contains atoms blasted into space by stellar explosions that blazed brighter than a billion suns. Every book you read contains atoms blown across unimaginable gulfs of space and time by the winds between the stars … If the atoms that make up the world around us could tell their stories, each and every one of them would sing a tale to dwarf the greatest epics of literature …The iron in your blood, the calcium in your bones, the oxygen that fills your lungs each time you take a breath – all were baked in the fiery ovens deep within stars and blown out into space when those stars grew old, and perished. Every one of us is a memorial to long-dead stars. Every one of us was quite literally made in heaven … For thousands of years, astrologers have been telling us that our lives are controlled by the stars. Well, they were right in spirit if not in detail. For science in the 20th century has revealed that we are far more intimately connected to events in the cosmos than anyone ever dared imagine. Each and every one of us is stardust made flesh …'
[*The Magic Furnace*, Marcus Chown]

Heady stuff, but Chown isn't the only one to hammer home the fact that the atoms of 20th century science are the same as those referred to in the early atomistic theories of Democritus and Lucretius. When Lawrence Krauss formulated the idea for *Atom*, he chose to use an atom of oxygen, located in a drop of water, to tell the story … *'because atoms, like people and dogs, and even cockroaches, have individual histories'*. This single atom could have been present in the cup of water taken by Ramesses II as he watched the construction of his mighty monuments. It could have been in a drop of sweat on Antony's brow as he waited in the marketplace for the arrival of Cleopatra, or the very first lap of floodwater to register on the original Nilometer. Or as Krauss would have it … it could have been part of Julius Caesar's last breath.

At first this comes across as fanciful thinking, but imagine for a moment that the oxygen atoms we are breathing now are being continually redistributed again and again throughout the atmosphere on a time-frame of centuries (**Nothing can arise out of nothing; nothing can be reduced to nothing**). Remember that each oxygen atom in the breath we are taking at this very moment in time has had a unique history. Some histories are exotic, and others are not. For example: the ancient poetry of Amhairhin, a Druid poet who lived c400AD, shows how we are connected, each time we breathe in and out, to almost all the rest of life on Earth, today, and in the past. And before the Earth was formed, to the stars … And by the same token, we are equally linked to the future …

I am an estuary into the sea.
I am a wave of the ocean.
I am the sound of the sea.
I am a powerful ox.
I am a hawk on a cliff.
I am a dewdrop in the sun.
I am a plant of beauty.
I am a boar for valour
I am a salmon in a pool.
I am a lake in a plain.
I am the strength of art

A similar analogy was made by the renowned British astro-physicist, Sir Arthur Stanley Eddington: *'Take a cupful of liquid, label all the atoms in it so that you will recognise them again, and cast it into the sea; and let the atoms be diffused throughout all the oceans of the earth. Then draw out a cupful of sea-water anywhere; it will be found to contain some dozens of the labelled atoms.'* So, life begins with the process of star formation: we *are* made of stardust as the ancient Egyptian believed, but we still have to find the key to unlock the door of this ancient wisdom.

Exercise: Meditation on Creation

Sit quietly or lie down in the sacred area near your shrine. Imagine water in all directions. Water rippling gently like a giant pond with the wind fluttering over its surface. Apart from water there is nothing. There is no sky, just a featureless, grey above, which stretches to infinity. It is neither light nor dark, but a strange astral light by which you can see but not clearly. The water is featureless and flat. It reflects nothing, for there is nothing to reflect; it might as well be mercury or liquid steel moving languidly in a grey fluid motion.

Gradually forms begin to coalesce out of the silver-grey astral light. At first you feel it could be a trick of your brain, tired with gazing at infinite nothingness. But soon there is no doubt that there are eight figures, smoky but solidifying, but still fluid in form. They form a circle and you see they alternate frog, snake, frog, snake ... four frogs and four snakes. Four gods and four goddesses: they are all that IS within the world. They are Water, they are Infinity, they are 'That Which Is Hidden', they are Darkness. Are they creatures? Or do they have human form? They stretch out their arms and move away ... away from each other ... away from the centre ... away, over and through the all enveloping water.

And as they move outwards and away, at the centre of their circle is an area of complete stillness in the rippling waters. No ripples here, yet they seem to bunch up around the centre as if something is holding them back. The ripples leap like frightened fish within an encircling net, as gradually the area of stillness expands and grows, as the gods move ever outwards and away. The centre becomes sleek and gains solidity, like the sleek sheen of a seal's back as it breaks the surface of the sea, the sleek, shiny mud of the Mound of the first earth breaks through the surface of the infinite ocean. And the wavelets and ripples bunch and retreat further and further, as more and more of the Mound grows through the waters and pushes them back.

The power of the individual gods grows and strengthens, bringing dry land from the waters. The Mound is prepared – reflect on it for a moment and then withdraw from the scene. Have a hot drink and sit quietly for a while to 'earth' and disperse the psychic energies.

The Mound is an integral part of the Egyptian religion since all temples, right from the very early period were designed to reflect this concept ... and plays an important part in the Egyptian Mysteries.

If the Key Fits ...

Although Aleister Crowley believed that magic was the alchemical product of science and art, there was an extremely valid reason why he continued to use what might be viewed as the outdated symbols of sorcery and superstition, as Kenneth Grant explained in *Hecate's Fountain;* which echoes George St Clair's observations outlined in Part Three, and the doctrine of Jung's collective unconscious contained in Part One.

> *It may be asked, why then do we not abandon the ancient symbols in favour of the formulae of nuclear physics and quantum mechanics? The answer is that the occultist understands that contact with these energies may be established more completely through symbols so ancient that they have had time to bury themselves in the vast store-*

house of the racial subconsciousness. To such symbols the Forces respond swiftly and with incalculable fullness, whereas the pseudo-symbols manufactured in the laboratory possess no link with elements in the psyche to which they can appeal. The twisting and turning tunnels explored laboriously by science lead, only too often, away from the goal. The intellectual formulæ and symbols of mathematics have been evolved too recently to serve as direct conduits. For the Old Ones, such lines of communication are dead. The magician, therefore, uses the more direct paths which long ages have mapped out in the shadowlands of the subconsciousness.

The mistake that is often made in assimilating modern magic with Egypt's ancient past, however, is that too many outside (or alien) influences are allowed to creep into the equation. Egypt's stellar-cult, as much as it may have influenced *subsequent* thinking down through the centuries, was not influenced by anything other than the home-spun philosophy of the indigenous gods of the early Nile people, with all its attendant symbolism. From that very early period, the astronomer-priesthood *'not only understood astronomical science so well that they recognised the precession of the equinoxes, but also that they founded every aspect of their civilisation upon a star-orientated, religio-mystic culture derived from such knowledge'* [*The Land of the Fallen Star Gods*]. But let us return the baton to George St Clair for a moment:

The basis of the Egyptian Religion was Astronomy and the Calendar; the Divine Order in the heavens suggesting the rule for the life of man ... the men who framed this system had ceased to be savages and had attained to considerable knowledge in observational astronomy. They may have received an inheritance of custom and fancy from savage ancestors, and continued to use the language and ideas of it to some extent, but a higher revelation had come to them through the study of the stars. Hence the early

*astronomers became priests, and the religion of mankind was lifted
to a higher platform than that of mere animism.*

We may search for evidence of Egypt's stellar-cult in the writings
of later civilisations, but this will always be a drastically diluted
affair. One the other hand, it is unwise to view Egypt as the 'fount
of all wisdom', and harbour a belief that subsequent or parallel
cultures were magically or scientifically inferior. As we now
realise, the social, religious and magical elements of Egyptian life
were inextricably interwoven, and therefore it is impossible to
view any aspect of one without the others. But, by the time the
indigenous stellar-cult had been wholly integrated within the
developing solar-cult during the pyramid-building era, Egypt
itself was on the brink of social and religious revolution. The
stellar-priesthood went into the shadows ... but this did not
necessarily mean that the cult disappeared completely, since
there *is* evidence of it persisting, albeit as part of the Inner
Mysteries, right up until the advent of the Ramesside family of
Dynasty XIX (1293-1185BC).

In *The Setian*, Billie Walker-John reveals how, hundreds of
years after the end of the Pyramid Age, the Ramesside dynasty
brought about a 'Setian revival' following the ascent of Seti I to
the throne. The family are believed to have been descendents of a
Set priest from an area where this indigenous god had long been
worshipped: Seti I's birth-name means 'He of the god Set' and he
retained his Set-name throughout his reign. If Seti I were the only
king to show Setian leanings, the Setian revival could be
dismissed as wishful thinking ... but this was not the case.

If his father's references to the ancient Mysteries were veiled,
Ramesses II was much more up front about his family's association with Egypt's oldest god. It was Ramesses the Great who
brought Set worship out into the open and paid homage to his
own ancestors who had preserved the ancient Mysteries of the
Set-Horus psychopompos, as we can see from the famous statue

in the Cairo Museum. It also confirms that the worship of Set was still an important and integral part of the Mysteries, which spanned over three thousand years of continuous loyalty from an 'inner' or underground priesthood. This priesthood kept those Mysteries alive despite civil unrest, religious upheaval, invading armies, foreign rule and the adverse publicity of having their god turned into a reviled assassin by a rival cult.

The main difficulty in trying to tie all these 'stellar strands of 'Khemeticism' together as one coherent whole, is the conflicting disciplines of history, science, theology, philosophy and magic.

History is concerned with that which can be proved via the discovery of ancient artefacts and writings, and is often interpreted quite literally, rarely taking into account that ancient esoteric beliefs (exactly the same as modern ones) relied heavily on allegory and metaphor, which were the main methods used in both the magical thinking process and its outward expression.

As Alexandre Piankoff, a well-known translator of Egyptian texts wrote:

> ... the approach to the study of Egyptian religion has passed without transition from one extreme to another. For the early Egyptologists, this religion was highly mystical and mysterious ... then came a sudden reaction; scholars lost all interest in the religion as such and viewed the religious texts merely as source material for their philological-historical research.

Science, on the other hand, regularly discards one theory in favour of a better one and by using approved 'scientific methods' of radiocarbon dating and DNA testing, boundaries are pushed further and further back in tracing the origins of the earliest Egyptian cultures. But science and history have always made uneasy bedfellows as the debate about the *geological* dating of the

Sphinx and its surrounding mortuary temples will testify. But as Eliphas Levi wrote: *'without faith, science leads to doubt; without science, faith leads to superstition ...'*

Needless to say, **Theology** [faith] is *always* a minefield, whether ancient *or* modern, since incoming beliefs, more than often than not, absorb or obliterate any existing ones. The original religion of the early Egyptians (i.e. the stellar-cult) is as far removed from the solar-beliefs of the later dynasties, as the latter are from contemporary Islam and Christianity. The modern view of the Egyptian gods is that they all fit snugly into a one single, internally coherent and self-contained pantheon, without taking into account the mighty deities of the pre-dynastic era, who were marginalised and trivialised by the incoming priest-hoods (with the exception of those pertaining to the Inner Mysteries). Egyptian magico-religious psychology is indeed complicated, and our present-day enumeration of 'body, soul and spirit' is quite insufficient as parallel concept.

According to the entry in the *British Museum Dictionary of Ancient Egypt*, the Egyptians considered that each individual person was made up of five distinct spiritual parts, separate from the physical body: the *ba*, the *ka*, the *ren*, the *shwt* and the *akh*.

- The *ba* has similarities with our concept of 'personality'. In other words, it comprised all those non-physical attributes that made one human being unique, although the concept of *ba* also referred to a power, which could be extended to gods as well as inanimate objects. In order for the physical bodies of the deceased to survive in the afterlife, they had to be reunited with the *ba* every night. Far from corre-sponding to the modern western concept of a 'spirit', the *ba* was closely related to the physical body, to the extent that it too was considered to have physical needs for such pleasures as food, drink and sexual activity.
- The *ka* is an almost untranslatable term used by the

Egyptians to describe the creative Life-force of each individual, whether human or divine, and was considered to be the essential ingredient that differentiated a living person from a dead one. It came into existence at the same moment that the individual was born; when the individual died, the *ka* continued to live, so long as it was provided with sustenance in the form of prayers, offerings and remembrance.

- Egyptians set a great store by the naming of people and objects, and the name or *ren* was regarded as an essential element of every human individual. The *ren* was regarded as a living part of each human being that had to be assigned immediately after birth, otherwise it was felt that the individual would not properly come into existence. The symbolic importance of the *ren* also meant that the removal of personal names from monuments was considered to be the equivalent to the destruction of the very memory and existence of the person to whom the name referred as revealed in the example given in Part One: *'To speak the Name of the dead is to make them live again. It restoreth the breath of Life to he who hath vanished.'*

- The shadow, or *shwt*, was also regarded as an essential element of every human being, and was considered necessary to protect its owner from harm. Funerary texts describe the shadow as an entity imbued with power and capable of moving at great speed, but the Egyptian word for shadow (*shwt*) also had the connotations of 'shade' and 'protection'.

- The *akh* was the fifth principal element that was considered necessary to make up a complete personality. The *akh* was believed to be the form in which the blessed dead inhabited Otherworld, and also the result of the successful reunion of the *ba* with its *ka*. Once the *akh* had been created by this reunion, it was regarded as enduring and unchanging for eternity.

As shown in Part One, a broad overview of the religious history of Egypt will tell us that there were several pantheons, all of them very confusingly cross-related, which carefully concealed the enduring Inner Mysteries. The fact that many of the gods had half a dozen alter egos, all with different animal heads or crowns, or other headgear and apparel to match, is in itself a source of endless confusion to the uninitiated. For all the multiplicity of gods and goddesses in the pantheon, however, the regard for Atum-Re was consistent throughout the long history of the Nile Valley. For the Egyptian, he was that 'Unseen' omnipresent Life-force in every microscopic fragment of the cosmos, with the Sun being the visible expression of his Being made manifest.

I am the Creator of what hath come into being and I myself came into being under the form of the god, Khepera in primeval time and formed myself out of primeval matter ... My name is ... who is the essence of primeval matter ... I appeared under the form of multitudes of things from the beginning. Nothing existed at that time and it was I who made whatever was made ... I made all the forms under which I appeared out of the god-soul which I raised up out of Nu, out of a state of inertness.
[Egyptian prayer]

When it comes to **Philosophy**, that 'pursuit of wisdom and knowledge: investigation of the nature of being; knowledge of the causes and laws of all things; the principles underlying any department of knowledge', we find little in terms of written texts when it comes to ancient Egypt. Philosophy is bound up in what we know, tempered with what we hypothesise, blended with what we would like to believe makes up an ideal society. Much of what we 'know' comes from other philosophical writers and according to Schwaller de Lubicz in *Sacred Science*, and Jane B Seller in *Death of the Gods in Ancient Egypt*, the Egyptian astronomer-priesthood *was* fully aware of the phenomena of the

25,920 year cycle of the precession of the equinoxes, even if they didn't understand the root cause.

And it is here that we can slide into the realms of fantasy (i.e. the Atlantean theory) if we pay too much attention to contemporary hypothesists, or to the classical historians who swallowed these tall tales. For example: Herodotus opined that whether the origin of the Zodiac is Aryan or Egyptian, it is still of immense antiquity. Simplicius (6th century AD) writes that he had always heard that the Egyptians had kept astronomical observations and records for the last 630,000 years ... Diogenes Laertius carried back the astronomical calculations of the Egyptians to 48,863 years before Alexander the Great. Martianus Capella corroborated the same by telling posterity that the Egyptians had secretly studied astronomy for over 40,000 years before they imparted their knowledge to the world ... Diodorus Siculus (1st century BC) was told by the Egyptian priests that the Gods and Heroes had ruled over Egypt for slightly less than 18,000 years, while mortals had ruled for just under 5,000 years!

Magic, of course, has always been an 'occult' (i.e. hidden), science and it takes an experienced magician to tease some semblance of order out from all the tangled skeins of history, science, theology and philosophy. The Egyptians believed in everything in the universe following a single, repetitive pattern ...

It was this, inherently, which underlay the principle of hierarchy and the need for it in maintaining perfect harmony throughout the cosmos ... It was because of their understanding of the divine origin of everything on Earth and of its hierarchically organised place in the scheme of things, that science and art – the very foundations of all objective culture – originally came to exist and be practised in Egypt, always with prior dedication to a particular divinity ... The ancient Egyptians did nothing without it having an esoteric significance, and this must also apply to their architecture. Each aspect of

proportion, acoustics, light and darkness, number and style of columns tells us something about the nature of the deity and the way in which it was to be approached and/or worshipped.
[*Land of the Fallen Star Gods*, J S Gordon]

Exercise: Personal Preparation

While you are washing or bathing before taking part in a ritual, it can be appropriate, and helpful, to add traditional herbs or oils to your bath water. Both rosemary and hyssop have been used for psychic purification for thousands of years and can be infused in your bath water; as can thyme or marjoram – all of which were used in ancient Egypt. To avoid having bits of floating herb sticking to your body put them in a muslin bag or tie them up in a handkerchief.

- The physical cleansing of your body, however, is only half the job. You also need to shed all every-day worries, faults and troubles during your preparations. This is done by imagining all of these unwanted emanations in the form of grey smoke clinging to your body and suffusing your aura.
- Close your eyes and relax in your bath as you visualise this. Using a bowl or a jug to scoop up the bath water, pour it over yourself and as the water flows over your body visualise it washing away all those grey, misty problems.
- As they dissolve into the water your body and aura are left cleaner than you have ever experienced before. When the grey smoke has completely dispersed, your body and aura will be literally shining with magical purity.
- When you have finished bathing and dried yourself, you may now wish to anoint yourself with oil, either to simply confirm your state of magical/spiritual readiness and purity; or to celebrate the ritual you are about to enact; or to attune your body and aura to a spell you are about to perform.

A simple, but effective all-purpose anointing oil can be made using pure virgin olive oil as the carrier oil: rose perfume was one of the most widely used in Egypt. If you prefer to buy this traditional Egyptian perfume, then substitute a good quality rose essential oil – after all the Egyptians would have bought it in the marketplace! Keep the oil separate from your everyday toiletries and use it for a general perfuming of the body prior to magical working – you can even add a couple of drops to your preparatory bath.

Learn The Secret That Hath Not Yet Been Revealed
Liber AL Vel Legis pt2v2

Much of what the ancient Egyptians perceived as having magico-religious significance appears to have been what was appearing in the heavens at the time of recording. For example, among the natural cosmic phenomena that affect the weather patterns here on Earth are the regular cycles of sunspot activity that peak every eleventh year, and which were first recorded by Chinese astronomers well over 2,000 years ago. The solar winds caused by the eruption of 'flares' associated with sunspot activity, distort the magnetic fields of the Sun and the Earth, often playing havoc with modern-day, earth-bound technology and computers.

Unlike the magnetic field on Earth, where the lines run tidily from one pole to the other, the Sun's 11-year cycle begins with this pattern. But because the electrically charged gases at the Sun's equator flow faster than at the poles, the magnetic field crossing the Sun's middle is pulled out of shape. Some of these contorting field lines break through the Sun's surface producing *'hundreds of magnetic field lines which criss-cross the surface like a haphazard jumble of overlapping croquet hoops ... responsible for sunspots, prominences, flares and coronal mass ejections ...'* (*Encyclopaedia of the Universe*). And, for the Egyptians, all this solar activity was, of course, the province of Atum-Re.

Similarly, the 19-year period is also a crucial one. About every 19 years (18.64 years, to be exact), the sun-moon eclipses in the same point of the sky. The Chaldeans, who called it Saros and believed that its magic powers could cause the end of the world, knew of this phenomenon. We know that the combined gravitational pull of the sun and moon causes widespread disturbances in bodies of oceanic water, even accounting for climatic changes over the centuries. A study by hydraulic engineer, E. Paris-Teynac, also revealed a similar pattern for several large rivers, and especially the Nile. If the Chaldeans had recorded the fact that terrestrial life was controlled by astral phenomena, then the Egyptians too, would have made similar observations.

Data on the tides of the Nile are available as far back as four thousand years. The pharaoh, worshipped as the 'master of the growth of the waters', attached a great importance to exactly how much water there would be in the river each year, for it brought wealth and nourishment to his people ...
[*The Cosmic Clocks*, Michel Gauquelin]

Some strange facts about rivers emerge from these records. The great Egyptian river has followed clear rhythmic variations that approximate certain astronomical cycles and Paris-Teynac identified an 11-year variation that seems to be tied to the sun-spot cycle. More importantly, he showed that these 18-year periods, roughly corresponded to the Saros, which reflects the sun-moon eclipse intervals. In ancient Khem, the moon's influence was evident everywhere, continues Gauqueli:

It's waxing was called 'the opening of Horus' eye'. When the eye of the hawk-god was completely open, the moon was full. The twenty-eight-day lunar cycle was compared to a staircase with fourteen steps: first one ascended the staircase to the 'fullness of the eye', then one went down it until the eye closed ... Lunar eclipses were considered to be evil omens presaging sad events. Often the moon itself was seen as dangerous. Its crescent was sometimes seen as a knife, 'a golden sickle in the starry field'. An Egyptian manuscript asks: 'Isn't the moon a knife? It can therefore punish those who are guilty'.

The shapes and movements of the stars also gave rise to numerous myths and rituals. The sky was seen as causing the beneficial growth of the Nile because each year the waters increased when the brilliant star Sirius rose at the same time as the Sun. Not surprisingly, this suggested that the floods were due to the alliance between the propitious actions of the Sun and Sirius – an alliance that occurred only once a year. It was the time when the black soil of Khem spread across the Valley, and why the New Year was celebrated on the date that Sirius rose with the sun.

According to E. Zinner, in *The Stars Above Us*, the Egyptians believed that the:

fixed stars were lamps, suspended from the vault, or carried by other gods. The planets sailed in their own boats along canals originating in the Milky Way, the celestial twin of the Nile. Towards the fifteenth of each month, the moon god was attacked by a ferocious sow, and devoured in a fortnight of agony; the he was reborn again. Sometimes the sow swallowed him whole, causing a lunar eclipse; sometimes a serpent swallowed the sun, causing a solar eclipse.

'When human prevision fails, it is God's will that is being carried out,' says a text of Dynasty V. The people of Egypt didn't have the slightest idea *why* their world grew colder when the stellar cycle brought Orion rising in the east at twilight ... or *why* the world grew warmer again when Lyra rose at dusk, and Orion was no longer visible. As John V Cambell points out in *Analog*, 'When the *world is one vast collection of mysteries, the business of a wise man is to establish some sound, reliable correlations, letting the question of why go until he has more information.'*

Another celestial phenomena recently discussed in scientific circles are the storm-related 'red sprites' – upper atmospheric optical phenomena associated with thunderstorms. Although only barely detectable with the naked eye, the sprites are massive luminous flashes that appear directly above an active thunderstorm and are coincident with cloud-to-ground, or inter-cloud lightning strikes. To see them requires visual access to the region above the storm, unobstructed by intervening clouds and although rare, it seems likely that they have been a part of thunderstorms that have occurred over millions of years. Red-tinged 'sprites' rarely appear singly, usually occurring in clusters of two, three or more and would most certainly have been identified with Set and his followers, if these 'storm devils' were viewed from a distance across the vast reaches of the desert.

As we have observed, the Egyptian priesthood was familiar with all manner of natural occurrences in the heavens, which proved to them that all things came from, were influenced by, or caused by those powers that dwelt beyond the stars. To repeat, for example, that difference of 0.014173 days *per annum* between the sidereal year (according to the stars) and the tropical year (according to the seasons); that slippage of close to 14 days per millennium that is termed the *precession of the equinoxes*.

Duncan Steel's calculations concerning precession are based on the meteor showers of the Taurid and Leonid streams. *'The rate of precession of the Leonid stream is virtually identical to the precession of the equinoxes, both being 14 days per millennium, meaning that a thousand years ago the Leonid meteor storms would be expected to have been occurring near mid-October rather than mid-November, and this is borne out by historical records.'* When he applied the appropriate precession rates for the Taurids, he found that back in 3000BC they would have peaked in mid-July – 110 days earlier than they do today with the activity starting around mid summer. That is 22 days earlier per millennium.

Find a clear dark site one night and let your eyes become well adjusted to the low light levels. Then, by looking randomly across the sky, you may expect to see up to 10 meteors (or shooting stars) an hour. In fact, most people are asleep during the best time for viewing meteors (during the last hour or two before dawn), when the count rate is two or three times higher than in the late evening. *'On certain nights of the year a larger number of meteors will be seen in what is called a meteor shower. Most such showers occur annually on the dates that the Earth passes through a meteoride stream and each shower is usually distinguished by the constellation from which it appears to come. Because it takes about a week to pass through the stream, showers will continue to show pronounced activity for some days,'* he writes in *Rogue Asteroids and Doomsday Comets.*

The question we must again ask ourselves, of course, is *how* could the ancient Egyptian priesthood come to possess such knowledge?

Even on the surface, it would suggest that they must have perfected highly sophisticated levels of scientific astronomical evaluation, in order to be able to recognise and *make long-term comparisons* of this cyclical phenomena and astronomical activity. But these long-term comparisons would often require the studied observations across hundreds of years to establish recognised patterns, and men were not as long-lived as they are today. This means that the phenomena must have been carefully watched and recorded across several generations in, for example, the plotting and predicting the return of a comet. Neither is it far-fetched to assume they would be familiar with the pattern of 'cause and effect', even if they did not understand the precise nature of the 'cause' itself.

This ancient stellar knowledge would, of course, only be

known to select members of the priesthood and probably not even understood by the king himself, despite holding the rank of the highest High Priest. What is even more astounding, is that this stellar knowledge may probably be the surviving remnants from *zep tepi* – the 'First Time' of the Nile civilisation whose origins are lost beneath the proverbial sands of Time.

This was also the time of the Egyptian *Urshu*, that mysterious race of mystical beings that haunt the periphery of every culture, and all Adepts are familiar with the 'First Time' – the universal Golden Age during which the waters of the Abyss receded, the primordial darkness was banished, and humanity, emerging into the light, was brought the gifts of civilisation by these 'Watchers' or 'Light-bearers', who acted as intermediaries between the gods and men.

Needless to say, modern Egyptologists dismiss this 'First Time' as nothing more than myth, but the 'Building Texts' from the Temple of Edfu, appear to refer to a 'mythical temple that came into existence at the beginning of the world' (*The Mythical Origin of the Egyptian Temple* – E. A. E. Reymond) and are synonymous with the First Time, or Early Primeval Age. The texts record that the 'Seven Sages', the 'Builder Gods', the 'Lords of Light', the 'Senior Ones' brought light, i.e. knowledge, to the people – and the similarities between the Lords of Light of Edfu and the *shemsu hor* of the later Heliopolitan period, are so similar that they are probably all descriptions of the same shadowy brotherhood.

Exercise: Discovering God-Power

This is the *natural* psychic energy that every one of us has within; and so has every animate and inanimate object on this planet. The aim of the following exercise is to demonstrate that this energy is very real, and not imagined or wishful-thinking.

• Choose a quiet moment away from any distractions. Hold

your hands in front of you at shoulder level, with the palms facing towards one another.

- Gradually move the hands together – very slowly. At a certain point you will feel the power flowing between your palms as a cool, or a warm breeze, or some other sensation.
- You may also find that there is a slight resistance between your palms as if they are trying to push apart, or else it may feel as if they are pulling together, rather like the opposing poles of a magnet. Put the south (or north) poles of two magnets towards one another and they will repel each other. If you reverse one of the magnets, however, so that the south pole and the north pole face each other, the magnets will be drawn together.

Practise feeling the god-power emanating from your own body. If you cannot feel it on your hands, try moving a hand towards the other parts of your body that generate the energy flow. Does the power feel any different at these areas – stronger, weaker, etc? You may also find the results vary with the sun or moon cycles; women may notice a difference with the state of their fertility or menstrual cycle while men may experience marked changes around the equinoxes and solstices. As with all magical exercises, it is necessary to experiment with them at different times and under varying circumstances. This particular exercise can be likened to using litmus paper for testing your own psychic energy levels.

Extra-Terrestrial Intelligences

The central idea behind early Egyptian beliefs, is that the gods would literally (if properly invoked at the correct time) descend from the stars and waken the god-nature in the priest, or that the god would manifest through the consciousness of the individual. Again this is where fantasy can often take over with the suggestion that the *'appearance and disappearance of these seasonally returning hierarchies of hugely intelligent, spiritual or divine beings'* (*Liber Ægyptius*) can manifest to contemporary humans. Modern thinking, however, rarely gets beyond the concept that if these beings come to Earth and take a phenomenal form (perhaps sometimes akin to our own), surely they must travel in some form of spacecraft.

The answer is an emphatic *'No!'*

The traditions of the ancient Egyptian priesthood give us the answer to that question in the recognition of the soul-bodies (the **akh** and **ba**), which have for so long been regarded as almost, if not entirely mythical entities, then to be so ethereal as to have no real existence in our physical world. It is here, where we find the lengthy esoteric training of the Adept's mindset, that allows them to embrace the idea of interaction with those discarnate entities, or extra-terrestrial intelligences. Beings who can best be likened to a spirit version of the Bodhisattvas of Madhyamaka Buddhism, who can move between different planes, or levels of consciousness, in order to bring guidance or protection to those who are able to make the mystical connection.

This doctrine has filtered through to the present day in the concept of 'the Great White Brotherhood' of the Western ritual magical traditions, which Helena Blavatsky described as *'boneless, formless, spiritual essences called the Self-born ...'*

Whatever these ethereal beings are, for a more tangible example we need to turn first to Aleister Crowley and examine the most famous of his writings: *Liber Al Vel Legis*, or *The Book of the Law*. This beautiful prose poem is possibly his greatest achievement and, purported to have been dictated to him by what he identified as his 'Holy Guardian Angel', is reminiscent of the exquisitely beautiful eroticism of *The Song of Solomon* from the Old Testament. Compiled in three separate parts, each one honouring a different Egyptian deity – Nuit [Nut]; Hadit [Set] and Ra-Hoor-Khuit [an amalgam of the different aspects of the ancient falcon-god-child usually identified with Horus] –

although the choice of Egyptian names is pure arbitrary, and it should not imply that this philosophy is confined to Egypt.

Nevertheless, Crowley's subsequent Thelemic teaching honours the oldest deities in the Khemetic pantheon.

- **Nuit, Nu or Nut**, 'Our Lady of the Starry Heavens'
  Invoke me under my stars!
  Love is the law, love under will.
  Goddess of the night sky, frequently depicted by the Egyptians in the form of a woman arched over the earth, her body strewn with stars. This representation of the all-embracing, infinite goddess power is of vital importance in the Thelemic teachings.
- **Hadit,** her son/consort: The Chaldean form of Set.
  I am the flame that burns in every heart of man,
  And in the core of every star.
  Hadit/Set represents the infinitely small yet supremely potent point which, in union with Nuit, generates the manifest Universe (Ra-Hoor-Khuit) ... Set was the first and oldest of the gods and of supreme importance in Thelemic doctrine, being not only the name of the primal creative spirit but also embodying the essential formula of sexual magick.
- **Ra-Hoor-Khuit**: Lord of the Eastern Horizon, Hoor-paar-Kraat.
  Nu is your refuge as Hadit your light;
  and I am the strength, force, vigour, of your arms
  In magical terms he stands for the projection of energy which begets the 'child' formulated from the combined wills of Nuit and Hadit ... Horus, the Crowned and Conquering Child, Lord of the New Aeon, and the perfect manifestation of the magical Will in the form of the Universe. This is the magical/mystical offspring of the dual aspects of primordial and stellar power.

From this we can immediately understand why Crowley was (and still is) accused of devil-worship. By identifying Hadit/Set as the principal deity in his new Thelemic philosophy, he was allegedly honouring evil over good. Both the Crowley and Grant explanations could be dismissed as crackpot occultist theory except that these primitive forms in the ancient Egyptian pantheon are confirmed on an academic level by dozens of the world's leading Egyptologists, including Professor E. O James, who wrote in *The Ancient Gods:*

> *It would seem that Set was the god most widely worshipped among the indigenous population ... in prehistoric and early dynastic times ... Set was a Storm-god and a Rain-god originally personifying the sky and weather, and when Osiris was equated with the life-giving waters of the Inundation (the Nile), he had to be suppressed as a serious rival of the Osirian cultos ... in spite of his great antiquity and status ...*

With his inimitable honesty, Crowley wasn't afraid to admit in later years that much of *The Book of the Law* was still incomprehensible to him. He worked tirelessly in his attempts to interpret its meaning, but decided he was too close to the subject and, in the end, entrusted the task to his friend, Louis Wilkinson, who wrote:

> *In some one phrase or other of* The Book *there is direct message for every human being. The best way for the layman to approach this* Book *is to regard it as a letter written directly to himself. Even though he may not be able to understand some parts of the letter; he is sure to find other parts that are unmistakably addressed, in an intimately personal sense, to him.*
> *[The Law Is For All]*

Needless to say, Crowley's detractors claim that he made up *The Book* himself and passed it off as divine writing, but this does not account for the differences in the use of language. Who, or whatever Aiwass was, English was not his mother-tongue, but it *was* one that Crowley excelled in. *If* Crowley had invented *The Book,* his monumental ego would never have allowed him to publish such bad grammar and syntax – and if he hadn't believed it to be a genuine mystical document, he could never have resisted the urge to tinker with it.

The Book of the Law was dictated in Cairo between 8th-10th April 1904.

> *The Author called himself Aiwass, and claimed to be 'the minister of Hoor-paar-kraat'; that is, a messenger from the forces ruling this earth at present. How could he prove that he was in fact a being of a kind superior to any of the human race, and so entitled to speak with authority? Evidently he must show Knowledge and Power such as no man has ever known to possess. He showed his Knowledge chiefly by the use of cipher or cryptogram in certain passages to set forth recondite facts, including some that no human being could possibly be aware of them; thus, the proof of his claim exists in the manuscript itself.*
> [*Confessions,* Aleister Crowley]

Following the Cairo revelation, Crowley had the manuscript typed out, but took no further trouble to follow it up. Even admitting in *Confessions* that he deeply resented *The Book of the Law*, being bitterly opposed to its principles on almost every point of morality. *'The third chapter seemed to me gratuitously atrocious.'* Not only that, the real horror for a man who had been brought up under a strict magical conditioning, which forbade any publishing of even the least part of the 'secret knowledge', was that he was now being instructed to make public the 'Secret Wisdom of the Ages'. Up to that point, Crowley had been 'absurdly scrupulous' with regard to the secrets entrusted to him and was fully aware of the serious repercussions that had resulted by apparently trivial indiscretions on the part of others who had been less discrete.

Far from being proud of being chosen as the channel for such revelation, he admits to being reluctant and afraid. He found himself in the most invidious of positions. He was bound by oath to the most solemn of obligations and would never have dreamt of attempting to dodge his responsibilities, but it took a long time before Crowley accepted that the 'Masters' or 'Lords of Initiation' had other plans for him:

> *They had ordained that I should pass through every kind of hardship at the hands of nature, suffer all sorrow and shame that life can inflict. Their messenger must be tested by every ordeal – not by those that he himself might choose ... The Masters test every link in turn, infallibility and inexorably; it is up to you to temper your steel to stand the strain; for one flaw means failure and you have to forget it all afresh in the fires of fate, retrieve in a new incarnation the·lost opportunity of the old. I had got to learn that all roads lead to Rome. It is proper, more, it is prudent, more yet, it is educative, for the aspirant to pursue all possible Ways to Wisdom. Thus he broadens the base of his Pyramid, thus he diminishes the probability of missing the method which happens to suit him best, thus he insures against the obsession that the goat-rack of his own success is the One Highway.*
> *[Confessions]*

Crowley's method of resisting the pressure to publish the typescript of *The Book of the Law* was to kick it around until he lost it but the 'Masters' had other ideas. With hindsight he realised there was a powerful message contained within its pages but that the gods deliberately kept him away from coming to any great personal conclusions. In short, he was embarrassed by the whole thing and repeatedly found excuses for postponing the publication. For many years the typescript languished in the attic of his Scottish home at Bolskine and, despite his deliberate carelessness and the conviction that secrecy was necessary to a magical document, that publication would destroy its importance, it would not go away. Crowley both hated and feared *The Book* and tried desperately to escape from its influence; at one stage, convincing himself that the typescript had been well and truly lost. In a diary entry for 28th June 1909, he records the accidental finding of an old portfolio in the loft that contained the missing typescript

It is interesting to note that although much of Crowley's subsequent Thelemic philosophy is firmly rooted in stellar wisdom it may come as a surprise to hear him state that astronomy was a subject about which he knew nothing. *'In spite of innumerable nights spent under the stars, I can recognise few constellations except the Great Bear and Orion,'* he wrote, but could still continue to draw on stellar analogies within the framework of his own teaching Order, *Astrum Argentinum* or Silver Star.

Not all extra-terrestrial intelligences that come through to Earth, however, should be considered benevolent. This form of discarnate entity is what a magical practitioner (regardless of Tradition) calls upon, or communicates with, for mystical/ magical purposes. They are what others may refer to as deities or gods, demons or angels – they are what are summoned to the Quarters to protect the magician, invoked into the magician in order to channel magical energy, or to act as a 'Holy Guardian Angel'. As Bob Clay-Egerton wrote on the subject:

What we should never lose sight of is the fact that these energies/entities can be helpful or harmful, and should be treated with the greatest respect and caution. Remember these are cosmic energies on a very lowly level but they are far more powerful than we can ever imagine and as such can destroy us if treated in a cavalier manner. Keep in mind that once summoned, the entity requires your energy on which to feed (i.e. recharge its batteries) and if you do not keep it under firm control, or forget to close down

*properly, it may continue to feed/grow until it manifests into
something unpleasant and difficult to shift. This is not as rare as we
would like to think!*

*Whatever we wish to call these 'powers' they do have the
necessary link to the abilities and attributes that the magician
strives for in the hopes of finding all he seeks. If the invocation is
gone about in the right manner, there is no reason why this cannot
be achieved – but remember that they are not interested in your
development, only their own. Only by encountering these varying
aspects can the magician learn to differentiate between the
positive/negative, active/passive beings that exist out on the other
planes. Be careful with your preparations and protections, because
for every one that will help, guide and give advice, there are the same
number who will hinder, deceive and even destroy you, if they get
the opportunity.*

Again, we could view these instructions as further evidence of
crackpot New Age fantasy if it were not for the fact that in 1992,
NASA launched a major space project to search for extra-terrestrial intelligent life – namely the SETI programme: Search for
Extraterrestrial Intelligence. In his book, *Are We Alone?*, Professor
Paul Davies reflects on how little contemporary thought has been
given to the far-reaching implications of SETI on earthly philosophical issues, which stands in stark contrast to the speculations
of earlier generations.

*Contrary to popular belief, the possibility of extra-terrestrials was
often debated, and the ramifications analysed, in previous ages …
and the impact that the discovery of alien life forms would imply for
our science, religion and the beliefs about mankind.*

The concept that we may not be alone in the Universe is not a
new one, since the idea of the 'plurality of inhabited worlds'
dates back to the very dawn of rational thought and scientific

enquiry. Despite that, speculation about extraterrestrial 'fact' rested almost entirely on philosophical debate, in the 4th century BC the Greek philosopher Epicurus wrote to Herodotus:

> *There are infinite worlds both like and unlike this world of ours. For the atoms being infinite in number ... are borne on far out into space. For those atoms which are of such nature that a world could be created by them or made by them have not been used up on either one world or a limited number of worlds ... so that there nowhere exists an obstacle to the infinite number of worlds ... We must believe that in all worlds there are living creatures and plants and other things we see in this world.*

Justification for this belief in other worlds was closely associated with the philosophy of atomism and as Professor Davies points out:

> *There is a tendency to regard SETI as a space-age activity. In fact, as we have seen, belief in, and the search for, extra-terrestrial beings stretch back into antiquity. Today a separation is usually made between belief in extraterrestrial life forms and belief in super-natural or religious entities – i.e. between aliens and angels. Yet it was not always thus. For most of human history the 'heavens' were literally that: the domain of the gods. Beings who inhabited the realm beyond the Earth were normally regarded as supernatural. In spite of the fact that ET is now firmly in the domain of science, or at least science fiction, the religious dimension of SETI still lies just beneath the surface. Many people draw comfort from the belief that advanced beings in the sky are watching over us and may some day intervene in our affairs to save us from human folly.*

Even the eminent astronomer Sir Fred Hoyle maintained that life extends throughout the Universe and *'hints at the existence of advanced beings out there who have contrived to create in our cosmic neighbourhood the rather special physical conditions needed for carbon-based life. These alien beings fulfil a function similar to that of Plato's Demiurge ... a much more powerful 'super-intelligence' who directs these acts of intelligent design from the timeless advantage point of the infinite future.'*

Professor Davies warms to this powerful theme of alien beings acting as a conduit to the Ultimate.

The attraction seems to be that by contacting superior beings in the sky, humans will be given access to privileged knowledge, and that the resulting broadening of our horizons will in some sense being us a step closer to God. The search for alien beings can thus be seen as part of a long-standing religious quest as well as a scientific project. This should not surprise us ... As we have seen, it is only in this century [20th] that discussion of extraterrestrial beings has taken place in a context where a clear separation has been made between the scientific and religious aspects of the topic. But this separation is really only skin-deep.

In view of these comments from such eminent astro-scientists, is it mere co-incidence that the project – the Search for Extraterrestrial Intelligence – should be better known worldwide by its acronym of SETI? Has this universal, collective unconscious, been influenced by the long-dead Seti I, whose birth-name means 'He of the god Set', and who brought about the 'Setian revival' some 1,000 years after the old stellar worship went into the shadows, finally triumphed over obscurity? Can this 'super-intelligence' be the core of the old Khemetic star-gods, the 'Imperishable Ones ... who grow not weary'? Is *this* the 'privileged knowledge' that enabled the people of the Nile Valley to construct their pyramids and temples on such a monumental scale? **Was the ancient Egyptian astronomer-priesthood already plugged into the Divine?**

We have tentatively picked up the key to this ancient Wisdom, and even though *our* unpractised hand cannot yet unlock its secrets we have to remind ourselves that for the Egyptians:

- The study of the stars was unequivocally a priestly business;
- There were probably no astronomers who were not members of the priesthood;
- It is impossible to disconnect the Egyptian religion from astronomy;
- In order to unravel the system of mythology, knowledge of the astronomical clues is essential;
- The facts and ideas of the Egyptian astro-religious system are represented by emblems or symbols [hieroglyphs];
- The mythology of Khem is chiefly an allegory of the heavens and the calendar.

The next question, of course, will inevitably lead us to the brain-teaser of where do these ethereal beings reside if they are not hurtling around the cosmos in hi-tec spacecraft? Perhaps it is time to make a quantum leap of our own imagination and explore the possible associations of the parallel or multiple Universe, the string (or M-) theory, and the *practical* Qabalah of the Western Mystery Tradition.

Marcus Chown, as cosmology consultant for *New Scientist*, writes:

> *The idea that our Universe could, without our knowledge, be super-imposed on another, 'mirror' universe with its own light and matter and even stars and plants and animal life is an amazing concept. This idea that there exists a multiplicity of universes is not new. The most striking evidence that there is a multiverse comes from the fundamental laws which control the Universe. A very peculiar thing about these laws is that they appear to be 'fine-tuned' so that human beings, or at least living things, can exist.*

The notion that the Universe has four dimensions – three of space and one of time – has become a familiar scientific 'fact', but modern cosmologists suggest that the Universe may possess more dimensions than this. The string (or super-string) theory views the fundamental building blocks of all matter as ultra-tiny pieces of 'string' vibrating in a space-time of *ten* dimensions, and unifying all the forces of nature, including gravity. According to super-string theory, fundamental particles resemble tiny strings or loops that 'sweep out a two-dimensional surface in space-time and which can be likened to a film on a soap bubble'. According to Colin Ronan in *The Natural History of the Universe*: *'Super-string theory awaits confirmation. It is too soon to make sweeping judgements about it, but it holds the possibility that it is step towards the most fundamental basic of physics: a TOE, or theory of everything.'*

A few years after its initial explosion on to the theoretical physics scene, the super-string theory seemed to have stagnated. By the early 1990s there were a number of different versions of the theory and no one knew which one was correct. Then a US physicist, Ed Witten, proposed a solution that suggested the fundamental entities were membranes rather than strings and it became known as the membrane theory, or M-theory for short. Many in the field of physics liked to think of the 'M' as standing for Magic, Mystery or Mother, and since the study of the stars was unequivocally a priestly business it really would have been the cosmic-mother of all theories! Witten was able to unify the different versions of string theory into M-theory by requiring yet another dimension. Thus, M-theory is an 11-dimensional theory. *'It also has the advantage over the older super-string theories of allowing a more natural merging of gravity with the other three forces.'*

The 11-dimensions also fits more snugly into the theory or philosophy of the practical Qabalah (as opposed to the wholly Jewish theological philosophy), although this is *not, and has never been*, a part of traditional Khemetic teaching. Nevertheless, this system, probably more than any other mystical philosophy, has had a profound effect on Western occultism.

> *Like most forms of mysticism it describes the levels of consciousness*
> *and being between man and Godhead, but it is not for this reason*
> *that it has become the basis of modern magic. The Qabalah employs*
> *a complex symbol called the Tree of Life as its central motif, and it*
> *is because this Tree is such a pragmatic framework on which to base*
> *rituals and meditations that the Qabalah is relevant today.*
> [*The Occult Sourcebook*, Neville Drury and Gregory Tillett]

In Qabalistic terms, the whole of the manifested Universe originated in Ain Soph, the hidden and infinite God-Energy that is without qualities or attributes ... similar to how the early Egyptians saw their own Creator-God

> *...he neither increaseth nor diminished.*
> *He made the universe,*
> *The world, what was, what is, and what shall be ...*
> [*Osiris and the Egyptian Resurrection*, Vol I., E A Wallis Budge]

The Tree describes a type of 'crystallisation process' by which the *Infinite* gradually becomes *Finite*, the latter being the world as we see it all around us, with intermediary stages of mind or being, of energy or consciousness. The Ain Soph thus reveals aspects of its divinity to man and on the Tree of Life these are represented symbolically by ten major stages called *sephiroth* ... or 11 if we count Daath, the 'hidden' sphere. In modern magical usage, the *sephiroth* are best regarded as levels of consciousness, or different levels of being, both on the front and the reverse side of the Tree. Within ritual, the priest-magician begins at his present level of 'earth consciousness' and tries to retrace the sacred steps back to Godhead.

In the writings of Iamblichus we find that:

The Egyptian priests were accustomed to exhibit simulacra of the gods in circles and globes as symbols of the uniform principle of Life. Hermes Trismegistus compared Divinity to a circle, and the sublime description will be remembered, that its centre is everywhere and the circumference nowhere. The Pythagoreans regarded the circle as sacred and considered it as the symbol of the highest spiritual truth. It also represents very aptly all human progress, which is never in straight lines, but in circles returning on themselves as if advancing in ascending spirals, or retrograding in vortices tending downward.

Study of the Qabalistic Tree soon reveals that each of the *sephirahs'* levels of consciousness plays an important harmonising role in conjunction with that of its neighbours. Some of the *sephirah* have distinct personal attributes – the Father, Mother, Son and Daughter, etc., – while others are represented by more abstract forms. The re-occurring triad of paths and circles also represent the 'trinity' of fulfilment and sacred wisdom. In practical Qabalistic usage, the priest-magician takes account of the different 'gods' and 'goddesses' assigned to the individual *sephirah*, and endeavours to compare and correlate them in terms of the attributes, correspondences, sacred qualities and aspirations that they personify.

He considers the gods to be symbols of what he himself may become, and regards their mythology as a type of symbolic energy process deep in the spiritual areas of his mind. This is what Jung was implying in his theory of the Archetypes of the Collective Unconsciousness, but for the magician it is a pragmatic reality. He knows the gods are inherent in his mind and he devises rituals and meditations as aides for encountering them.
[The Occult Sourcebook]

As we have seen, all these symbols are so ancient that they are buried deep in the 'vast storehouse of the racial subconsciousness', responding swiftly and with incalculable fullness, along the more direct paths, which ages before have mapped out in the 'shadowlands of the subconsciousness'. Not only that, throughout the history of religion the 'company of gods' were repeatedly three in number, often formed by the local deity and two gods who were associated with him and who shared the focus of worship *with* him. In later times, two of the Triad were gods, one young one old, and the third a goddess who was, naturally, the female counterpart of the older god. The conception of the Egyptian Triad is probably as old as the belief in the gods themselves.

So, even in the most simplistic of terms, we can see that the Qabalistic Tree of Life could be used as a template for the whole Universe, in that the pillars, paths and *sephiroth* – and even the concept of the 'reverse side of the Tree' – correspond to the scientific theories of multiple and parallel universes, black holes, worm holes, cosmic membranes and vibrating strings. Of course, the Egyptians of the ancient Khemetic beliefs had none of this 'advanced' scientific theory, but to repeat a refrain – they recorded their concept of Life as coming from beyond the stars, and returning to the realms of the Imperishable Ones after death.

Unfortunately, because of Aleister Crowley's infamous reputation – much of it promulgated by himself – any reference to him as a prophet of stellar wisdom will be met with incredulity and the likelihood of downright hostility from some quarters. If we trawl through his voluminous writings, however, we find that the 'star' is a re-occurring theme. Esoteric author Robert Anton Wilson considered Crowley to be:

One of the most original thinkers of this era – right up there with such titans as Einstein and Joyce. Indeed, what Einstein did for physics and Joyce for the novel (and Picasso for painting, and Pound for poetry, and Wright for architecture), Crowley did for the mystic tradition. He swept aside all 19th century barnacles and

incrustations, redefined every concept, and created something that is
totally contemporary with our existence as 20th century persons ...
Crowley was always true to that inner 'governor' – that hidden star
in every human psyche – and followed it without flinching.

Much of Crowley's writings were concerned with the Great
Work: the transformation of man in the quest for self-discovery.
This 'quest' holds that:

...man has far vaster potentiality for know-ledge, and hence power
over his fate, than he ordinarily dreams of as possible ... that it is
possible to know – in a way that is completely different from the
mere accumulation of facts – man's essential nature and his true
relationship to the creative force behind the universe, and wherein
his fulfilment lies – that is what it is he values most highly when the
meaning of life is clearly seen.
[*Eye in the Triangle*, Israel Regardie]

The first steps towards the Great Work are, as every magical
practitioner knows, 'To obtain the Knowledge and Conversation
of the Holy Guardian Angel', or experience of the mystical
enlightenment in both vision and the waking state. And as Israel
Regardie observes:

It must be an occurrence of the greatest significance in the treading
of the Path because it appears always and everywhere as uncondi-
tional. It is an experience which defies definition, as well in its
elementary flashes as in its most advanced transports. No code of
thought, philosophy or religion, no logical process can bind or limit
it. It always represents, spiritually, a marked attainment, a liber-
ation from the perplexities and turmoils of life, and from nearly
every psychic complication.

At this point we need to ask ourselves:
  What exactly *is* a Holy Guardian Angel?
  And
  Does *everyone* have this guiding spirit watching over them?

In truth, the answer to the second question is 'No!' Superstition and the establishment religions would like everyone to bask in the religious certainty that there was a personal guardian angel watching over each and every one of us from birth to the grave, but in reality the answer is not so simple. These 'guardians' may watch over mankind in order to single out the 'promising students' in terms of spiritual development, but as each individual succumbs to the lure of earthly pursuits and material pleasures, so the guardians withdraw to concentrate their energies on those who stay the course.

This particular kind of cosmic bonding was *never* an option for all. It was the growing power of the incoming priesthoods that overthrew the early priest-astronomers, and who promised eternal and everlasting life to the common man. It might have been Karl Marx who coined the phrase that religion was the opium of the people, but he was not the first to have realised this – the concept was already being exploited by the Osirian priesthood as early as Dynasty VI. The elitist Old Order had been swept away and, in the place of direct communication with the cosmic entities, there was an ancient equivalent of happy-clappy evangelism that promised everyone would be welcomed into the embrace of the gods in the Afterlife.

As we have seen, however, the central idea behind early Egyptian belief was that the 'god' would descend from the stars and waken the god-nature in the priest, or that the god would manifest through the consciousness of the individual. Here the divine spirit is brought down into the priest-magician and as a result, 'familiar objects take on a divine radiance illuminated by an internal spiritual light'.

In *The Eye in the Triangle*, Regardie describes this process in these words:

All we can say honestly and simply is that the awakening comes. There is no certain method, no stereotyped set of stimuli or patterns, no standard set of responses. But when it is there, when it does come, the individual is never the same. It is rather like being brought to the Light, in the ritualistic sense, except that this is no ritual. It occurs in the most natural, and, in one sense, the most unsought way.

But this descent into the Mysteries does not confer automatic insight into the Will of the Divine.

These are the experiences and events which occur to every aspirant when initiation forces the realisation upon him, through the activation of the latent contents of his own psyche, that 'all is sorrow'. In fact, the existential criterion or hall-marks of successful initiation is the occurrence of these or similar experiences.

In other words, the more enlightened the seeker becomes, the more he (or she) comes to realise that:

...the whole universe, under the stimulation of the magical elements ... seems to tumble like a pack of cards crazily about one's feet. The significance of all this is to point to a higher type of consciousness, the beginning of a spiritual rebirth. It acts as a self-evolved link between the higher Self at peace in its supernal place, and the human soul, bound by its fall to the world of illusion, fear and anxiety. But until that self-awareness and acquired knowledge are tuned to higher and initiated goals, sorrow and anxiety are the inevitable results.

Here we find that direct contact with the Divine spirit following Initiation does *not* bring an inner peace and contentment ... in fact, the reverse is true. The Initiate is overwhelmed by a sense of futility and desolation; the 'innocence' of the pre-initiatory state cannot be regained, and the way ahead is uncertain and dangerous.

These were the lofty heights of Crowley's magical experience and experimentation, and why he could preach to his followers: *'I say to each man and woman, 'You are unique and sovereign, the centre of the universe ... Every man and every woman is a star!' You, being man, are therefore a star. The soul of a star is what we call genius. You are a genius.'*

And strangely enough, it is within Aleister Crowley's own Thelemic philosophy we find that elusive amalgamation of history, science, theology, philosophy and magic. *'The land of Khem is my spiritual fatherland,'* he wrote, *' ... my gods were those of Egypt,'* thereby linking the remote historical past with the scientific future's belief in and search for praeter-human intelligences [SETI]; and encompassing the receiving of knowledge derived from the investigation of nature through the senses and intellect. The bringer of *The Book of the Law*, Aiwass, claimed to be 'a messenger of the Lord of the Universe' and was revealing a method by which men may arrive independently at the direct consciousness of the universal Truth and *'enter into communication directly on their own initiative and responsibility with the type of intelligence which informs it, and solve all their personal religious problems'*.

When Crowley writes about religion, however, he is not referring to the doctrines of the established faiths when he goes out to prove the existence of 'god'.

The existence of true religion pre-supposes that of some discarnate intelligence, whether we call him God or anything else. And this is exactly what no religion had ever proved scientifically ... But there is no a priori reason for doubting the existence of such beings. We have long been acquainted with many discarnate forces ...

Especially in the last few years science has been chiefly occupied with the reactions, not merely of things which cannot be directly perceived by sense, but of forces which do not possess being at all in the old sense of the word.

Exercise: Creating a Sacred Circle

There is no evidence to suggest that the Egyptians used the Circle for protection but when experimenting with magic it is always best to be safe rather than sorry. The Circle is your protection against psychic attack; it's a tried and tested method of defence and should be looked upon as one of the essential magical 'tools'.

- The size of your Circle will depend on the amount of space given over to your sacred area. This is the boundary of your ritual area, the boundary between the everyday world and the planes of magic. Once inside the Circle you are said to be 'between the worlds'.
- Initially, the boundary of the Circle can be marked with chalk, with masking tape, or with a cord (1 metre of cord (approx. 3ft) will enclose a circle 0.3m (approx.1ft) in diameter, therefore you will need 3m for a circle 1m across, 5m for 1.5m (approx. 5ft) and so on). If using cord, choose a light colour that will show up well by candle light.
- Start at the eastern edge of the circle, inside the boundary – do not step over the boundary until you close down the operation. Make sure you have everything within the circle you might need.
- Hold out your strongest hand, palm down, over the boundary marker. Close your eyes and concentrate on feeling the god-power flowing outwards and downwards from you palm to empower the boundary of your circle. If you are able to half open your eyes as you do this, so much the better. Now begin to slowly walk clockwise (that is the direction the sun moves around the earth) around the

boundary. This means that you will be heading towards the south of your circle.

- It is far more important that you take the time to *feel* the god-power and build up your visualisation relating to the influence of your new Path – this will get easier with practice so that you are able to walk more normally around the Circle. Pause at the south and close your eyes if you have to, so that you can both 'see' and feel the god-power glowing through the arc of the circle you have completed. Then continue towards the west in the same way. Visualise the flame like the low blue flame in a gas oven.

- If you lose the visualisation, don't panic. Just pause and bring your mind gently back to the task. Wait until you have regained the feel of the god-power in your palm and picture in your mind of how your Circle looks so far. Pause again at the west to build up the visualisation then continue to the north.

- Pause again at the north and then carry on to the east. You must continue to the east or your Circle boundary will not be complete. When you reach the east again, visualise the power spreading from the boundary above and below you, so that you are completely enveloped in a blue bubble, or sphere. Now close your hand and this will cut off the power and leave the bubble intact.

- Go to the centre of your Circle and sit down, facing north. As a guide, initial magical exercises should be performed facing towards the north. There are always exceptions to this rule, and others may find that facing south – the direction of Egypt – is more productive.

- Sit for a while in peace and quiet. See if the atmosphere within the Circle begins to feel any different to you. If you find that it is easier to visualise with your eyes closed, then do so. Use this exercise for meditative purposes and

expand your psychic exercises by reflected on a consecrated figure from your pouch – a solar disk, scarab, ankh,
cobra, etc.

- When you feel ready to leave the Circle, stand up, stamp
your feet or clap your hands (this makes sure that your
astral and physical bodies are aligned correctly) then
simply step over the boundary of the Circle. Stepping over
the boundary will 'pop' your circle like a soap bubble.
Have a hot drink and a sweet biscuit to earth you energies.

Do not expect everything to work for you immediately since you
are working with new energies and a completely different focus.
Conversion to a new religion, Path or Tradition should never be
taken lightly, so don't become disheartened if you encounter
barriers. All we are trying to do at this stage is to channel your
subconscious mind into accepting a different set of holy images
or 'correspondences'.

The Survivor

So here, in the magical writings of a 20th century magus, we find
reflected the observations of the ancient Egyptians in placing
their gods in the realms beyond the stars, but with whom *both*
could make direct contact by harnessing the power of the senses
and intellect. And here is the right place to repeat an earlier
extract, which observes that, however much we might like to
deny it, evidence of god – *or what is left of Him/Her/It* – *is* out
there. This may not be the benevolent, divine presence of the
religious textbooks, but current exploration produces a more
reasonable argument for the existence of God from the *scientist's*
point of view. By facing up to the future destruction of the planet
by natural forces, rather than confirming the *non-existence* of God,
science actually proclaims long and loud that there is proof of
everlasting, regenerating life ...

But what do we mean by 'what is left of God'? In his novel,

The Survivors, Simon Raven has one of his characters put forth the theory that God had actually destroyed himself. It is, of course, pure fiction but it raises a few points to ponder if we are of a mind to do so; if we allow ourselves to travel backwards in time, just as the this character had done and the subsequent conversation in which a friend describes his vision to another:

In his dream-vision he'd been catapulted back in time to witness what had happened before space and time began ... where there was Nothing. Not even emptiness, for there was not yet any form of space to be empty ... But how, he'd asked himself, had existence sprung from this nothingness. Because there was total nullity, nothing whatever could have been born in it or emerged from it. He had seen the explosion, and now he was seeing the nullity that had preceded it, and out of which, 'it' must have come.

What he'd seen, he convinces himself was God's death. *'For there could only be one explanation ... The nullity which preceded the universe only commenced when there was a universe to precede. The explosion which was the birth of the universe had created nullity in retrospect. Before the universe began there must have been something, which we may call God. But God, in creating the universe, had destroyed himself – he had become the universe, and so left a blank, a nullity, where he himself had once been.'*

His companion, obviously a sceptic, observes cynically that if he'd been privileged enough to travel back that far in time to where the Universe began, he must have encountered God, or whatever there had been there before God existed. *'No. In becoming the universe God abdicated. He destroyed himself as God. He turned what he had been, his true self, into nullity and thereby forfeited the Godlike qualities which pertained to him. The universe which he had become is also his grave. He has no control in it, or over it. God, as God, is dead.'*

The companion persists in humouring his friend by asking

why had God in effect, committed suicide. *'The only person who could answer that question,'* came the reply, *'would be the true God who no longer exists to answer it. It is conceivable that he got bored with his own perfection.'*

[*The Survivors* from the 'Alms for Oblivion' series, Simon Raven]

Heady stuff and pure speculative fiction ... but there are more than a few atoms of truth in that speculation. What if the Big Bang, as well as being the birth of the Universe as we know it, was also the death of its Creator in the true spirit of the original Sacrificial/Dying God? And what if the atoms of his corpse, catapulted across time and space gave form to those discarnate, or extraterrestrial intelligences that both science and magicians believe to exist? We might accept that God is very much dead, but we must also consider the possibility that the atoms of his 'wisdom' were blasted across the cosmos in much the same way as the debris from an exploding supernova.

To return again to Eliphas Levi:

Without faith, science leads to doubt; without science, faith leads to superstition. Uniting them brings certainty, but in so doing they must never be confused with each other ... The science of the Qabalah makes doubt, as regards religion, impossible, for it alone reconciles reason with faith by showing that universal dogma, at bottom is always and everywhere the same, though formulated differently in certain times and places, is the purest expression of the aspirations of the human mind, enlightened by a necessary faith.

By now, it should be apparent that the stellar path is the path of the individual and reached only after long years of magical journeying. It may often mean walking away from the group confines of a particular Tradition, while always remaining true to one's own roots regardless of how far we may travel ... still part of it, but no longer belonging. And if we wish to take our quest further into the uncharted, esoteric regions of the cosmos, it will be necessary to rid ourselves of the altruistic ethos of modern pagan thinking and reflect upon Aleister Crowley's own brand of stellar wisdom.

In a galaxy each star has its own magnitude, characteristics and direction, and the celestial harmony is best maintained by its attending to its own business. Nothing can be more subversive of that harmony than if a number of stars set up in a uniform standard of conduct insisted on everyone aiming at the same goal, going at the same pace, and so on. Even a single star, by refusing to do its own Will, by restricting itself in any way, would immediately produce disorder.

In other words: the Will of Set as opposed to the Order of Ma'at. For as we have seen, Set was the god of Chaos, pure primordial energy that fuelled the Will of the individual, as opposed to that of Ma'at (order and harmony). Unequivocally, the seeker needs to be able to differentiate between the need for social order and the freedom of the individual, for there is nothing altruistic about the pursuit of mystical enlightenment.

What is needed to turn the key is the right mindset, and this means adopting a completely different concept in terms of philosophy and morality. But as our sympathetic scholar, George St Clair, observed, the discovery of the key does not mean that 'all the doors can be unlocked at once by an unpractised hand'. Neither does it take much of a flight of fancy to make the link between the ancient stellar gods of Khem; those known as the Great Old Ones, who control the destiny of this planet (and many other celestial realms), radiating their influence through the stars; and the SETI quest for extraterrestrial intelligence in deepest space.

The mystic in pursuit of these celestial contacts will, at some stage in his life, be unexpectedly offered the opportunity to undergo a magical or mystical ordeal: the main test being the recognition that the incident is of paramount importance. Crowley wrote:

> *I announced that since 'Every man and every woman is a star', each of us is defined and determined by a set of co-ordinates, has a true will proper and necessary, the dynamic expression of that nature. The conclusion from these premises is that the sole and whole duty of each of us is, having discovered the purpose for which he or she is fitted, to devote every energy to its accomplishment.*

It should also be obvious by now, that the religious doctrines of the world-dominant monotheistic religions would be more than anxious to suppress any philosophy that exalted the Will of the individual as opposed the social obligation of order and harmony … and excluded the vast majority of its followers. Needless to say, this does not mean that the magician should ride roughshod over the rest of humanity, but it does mean that he (or she) has an obligation to discover their own true Will and act in harmony with it to the best of his (or her) ability – in other words: *'Do What Thou Wilt Shall Be The Whole Of The Law.'*

It also explains the measures such opposing theologies will take to invalidate any suggestion that there are elements of their faith that are not normally revealed to the man or woman in the street. In fact, as far back as the end of the Pyramid Age, this promise has been used to strengthen the hold of the new religious establishments of the time, so can we even begin to imagine public reaction if it were given out officially that everlasting life was *not* for everyone?

Much of the problem of embracing new philosophies lies in the fact that most theologians (of any faith) are some 100 years behind the times with their visions of God. If they were to be more open and honest about the vast, glaring chasms between contemporary religious teaching and scientific advancement, people might show more respect, but for most, the theologians are still pre-occupied with the question of obedience, suffering and self-sacrifice, which enlightened seekers see as undermining present society. Crowley, of course, had something to say on the subject that should make everyone sit up and think before they consider themselves right for the stellar Path.

We have a sentimental idea of self-sacrifice ... it is the sacrifice of the strong to the weak. This is wholly against the principles of evolution. Any nation which does this systematically on a sufficiently large scale, simply destroys itself. The sacrifice is in vain; the weak are not even saved. We should not protect the weak and the vicious from the results of their inferiority. By doing so, we perpetuate the elements of dissolution in our own social body. We should rather aid nature by subjecting every newcomer to the most rigorous tests of his [or her] fitness to deal with his environment. The human race grew in stature and intelligence as long as the individual prowess achieved security, so that the strongest and cleverest people were able to reproduce their kind in the best conditions. But when security became general through the operation of altruism the most degenerate of the people were often the offspring of the strongest.

Obviously, scientist and theologian Dr David Wilkinson does not share this view, but he does believe that the importance of the expanding universe has yet been recognised by the theological community.

If the universe keeps on increasing its acceleration rate, then it will eventually lose energy, everything will cool down, there will be no life, no light, no warmth. That poses a number of theological questions. For example, why did God create a universe which was destined to futility? What does this tell us about God's purposes for the future? If the universe is winding down, and is a lost cause, what's the point of it all? A transformation of the cosmos is going on. The creation of a new heaven and a new earth is not simply the result of the evolution of this universe, but a sovereign act of God. Some people have thought that God can destroy the earth and then create a new earth in the midst of this cosmos. I think the cosmos is telling us that view is much too limited, much too anthropomorphic.

But, however Dr Wilkinson chooses to word it, it is obvious that the Earth is going to run out of steam and, even if science had made the journey possible, it would not be physically viable to transport every man, woman and child on the planet to the new 'Earth'. Even here, behind the words of comfort, the message is veiled, but clear: the Path is not for everyone!

Again, the difference between science, theology and mysticism is that the priest-magician is always willing to risk his (or her) life and sanity in pushing the boundaries of the mystical experience in pursuit of 'truth'. In order to understand something of the process and ethos of mystical Initiation, we have to bear in mind that the aim is to help produce a spiritually self-conscious and self-sufficient individual. In order to achieve this, the individual has to be a well-equipped 'all-rounder', not just someone with highly developed 'occult' powers.

Exercise: The Personal Deity

Using the Egyptian *Book of Days* select which seems to be the most compatible deity for you and, in order to follow the Old Ways, it is easier to understand if we use the three separate approaches given in Part One:

- The Stellar Path that deals with the primeval/primordial forces of the universe usually aligned with ritual magic and inner temple working; pre-dynastic and Old Kingdom.

For example: Set, Nut, Horus the Elder.

- The Solar Path that offers a more intellectual, spiritual or mystical approach; Middle Kingdom. For example: Atum-Re, Hathor, Amum.
- The Lunar Path, which concentrates on the purely devotional aspects and the ability to move between the worlds, i.e. different planes of consciousness. New Kingdom. For example: Thoth, Isis, Osiris.

Make a note in your diary of the forth coming feast days for your chosen deity and meditate on their image in Circle to celebrate that festival.

In recent years, so much has been made of the issue of Initiation into the Mysteries that people tend to forget about the very necessary and very extended prior training, the latter in itself being no guarantee of success for the individual. Successful accomplishment of mystical advancement, however, offers a chance to walk between the worlds and attain, in esoteric terms, 'Conversation with the Holy Guardian Angel'.

Once the Initiate has stepped through the portal, there is no going back and it alters the perspective on almost everything that we once held to be of worth and consequence. Even family and friends assume a lesser degree of importance when compared with the quest upon which we have embarked. This is why the first steps on the Path should never be taken lightly, or without due thought about the consequences. We must accept that those we care about cannot lay claim to 'everlasting life' whether it be a Christian or Pagan Afterlife, and that we may never again cross paths with those we've considered to be our soulmates. There can be no retracing of our steps once we have stepped through the gate.

This stellar-path is not for the faint-hearted. Nevertheless, if we fail to grasp the importance or appreciate the opportunity at its full value, we will have missed the supreme chance of our spiritual life and the gateway (or Stargate) to another world will be shut to us, at best for this lifetime, at worst – forever.

Part Five

Liber Ægyptius

Let my servants be few and secret.
[*Liber AL Vel Legis pt1.v.10*]

It flows through old hushed Egypt and its sands,
Like some grave mighty thought threading a dream,
And times and things, as in that vision, seem
Keeping along in their eternal stands.
[*The Nile*, James Henry Leigh Hunt (1784-1859)]

It should now be apparent to the genuine seeker that the stellar wisdom of ancient Egyptian disciplines was never intended for those outside the inner sanctum of the temple. And from archaeological sources we can glean several plausible reasons why the Nile Valley was plunged into civil unrest at the end of the Pyramid Age. Despite hundreds of years of stability and prosperity, and from the advantage point of hindsight, we can see how a magically *inferior* priesthood might be willing to sanction the destruction and even murder of the old stellar priesthood, on whom they could apportion blame for the misfortunes of the State.

Liber Ægyptius, the *Book of Egypt*, offers only a tantalising glimpse into the fiery brilliance of the distant past, just as it can only suggest what lies behind the star-spangled veil of the future. The old stellar wisdom has been inert for too long for it to suddenly burst upon the consciousness like a supernova. To quote Crowley: *'In all systems of religion is to be found a system of Initiation, which may be defined as the process by which a man comes to learn that unknown Crown. Though none can communicate either the knowledge or the power to achieve this, which we may call the Great Work, it is yet possible for initiates to guide others.'*

These first guided steps, therefore, come in the form of a series of pathworkings that differ each time the seeker performs them.

Stellar, Solar and Lunar Pathworkings

It is important that a full and accurate account of each exercise is recorded in a Magical Journal for comparison. There is sometimes confusion over the term 'pathworking' because often this is mistakenly referred to as 'visualisation'. There is a difference between the two applications but here visualisation is the relaxed and controlled state that is *the lead-in* to pathworking proper. Most magical practitioners will be familiar with the moon/earth tides and so we begin by exploring the natural lunar energies.

The Lunar Pathworking

Choose the phase of the moon when your *personal* magical energy is at its strongest. Check on the time of moon-rise, and unless you are going to work on the dark phase, you should try to ensure that the moon is visible throughout your pathworking. For this first, simple exercise we are going to bathe in moonlight and let its rejuvenating powers wash over us, and because this is a very individual exercise there are no instructions other than to go with the flow. For all moon phases, sit in the moonbeams, watch them as they glow all over and around you like shimmering silvery mercury. You can pick handfuls up and watch it stream through your fingers like fine sand or silvery water.

How does that make you feel?

If you are using the dark phase, simply gaze up into the dark sky above, and allow yourself to drift out into the comforting darkness; visualise yourself slipping deeper and deeper into the void. There is no danger here and you can return whenever you wish. Let yourself drift out into the softness, where it feels like sinking into beautiful velvet or the softness of unseen feathers. It is gentle, soft and welcoming.

How do you feel in this black, silent world?

The Solar Pathworking

We may not, however, be as familiar with solar energies, since most magical practitioners channel their activities under the cover of darkness. By contrast, the Egyptian priesthood performed their devotions during the hours of daylight: at dawn, noon and dusk – see the *Book of Days*.

Try this as a *daytime* pathworking by sitting in a patch of strong sunlight either outdoors or indoors. Make yourself comfortable and concentrate on a candle flame burning in a shaft of direct sunlight, which will give a completely different effect to that which we usually experience in a darkened room. You are working with the element of fire through the sunlight and flame.

Imagine that you are being drawn gently into the candle flame. Feel the warmth as you pass into the centre of the flame. Allow your being to dance in the flame; you are one with it. If you feel your eyelids drooping let them close but keep your mind focussed within the candle flame. See what happens … maybe nothing will, but this is a form of lucid dreaming that can often produce some interesting results. If the working can be performed around the time of one of the solstices or equinoxes, then so much the better. Sunday would be a good day to try this, as it is traditionally the day of the Sun.

The Stellar Pathworking

Before embarking on the stellar pathworking, spend some time studying the placement of the circumpolar stars in any beginners' guide to astronomy. Over time, we *must* become familiar with the stars – and not with an astrologer's eye – but from an astronomer's perspective.

This exercise should be performed outdoors on a clear night

before or just after the dark of the moon. [If you cannot perform this outdoors, sit at an open window with the interior lights switched off.] Your eyes will need 20 minutes to adjust to night vision so use the time to make yourself comfortable. Ensure that you are wearing something warm if you are doing this in winter. As you will need to spend some time with your head tilted back, it is a good idea to spend this waiting time arranging cushions or setting a reclining chair so that you can gaze at the heavens in comfort.

To begin, you will need to identify two star constellations; **Ursa Major** (the Plough) and **Cassiopia** (with its `W` formation). These are known as circumpolar stars as they perpetually revolve around the Pole Star (Polaris), and can be seen as symbolising the male and female cosmic energies. They are both easy to identify.

After 20 minutes, look up into the sky again, and you will be surprised how many more stars you can see now that your eyes have made the adjustment. Watch Cassiopia and Ursa Major in their slow heavenly dance and think about the energies of male and female weaving their magical dance across the night skies. Let your eyes be drawn towards the brightest star that you can see and concentrate all your effort into reaching out to this star with your mind. Let the charm *'listen and glisten'* run repetitively through your mind over and over again the whole time …

See what happens … make notes on your return.

These elementary exercises are useful tools in that they focus and draw the seeker's attention away from the stereotypical planetary influences, and out into deep-space. Do not attempt to work them one after the other, but spread them over the course of a month to get the best from your efforts. The results will *always* vary, but the end-product will be a greater understanding as the journey deepens.

Despite claims to the contrary, the origins of the constellation patterns are not known with any certainty. Both the ancient

Chinese and Egyptians drew up fanciful sky maps (as we know, two of the Egyptian constellations, for example, were the Crocodile and the Hippopotamus). The template followed today, however, is based on that of the ancient Greeks (see Part Seven – 'The Book of Nights'), and all of the 48 constellations given by Ptolemy in his book the *Almagest*, written about 150AD, are still in use. Ptolemy's list contains most of the important constellations visible from the latitude of Alexandria in Egypt. Among them are the two Bears, Cygnus, Herculus, Hydra and Aquila, as well as the 12 zodiacal groups. There are also some small, obscure constellations, such as Equuleus (the Foal) and Sagitta (the Arrow), which are surprisingly faint and, one would have thought, too ill-defined to be included in that original 48.

It has been said that the night sky is a mythological picture book, although none of the original Egyptian myths have been preserved in the telling. But it is interesting that an early reference in the Pyramid Texts identifies Sopdu, an early hawk-god who personified the eastern frontier of Egypt, as a star who was born from the union of Orion (Sah) and the Dog Star (Sopdet). He later became associated with the more important hawk-god Horus, and the Triad of Sopdet (Sirius), Sah (Orion) and Sopdu was later paralleled by the divine family of Isis, Osiris and Horus.

As we have already discussed, the Greeks – despite creating the 'modern' star-maps – actually accredited the Egyptians with recognising the existence of the *movement* of the stars. Thales, who lived in the 6th century BC, was the first of the Greek philosophers to bring back to Greece the knowledge and records of the Babylonians and Egyptians, and put forward theories that lay somewhere between the 'mythologies of the past and future scientific discoveries'. But it was Ptolemy of Alexandria who drew together centuries of Babylonian observations of the motions of the planets to support his theory of an Earth-centred universe and it was his system that ruled the world of astronomy for nearly 1,500 years.

Perhaps it is not surprising that Egyptian 'mythology' failed to play a major role in these theories since, by that time, there was little preserved of the ancient religion, and the Greeks had already associated most of the old Egyptian gods with their own home-grown myths and legends. Despite trying to explain why natural events occurred without reference to supernatural causes, the Greeks appear to have little concept of the stellar energies of deep space that played such an important part within the Egyptian Mysteries.

Perhaps because the Graeco-Roman Mystery traditions tended to be chthonic rather than cosmic, they were dismissive of the strange anthropomorphic gods of a distant and long-dead civilisation. In addition, apart from the various creation-myths, there is very little by way of folklore preserved in the literature of Egypt. According to the entry in *The British Museum Dictionary of Ancient Egypt*, the Middle Kingdom was particularly characterised by the introduction of 'fictional' literature, all of which *purport* to be historical accounts, although many of the details of the narrative indicate that they were fantasies designed to entertain rather than record actual events. The Greeks probably considered them unworthy of consideration and, as a result, the modern astronomical references are devoid of any link to an older Egypt.

The Imperishable Ones

Before attempting to travel out into the cosmos, however, the seeker needs to return to the concept of the 'Imperishable Ones' – the circumpolar stars that provided the fundamental basis for the archaic religion. These are the stars that never set, but seem to circle around the celestial Pole or North Star, which in our time is Polaris in the constellation of Ursa Minor. This star is easily located by taking a straight line from the stars Merak and Dubhe in Ursa Major to the last star (Polaris) in the Little Bear's tail.

Once you have got used to locating the Pole Star, use it as a focus for the stellar pathworking.

Polaris, however, has not always been the Pole Star. When the pyramids were being built around 4,800 years ago, during the Old Kingdom, the north-pole star was Thuban – Alpha Draconis in the constellation of Draco. Thuban was at its closest to the pole in 2830BC and there have been many academic discussions about the celestial pole and the alignment of the pyramids. Despite having no outstandingly bright stars, Draco sprawls across the sky and is the largest of all the constellations, occupying over 1,000 square degrees of the sky. Thuban, today, is only the eighth brightest star in Draco and can barely be seen with the naked eye in an unpolluted night sky, but it is not surprising that this large, rambling star-grouping was identified with Nut, the 'Mother of Set'.

Similarly, those seven stars of Ursa Major cannot be mistaken and the sacrificial offering – the 'thigh' – is easily identified from the zodiacal ceiling in the Temple of Hathor at Dendera. These are the seven stars that have long been associated with Set. Almost opposite Ursa Major is the distinctive constellation of Cassiopeia, which corresponds to the figure of the hippopotamus – Tauret, goddess of childbirth.

These four constellations: Ursa Major, Ursa Minor, Draco and Cassiopeia contain the principal stars with which the Egyptians identified as being the 'Stars That Grow Not Weary'. Or the place to where the king journeyed after death; to be reborn and returned to earth as an embodiment of the living god. Without the aid of telescopes, it *is* possible to watch and study these brilliant specks of light, which will eventually become the focus for future pathworkings and the first step on the stellar path.

In his extensive writings, Aleister Crowley has provided us with examples of his own pathworkings in order that we may try for ourselves, those first tentative steps in linking magically and intellectually with the universal energies so hungrily sought by men of science and faith from the beginning of time. In his own *Confessions*, he gives an insight into a meditation technique used for the purpose of projecting the Will.

The 'Star-Sponge' Vision

I lost consciousness of everything but a universal space in which were innumerable bright points, and I realised this as a physical representation of the universe ... I concentrated on this vision, with the result that the void space which had been the principal element of it diminished in importance; space appeared to be ablaze, yet the radiant points were not confused ...

This vision led to an identification of the individual blazing points of the stars, and he perceived that each star was connected by a ray of light with its neighbour, and that certain stars were of greater magnitude and brilliancy than the rest ... The next step is to attempt to combine the previous stellar pathworking with the 'Star-Sponge Vision' and see what kind of reaction can be obtained by focussing on Polaris ... *'listen and glisten'* ... Does the star glow bigger and brighter? Does it draw you toward it? Or does it cast you deeper into space on one of its rays of light?

All we are doing is opening up our minds to the power of cosmic forces. What is important to realise, is that this is only very elementary pathworking and, no matter how intense, illuminating or frightening the imagery, **these are merely the steps of a relatively humble beginner.** We cannot, however, afford to *over*-estimate the effects of this simple psychic probing, simply because we could be laying ourselves wide open to attack from extra-terrestrial intelligences before we are ready to cope with them. And be warned, there *are* dangerous energies at large out there for the uninitiated. No matter how profound the experience, nor how intensely charged we *believe* ourselves to have become, we are not yet ready to claim the title of Master of the Universe!

The opening and closing verses of Crowley's famous poem, *One Star in Sight* becomes an allegory for the metaphysical transformation of the seeker. At the start of the journey the seeker's head and feet are held fast, imprisoned in ignorance of what lies beyond the veil.

Thy feet in mire, thine head in murk,
O man, how piteous thy plight,
The doubts that daunt, the ills that irk,
Thou hast nor wit nor will to fight –
How hope in heart, or worth in work?
No star in sight!

Few do have the 'wit nor will' to challenge this state of ignorance or push the boundaries of Knowing and, as a result, most will remain fettered by spiritual doubt and uncertainty. But along with Knowledge and Wisdom, comes Understanding.

To man I come, the number of
A man my number, Lion of Light;
I am The Beast whose Law is Love.
Love under Will, his royal right –
Behold within, and not above,
One star in sight

Before we can 'behold within', there are many paths to travel and other worlds to explore. To repeat Crowley's words: *'Though none can communicate either the knowledge or the power to achieve this, which we may call the Great Work, it is yet possible for initiates to guide others.'*

This guiding towards the rediscovery of the old stellar wisdom can only be in the form of general pathworking and visualisation, simply because each person's journey will take a different route. Some methods will appear as easy as following stepping stones across a stream, while others will plunge the seeker into the Abyss. Added to this, we still have no way of knowing how the earliest Egyptians acquired their knowledge of other worlds, but it is safe to assume that certain members of the priesthood would have closely studied every movement of those stars on which their beliefs were focused. Needless to say, that ancient night sky with its vast panorama stretched out across the open desert, would have offered a far greater stellar vista than our own present-day polluted sky-scape.

Three poems by Walter de la Mare refer to the stars that are visible from the northern hemisphere. The first extract from *Stars,* helps to identify those that make up the formation of Orion – the constellation that played such an important part in Egyptian beliefs. Look for Orion around the Winter Solstice ... and follow the instructions ...

If to the heavens you lift your eyes
When Winter reigns o'er our Northern skies,
And snow-cloud none the zenith mars,
As Yule-tide midnight these your stars:
Low in the South see bleak-blazing Sirius;
Above him hang Betelgeuse, Procyon wan;
Wild-eyed to the West of him, Rigel and Bellatrix,
And rudd-red Aldebaran journeying on.

Similarly, *The Ride-by-Nights* can easily be adapted for a simple visualisation once you've deciphered the cryptic clues in the poem for the real names of the constellations: choose a clear, moonless night around the Winter Solstice to locate where they are. Now visualise yourself zooming through the night like a shooting star ... beneath Charlie's Wane (the Plough or Ursa Major) and under the Dragon's Feet (Draco). The air is cold and crisp and thousands of stars hurtle past, as you wheel and turn in a helter-skelter ride along the Milky Way. Imagine yourself soaring among the twinkling beads of light and between the legs of the Chair (Cassiopeia) and out past Leo. The unmistakeable form of Orion, with Sirius following behind, looms large ahead but you accelerate and fly between the legs of the Hunter before heading back home.

This is a simple exercise that can be repeated whenever there is a clear, moonless night ... and may just lead to a revealing pathworking, despite the fact that the imagery is one of British witchcraft, rather than the Egyptian Mystery Tradition!

Planetary Pathworking

The third poem, *The Wanderers,* focuses the mind on the planets, even though the Egyptians were not aware of the two furthest – Uranus and Neptune.

And through these sweet fields go,
Wand'ers mid the stars
Venus, Mercury, Uranus, Neptune,
Saturn, Jupiter, Mars.

Nevertheless, as we have seen earlier in this book, those with which they were familiar were assigned to the various gods:

- Horus 'who limits the two lands' – Jupiter
- Horus of the Horizon – Mars;
- Sebegu (a god associated with Set) – Mercury
- Horus 'bull of the sky' – Saturn
- Re or Osiris with Venus ('the one who crosses' or 'god of the morning').

Around 1590BC an anonymous Egyptian scribe wrote: *'Do you not know that Egypt is a copy of heaven and the temple of the whole world?'* Today, our 'temple' reaches out into space and, like all true seekers of the Mysteries, we need to understand the perils of the Path that draws us ever onward. In the 21st century we are no longer reliant on blind faith simply because we now have a wider view of the cosmos, and a greater belief in the Source of all life, as a continuing and self-perpetuating concept. Visualise the rebirth of another world ...

> From out of nowhere, through the swirling fog, a world the size of the Earth's Moon looms into view. Its surface is glowing with lakes of bubbling lava, and a torrent of impacting meteorites sends white-hot rock spraying high up into its wispy jacket of sulphur-green clouds. The bombardment is relentless and stone by stone, rock by rock, boulder by boulder, the growing planet absorbs anything that dares stray into its path. Originally, just one of a huge army of rocks circling an embryonic Sun, this world has grown large. It has swallowed up countless smaller rivals. Others, which narrowly escaped its draw, it threw off course and sent to a fiery death in the heart of the Sun. The odds of this young planet surviving are slight – at any moment it could be torn apart in a cataclysmic collision with another large ball of rock. There are scores of others like it in this young Solar System, and only a handful will make it. Yet somehow it does survive. In 100 million years it will grow large enough to hang on to a thick layer of gas and cloud. Its surface, now hot enough to melt rock, will cool to a temperature where water will condense into oceans and, one day, it will develop life ...
>
> [Extract from *The Planets*, McNab & Younger]

By using the 'birth of a planet' sequence above, create your own pathworking in order to visit other worlds. To put your 'journeying' into perspective, bear in mind that unlike Ptolemy's theory of an Earth-centred universe, we now know that our Earth is situated in a remote backwater of the Milky Way galaxy. In fact, the Earth is on the middle arm of three great spirals – known as the Orion Arm. Taking this as our cue, we now are going back even further than the birth of the planet, because the Stellar Path is all about pushing the boundaries. ... By now our own galaxy was already billions of years old and full of stars, and using the following as a basis for visualisation, see where this journey takes you ...

From the centre of our galaxy, a massive cloud was gently drifting through space As this cloud floats between the distant star fields, being pulled first this way then that by gravitational tugs of other stars, pockets of gas in the cloud started to collapse inwards on themselves. As these imploding pockets reached a critical density, their cores heated up and ignited: stars were born. If we could watch the process of aeons speeded up into minutes, we might see small points of light flickering into life as stellar neighbourhoods sprang up throughout the cloud. Most of the smaller lights might glow steadily for several tens of seconds before slowly burning themselves out. But as the rash of stars spread throughout the cloud, a few of the lights – the largest and brightest – would flare for just a few brief seconds before disappearing. These are giant stars that burn for just a fraction of the lifetimes of their smaller, steadier siblings ... Deep in the twinkling parent cloud another light flickered on – it was our Sun.

[Extract from *The Planets*, McNab & Younger]

The Realm of Chaos

Chaos: the shape of matter before it was reduced to order

If we want to work with *real* chaos energy, then it is necessary to have some idea of those naturally occurring phenomena that happen in space and yet have serious repercussions here on

Earth. The solar pathworking given at the beginning of this section, is an exploratory exercise but if the more experienced practitioner wishes to work with *real* solar forces, then a basic scientific understanding of the type of energy manifesting in the form of solar winds and sun-spots – first discovered by the Chinese 2,000 years ago – is essential.

Sun Spots

The Sun is so brilliant that it can damage the eye within seconds and so we should *never* look at it directly through a telescope or binoculars, nor stare at it with the naked eye. If we *were* able to view the Sun direct, it would be possible to see small dark spots, just a few hundred kilometres across, where strong magnetic fields emerge through the Sun's surface. Some last for just a few hours, while others grow quite large, perhaps 10 times the size of the Earth, and last for months.

The number of sun-spots wax and wane over an 11-year period, in what is generally referred to as the 'sun-spot cycle'. In addition to the sun-spots, the cycle also produces a host of other activity on and above the Sun's surface. The *Encyclopaedia of the Universe* informs us that: *'Among the more violent events associated with active regions, where the magnetic field is twisted and complex, are flares, in which a huge amount of energy is released – the equivalent of 10 billion one-megaton bombs in a large one ... creating shock waves and producing strong bursts of radio emission.'*

Another manifestation of this type of solar activity is where 10 billion tonnes of hot gas are ejected into interplanetary space, pulling with it elements of the coronal magnetic field. As we should now expect: Earth is not isolated from these violent events – the storms of energetic particles shot out by the Sun often wash the near-Earth environment, affecting power lines and communications, generating auroral displays in the ionosphere around the north and south poles, and damaging sensitive equipment on spacecraft.

Solar winds

Close to the maximum of the sun-spot cycle, a steady flow of atomic particles of ionized gas streams out from the Sun in all directions. This activity is estimated to carry off 50 million million tonnes of material per year and the material flowing away from the Sun, at a few hundred kilometres per second, produces the solar wind. The intensity of solar wind is enhanced during solar storms but the average velocity as it passes the Earth is 300-400 kilometres per second! These wind-speed variations buffet the Earth's magnetic field and can produce storms in the Earth's magnetosphere, and are responsible for the Aurora Borealis, or Northern Lights.

However, a burst of radiation on 20th January 2005 accompanied a huge solar flare tripped radiation monitors worldwide and scrambled detectors on spacecraft, marking the 'largest solar radiation signal *on the ground* in nearly 50 years'. Normally, it takes two or more hours for a dangerous shower of positively charged protons to reach maximum intensity at Earth after a solar flare, and between one and four days for ejected solar material to arrive. But the particles from this vast flare peaked about 15 minutes after the first signs. So the next time you hear a chaos magician talking about butterfly wings flapping on the other side of the planet, just take a leaf out of Crocodile Dundee's book and think to yourself: *'Nah! THAT'S Chaos!'*

Needless to say, no one in their right mind would ever attempt to harness such uncontrollable power but it does serve as an example of bringing the might of the cosmos right to our doorstep. It also acts as a lesson in understanding that *'learning does not consist of knowing what we must or can do, but also of knowing what we could do and perhaps should not do'*. [Umberto Eco]

North Wind Meditation

As a workable substitute, a highly experienced member of the Temple of Khem's priesthood, following a guided exercise in working with elemental quarters, wrote the following meditation. Perhaps the results were produced because the spiritual or magical focus of Egyptian working is geared towards the North (i.e. the Imperishable Ones), or simply because North is always regarded in esoteric terms as the 'Place of Power', but this came through as extremely powerful imagery:

The first wind that seemed to capture my attention was the North Wind. Before me stretched a vast expanse of dark space lit by the cold blue/white twinkling of the stellar bodies. The scene was cold and void and I loved every aspect of it, because I knew that somewhere out there was a mighty power waiting to be called and welcomed back to these realms. Between the archaic galaxies, a chill wind started to blow towards the circle and me. It's icy sharpness cut the surface of the skin like a thousand minute fine needle-points. There was a sensation of knowledge and enormous power, but also of destruction, darkness, fear and chaos. It was as if the Great Old Ones who created humanity had decided to return and see how their work was progressing. I experienced a total lack of sentiment, as we usually know it, and in its place was a feeling of the end of all time when false forms are cast off and you stand face to face with eternity. Perhaps when death itself has died.

Slowly I tried to channel the North Wind down from its lofty regions to the Earth plane, and gain mundane knowledge of it. The home of this wind on Earth is the high snowy mountain passes, or the tumbled chaos of the icefields of the Arctic or Antarctic. When working with this wind I was intolerant to people and noise, and longed for the freedom and solitude of those isolated places. I was reminded of the peoples of the Andes and Tibet as well as the Eskimos. My parting experience of this wind was that it was a wind of freedom and transformation that offered much to those who were committed to learning and service to magic. To me a good title for this wind is the Elder Wind because it brings change.

This pathworking is not, of course, without its risks and should not be undertaken merely for the thrill of the experience. And yet it is just another small step towards making that 'giant leap for mankind' in terms of a spiritual quest.

Batrachophrenoboocosmomachia

By contrast, in *The Complete Astrological Writings*, Crowley detailed a series of highly complicated exercises aimed at improving the capabilities of the seeker's mind. The final one being an extremely complex planetary pathworking that would take many years to master, involving the building up of the solar system within the mind's eye. Beginning with the Earth and the Moon, keeping in mind the relative sizes of, and the distance between, the planet and its satellite, the seeker will then add in turn Venus, Mars, Mercury and the Sun. At this stage it may be advisable to change the viewpoint to the centre of the Sun, since this makes it easier to add the Asteroids, Jupiter, Saturn, Uranus and Neptune.

The utmost attention to detail is now necessary, as the picture is highly complex, apart from the difficulty of appreciating relative size and distance ... Let this picture be practised month after month until it is absolutely perfect.

Once the exercise has been mastered, the practitioner should:

... recommence the picture, starting from the Sun, and adding the planets one by one, each with its own proper motion, until he has an

image perfect in all respects of the Solar System as it actually exists.
Let him particularly note that unless the apparent size is approx-
imate to the real, his practise is wasted. Let him then add a comet to
the picture; he may find, perhaps, that the path of this comet may
assist him to expand the sphere of his mental vision until it includes
a star. And thus, gathering one star after another, let his contem-
plation become vast as the heaven, in space and time ever aspiring to
the perception of the Body of Nuit ...

The Urshu – Lords of Light

The *Urshu*, the old Great Ones of *zep tepi* – Egypt's 'First Time' –
also have parallels in other esoteric cultures in the form of the
Watchers, or Light Bearers – great cosmic beings who acted as
intermediaries between gods and men, and played an important
role in developing human affairs. The concept of these celestial
beings appears to have originated in the Middle East, and entered
the Western ritual magic tradition via the legend of the *Grigori*, or
Watchers.

These were the Hebrew 'fallen-angels' or Ben Elohim, who
mated with human women and taught them the magical arts, and
from whom all esoteric traditions and occult knowledge are said
to have sprung. This would not be the first 'idea' to have been
hijacked by subsequent Middle Eastern cultures to add credence
to their own burgeoning religious doctrine. Just as the Urshu
became identified with the Ben Elohim, so the notion of the 'holy
family' passed into Christian tradition, having already metamorphosed once within Egyptian history, from the early Triad of
Sopdet (Sirius), Sahu (Orion) and Sopdu to the later divine family
of Isis, Osiris and Horus.

In the book *Liber Ægyptius*, the suggestion was made that the
Urshu decamped following the destruction of the stellar
priesthood; repulsed by the excesses of mankind when they
witnessed first-hand its capacity for self-destruction. Their
continued presence as shadowy beings on the periphery of

human consciousness has only added to the growing belief in guardians, angels and fairies within esoteric circles. When Crowley encountered Aiwass in that hotel room in Cairo, it was not a visitation by a 'good fairy' ... the Guardians are no longer kindly disposed towards humankind *en masse*. And we only have to read *The Book of the Law* to understand that there is even a certain amount of hostility towards those who remain impervious to the warnings.

Now let it be understood that I am a god of War and Vengeance ... I will give you a war-engine. With it ye shall smite the peoples; and none shall stand before you ... let blood flow to my name. Trample down the Heathen ...

Even up to his death in 1947, Crowley still found parts of *The Book* distasteful. This supposedly heralding in of the New Aeon in Part III of *Liber AL* proclaims *'an end to the humanitarian mawkishness that is destroying the human race by the deliberate artificial protection of the unfit'*. Are we to understand from such words, that no favours are to be expected from these extra-terrestrial intelligences that inhabit the 'world between worlds', seeking out receptive channels for their teachings? And, as if to endorse such musings, perhaps we should recall the results of the ToK priest's meditation, where he 'experienced a total lack of sentiment' when he encountered the Old Great Ones.

For next stage of preparation, we need to reflect on the meaning behind the oldest religious writings in the world. *'The texts can be understood through knowledge of the ancient Egyptian mythology and symbolism, which explain the origin, function and qualities of the natural laws,'* writes Dr Ramses Seleem. *'Someone who reads the texts without comprehension of the mythology and symbolism is like a deaf person trying to listen to the music of Mozart ... The Egyptian sages, through the mythology, mapped the path of eternity in detail ...'* As we know, the Egyptian New Year was marked by the helical rising of Sopdet (the Dog Star, or Sirius). In the early Egyptian myth, it says that the newborn child, Sopdu, fathered by Sahu (Orion) came forth from the thighs of Sopdet. In death, the deceased then rises as a 'Sahu', or as a spiritual body, waiting to be reborn.

Star Thrall

Orion has been recognised as a distinctive group of stars for thousands of years. The Chaldeans knew it as Tammuz, named after the month in which the familiar belt of stars first rose before sunrise. The Syrians called it Al Jabbar, the Giant, and to the Greeks it was Orion, the great hunter. For the Egyptians it was Sahu.

Faulkner's analysis of the Pyramid Texts shows two distinct strata. One, the circumpolar stars and the northern sky, which appear as the abode of the gods and the illustrious royal dead; the other with the constellation of Orion and Sothis. *'Orion is either a companion of the King, and is joined by him, making with Sothis a celestial trio; the King may thus be thought of as sharing in the responsibility for regulating times and seasons.'* As fragmented as these details are, the power of the archaic stellar-cult was still making itself felt, if not wholly understood, well into the Pyramid Age and beyond. By this time, the Osirian cult was already transposed onto the earlier Sahu (*S3h*) – Sopdet (*Spdt*) – Sopdu (*Spdw*) Triad, the latter disappearing almost entirely. In Faulkner's 1969 translation of the Pyramid Texts, Osiris has already *become* Orion in the funerary texts.

Pyramid Texts

In Utterance 216 [151], for example, the king is represented as a star fading at dawn with the other stars:

Orion is swallowed up by the Netherworld,
Pure and living in the horizon.

Sothis is swallowed up by the Netherworld
Pure and living in the horizon.

In Utterance 218 [186] the king is identified with Osiris (Sahu):

In your name of Dweller in Orion, with a season in the sky and a
season on earth.

In Utterances 273-4 [408] ...

For the King is a god,
Older than the oldest.
Thousands serve him,
Hundreds offer to him,
There is given to him a warrant as Great Power
By Orion, father of the gods.

In Utterance 412 [723], a 'resurrection' text:

You shall reach the sky as Orion, your soul shall be as effective as
Sothis [Sopdet] ...

In Utterance 442 [819-21] the dead king becomes a star:

Behold, he has come as Orion, behold, Osiris [the king] has come as
Orion ... O King, the sky [Sopdet] conceives you with Orion [Sahu],
the dawn-light bears you with Orion ... You will regularly ascend
with Orion from the eastern region of the sky, you will regularly
descend with Orion into the western region of the sky, your third is
Sothis pure of thrones, and it is she who will guide you both on the
goodly roads which are in the sky in the Fields of Rushes.

In Utterances 466 [882-83] the king is again referred to as a star:

O King, you are this great star, the companion of Orion, who traverses the sky with Orion ... The sky has borne you with Orion ...

In Utterance 471 [[924] there is the 'ferryman' text:

I have come that I may glorify Orion ...

In Utterance 582 [1561] there is the 'ascension' text:

May Orion give me his hand, for Sothis has taken my hand ...

In Utterance 625 [1763] – As last:

I have ascended among the [Great Ones]; *I have gone up the ladder with my foot on Orion and my arm uplifted ...*

Even though the Osirian-cult has superseded the old stellar-cult of early times, it can still be seen how the ancient Mysteries were preserved within the doctrine of the new Egyptian religious beliefs.

Coffin Texts

These later funerary texts take their name from the fact that they were inscribed in ink on the inside walls of the wooden coffins during the Middle Kingdom. By this time, the Old Ways would have been forgotten, 'for there are none that now live who remember it'. The 'Spells' were added to and amended; and repeated by rote since the old priesthood had long since departed.

The Spells lack the mystery and majesty of the Pyramid Texts, and were probably 'dumbed-down' in order to appeal to the lower classes, who now had access to everlasting life. For example, Spell 44 [188] has faint echoes of the earlier texts, although there is the suggestion that the Spell no longer refers to the person of the king, but to anyone who could afford the funerary rites, as archaeological discoveries have shown:

May [Name] *be encircled by Orion, by Sothis and by the Morning Star, may they set you within the arms of your mother Nut ...*

Spell 227 [263] also reflects some of the old mystery ...

I am Orion who treads his Two Lands, who navigates in front of the stars of the sky on the belly of my mother Nut ...

As does Spell 236 [304]:

I ascend to the sky with Orion, I receive food-offerings with the Great Ones, my abode is at the high portals of the Entourage of Re ...

The Egyptians obviously retained the concept of the dead going to 'heaven', i.e. the abode of the stars, but this appears to be a purely collective religious belief, rather than a magico-religious one where the king assumes his moral obligation to transcend death to be reborn again as protector of his people and the State. The differences between the Pyramid Texts and the Coffin Texts can be seen as the demarcation of religion and the Mysteries, leaving what can best be identified as an 'Osirian death-cult' in the public domain.

Book of the Dead

Or to give the texts the correct name: 'The Chapters of Coming-Forth by Day', refers to the later collections of religious and magical texts, dating mostly from c1500-250BC. The texts from this period are dominated by Osirian references, with only vague, infrequent mention of the original stellar-related beliefs.

For example:

> ... *may I see the Sektet boat of the sacred Sahu* [Orion] *passing forth over the sky ...*
> ... *triumphant are the fingers of Orion ...*
> ... *to Osiris-Orion (Sah) ...*
> *Thou risest up like Sah (Orion) ...*

We still have casual, fleeting glimpses of the old religion that had its roots in the belief in, or knowledge of, the unseen powers of the Universe, and knowing the order and the structure of things – i.e. the concept of Ma'at. The importance of the Mysteries, and knowledge that all things in the Universe are dependent on each other, however, appears to have been lost. This understanding is not, however, exclusive to the ancient Egyptians.

> Reflected in many sacred systems of knowledge is the idea that the world is a mystery and yet, at the same time, operates according to strict, ordered relationships. Some questions can never be answered with a single answer and others can be answered simply by observing various cycles day after day, year after year ...
> [*The Sacred: Ways of Knowledge, Sources of Life*]

But to return to the obvious link between the star-grouping of Orion and Sirius, and the ancient Mysteries. In January 2003, a claim was made by Dr Michael Rappenglueck, renowned for his pioneering work locating star charts painted on the walls of prehistoric caves, that the oldest image of a star pattern had been recognised as the constellation of Orion. Carved on an ivory tablet, *some 32,500 years ago*, this tiny sliver of mammoth tusk shows a carving of a man-like figure with arms and legs outstretched in the same pose as the stars of Orion. It was found in a cave in the Ach Valley in Germany and the proportions of the man correspond to the pattern of stars that comprise Orion, despite the fact that these stars were in slightly different positions 32,000 years ago. Astronomical confirmation of the archaeological dating came from a computer reconstruction, which found evidence that Orion appeared completely above the natural horizon of the cave between 32,000 and 33,500 years ago! *'The appendix between the legs would show a phallic star creature, in line with ancient ideas that Orion may be responsible for the celestial insemination of Earth, and for cosmic fertility.'*

Orion is the most striking of all the constellations and has had a special significance for many cultures throughout history, throughout the world. Perhaps this is where we should begin our search for ancient knowledge: in the stellar nursery of the Orion Nebula. Easily visible to the naked eye, as the central object in the 'sword' of Orion, this is a region of ongoing star formation. But ... and it really *does* depend very much on how you like your magical energies served. If you *are* satisfied with that plain, wholesome fare with few surprises; if you prefer a satisfying but unchanging (and unchallenging) recipe in your ritual; or if adventure plays no part in your quest, then stellar magic certainly isn't for you.

On the other hand, if you *can* look beyond the picturesque seasonal life-death-rebirth cycle of planet Earth and out towards the stellar nurseries of deep space, then you might confront your Holy Guardian Angel on his own turf! As we have seen, the pursuit of stellar wisdom is, literally, as old as time. It has its roots in all the ancient creation myths – those primordial, indigenous forces – and to come full circle, *The Atum-Re Revival*, ends where it all began: with those Khemetic stellar beliefs of ancient Egypt:

The Path to Immortality is hard and only a few find it. The rest await the Great Day when the wheels of the universe shall be stopped and the immortal 'Sparks' shall escape from the sheaths of substance. Woe unto those who wait, for they must return again, unconscious and unknowing, to the seed ground of the stars, and (there) await a new beginning.

[From The Divine Pymander of Hermes Trismegistus]

Part Six

The Book of Nights

Astrology was foreign to the ancient Egyptians, and even among the Greeks, it only reached its prime in the later Hellenistic Period ... What is plainly lacking in the pharaonic period is belief in the influence of the planets and their alignments.

[The Secret Lore of Egypt: Its Impact on the West, Erik Hornung]

Like magic, gnosis and alchemy, astrology outlasted the victory of Christianity, but if we turn to *Calendars and Constellations of the Ancient World*, we find that zodiacal signs with which we are familiar are also out of alignment with the 'star signs' of the ancient world. Those early calendar makers believed that in making the beginning of the year dependent on the Sun's entry into the constellation of Aries, they were also binding it to the season of the Winter Solstice and the re-birth of the Sun. As the centuries rolled by, slowly the stars of Aries receded from the Winter Solstice until they arrived at the Spring Equinox – which is where our zodiac begins today.

As a result, there is a large amount of conjecture and speculation in *The Book of Nights*, which is unashamedly a blend of modern astrological symbolism, magical correspondences with genuine historical and astronomical references wherever possible. Needless to say, it should *not* be taken as a scholarly work, nor as a definitive approach to Egyptian astrology – but merely acts as a guide for those interested in establishing some semblance of compatible order within the Egyptian year – see *The Book of Days*.

Aket-Season (Inundation)

First Month – *Dhwty* (19 July-17 August)
Leo 24 July-23 August

The Sun enters Leo around 24th July just after the Egyptian New Year on the 19th July, and leaves around 23rd August. Leo is ruled by the Sun, being a predominantly masculine sign and representative of Elemental Fire. The Sun rose in Leo during the Pyramid Age when the Egyptian solar cult was in its ascendancy over the much older stellar cult and the sign can therefore be looked upon as a time for new ventures to coincide with the Egyptian New Year. Although traditionally a masculine symbol, the lion in the Egyptian pantheon was the emblem of the goddesses Tefnut and Sekhmet, the dreadful lion-headed daughter of Re. In ancient times, Leo was associated with the Summer Solstice and the rising of Sirius to herald the annual Inundation of the Nile.

For the Egyptians, the lion has been a symbol of kingship from pre-dynastic times and, since they lived on the desert margins, the animals were seen as the guardians of the eastern and western horizons, the place of sunset and sunrise. In this aspect Aker, the primeval earth-god presides over the juncture of the western and eastern horizons in the Otherworld. The god's motif consists of the foreparts of two lions, facing in opposite directions but joined in the middle. Aker opens the earth's gate (i.e. the grave) for the king to pass into the Otherworld, ready for his traditional rebirth.

Most leonine deities, however, were female, the most important being Sekhmet and Tefnut, whose cults were eventually merged with those of Bastet and Mut. Tefnut, with her brother/consort Shu, was part of the first couple created by the sun-god Atum, and often represented as a pair of lions. Sekhmet was regarded as one of the 'Eyes of Re' and in one myth was almost responsible for the annihilation of mankind following the mortal rebellion against Re. She was also believed to be responsible for plagues and sickness brought by the 'messengers of Sekhmet' and, on the assumption that she could cure as well as kill, she was later worshipped as the 'lady of life'.

Concept

For the Egyptian astrologers this meant that when the Sun was in Leo it was stronger than in any other sign. The symbol of the lion, whether in its male or female aspect, is one of loyalty, stability and a preserver of the status quo rather than revolutionary. The classic Leo has a strong sense of pride and individualism but in true Egyptian form, is equally content to work in tandem with his or her partner – providing their standards are compatible with their own. After all, in the wild it is the lioness who does the work and feeds the family! The ideal balance for the unstoppable energy of Leo is the calming influence of the lunar deity Tahuti/Thoth who was the only one with the ability to handle the volatile lion-goddess. Magically speaking this is the perfect partnership

Second Month – Phaophi (18 August-16 September)
Virgo 24 August-23 September

The Sun enters Virgo around the 24th August after the annual celebration of the Opet Festival and of the marriage between Osiris and Isis on the 18th. Virgo is the second largest of all the constellations and the most prominent in the evening sky around 8th May. For the Egyptians, the benevolent goddesses symbolised by Virgo could be identified as Hathor, Isis and Neith – although since this is the only sign attributed to the female we should also consider less familiar deities such as Nephthys, Mut, Tauret, Nut and Ma'at. Ruled by Mercury it is a feminine sign associated with Elemental Earth.

As with most cultures, the role of the female deities was identified with motherhood and/or protection, even if each individual had different facets to her character. Although Nut, Tauret, Mut and Isis were all symbols of motherhood it is important to separate the subtle differences between them. Nut is the most ancient and although she is the 'Lady of the Starry Heavens' and matriarch of many of the later gods, she is seen much more as an Otherworld deity than an earthly mother figure. Tauret is the patron and protector of pregnant women and children, while Mut's very name is the Egyptian word for 'mother'. Isis is the dynastic mother who is fiercely protective of her offspring, although she is often shown as cold and calculating – unlike Hathor, who is seen as gentle and fun-loving. Nephthys is a goddess of illusion and, despite being identified as the mother of Anubis, she shows few maternal qualities. Neith, one of the oldest of the Egyptian deities is portrayed as a hunter/warrior goddess, a protectress of her people. Ma'at, the goddess of justice, is a late-comer and was originally shown in abstract form as an ostrich feather; it was only much later that she was portrayed as a woman.

Concept

The Sun enters Virgo around the 24th August, which would be an ideal time for working towards harmony between the sexes. The symbol of Virgo is benevolence but at the same time rules the realm of the senses. For all their macho imagery, the ancient Egyptians were appreciative of strong women as the history shows, so the Egyptian Virgo will only be 'girly' if she's using her wiles in the manner of Hathor – to coax someone or something into action. The Sun currently occupies the same zodiacal degree as Spica on 14th-16th October and this offers another opportunity to bring any Virgoan traits into play, especially if the focus is on playing a supporting role or careful management of the material side of life, as it is a sign that needs to be useful.

Third Month – Athyr (17 September-16 October)
Libra 23 September-23 October

The Sun enters Libra around the 23rd September and leaves around the 23rd October. Its entry marks the Spring Equinox in the southern hemisphere (Autumn Equinox in the northern hemisphere), when day and night are of equal length. The scales, however, were not merely symbols of the equal balance between day and night in ancient Egypt – they symbolised the 'Weighing of the Heart' and were an important part of the rites of passage for the dead. Libra is a masculine sign, ruled by Venus and identified with Elemental Air.

According to Patrick Moore, in *The Observer's Year*, 'In March the Sun crosses the celestial equator, moving from south to north (20th March). Now (21st September), six months later, it is back to the equator, this time travelling from north to south, so we have the Autumnal Equinox.' In the southern hemisphere, in the land of Egypt, it was the Spring Equinox and the third month of Inundation when the waters of the Nile began to subside, leaving behind the rich deposit of a new layer of fertile silt. As far as the symbolism of the scales is concerned, this is associated with those gods whose presence is required for the Weighing of the Heart – Thoth (Tahuti), Anubis, Ma'at, Osiris and Ammut, the Devourer of the Dead.

Concepts

A time to focus on balance, harmony and equilibrium. The focal belief of the Egyptians was the importance of order or harmony, symbolised by Ma'at in the form of an ostrich feather. This 'order' should not, however, be viewed as *perfect* balance, since this has a neutralising effect and sterility of thought. If all things are weighed in equal proportion there is no room for movement and so things become stagnant or stationary. When viewing problems and difficulties, always try to look at the third alternative so that there is always a 'casting vote'. The Egyptian belief in the power of Triad, i.e. a grouping of three deities for religious, magical or political reasons, persisted throughout their history. The scales also represent the final judgement, when the deceased must make the 42 Negative Confessions before the gods. They are a permanent reminder that all things will be taken into account at the end of the day.

Fourth Month – Khoiak (17 October-15th November)
Scorpius 23 October-22 November

The Sun enters the sign of Scorpius around 23rd October and leaves around the 22nd November. A predominantly female sign of Elemental Water, it is nevertheless ruled by Mars in traditional astrology. This turbulent sign caused Ptolemy to write in his *Tetrabiblos* [2nd century AD] *'The sign of Scorpius as a whole is marked by thunder and fire. Its leading portion is snowy, its middle temperate and the end causes earthquakes. The north is hot and the south is moist.'* The Transformation of the Benu on 28th reflects this ancient concept of thunder and fire. It also refers to the phoenix, which personifies the everlasting sun-god and symbolises the receding flood waters that allows the re-emergence of the land with the newly enriched soil. The 'black' land is also representative of the primeval Mound, which is also closely associated with the benu-bird – the phoenix, usually identified as the blue heron

According to Professor Maria Betrò, author of *Hieroglyphics*, the classical version of the hieroglyphic of the goddess Selket shows the 'insidious outline of the frightening scorpion'. Abbreviated forms lacking both head and tail, were apparently preferred in the funeral texts, thereby magically reducing the sign, which was potentially animate and dangerous, to impotency. Selket (or Serket) belongs to the group of 'witch' goddesses associated with Isis and had a corps of specialists who could cure the devastating effects of the creature's sting. Although widely connected with the Egyptian funerary-cult, she has powers that can be used by the living to heal venomous bites and was patron of 'magician-medics' dealing with poisonous bites.

The earliest references to Selket occurs in Dynasty I at Saqqara and during the Pyramid Age she had a protective role around the royal throne. Her most famous image is part of the group of four protective goddesses (Selket, Neith, Nephthys and Isis) that guarded the gilded shrine of Tutankhamen.

Concepts
A time to focus attentions on those plans and dreams that have been formulating during those long hours of daylight. Here are the dual energies of change and transmutation as mirrored in the night sky, but with destructive undercurrents if the correct propitiatory observations are not carried out. Remember the ancient Egyptian magical method of neutralising the dangerous, before proceeding with any drastic alterations to either domestic and/or business situations. The energies of Scorpius are not, however, all destructive and a considerable amount of healing/protective power can be drawn upon should the need arise. This is a time for fearlessness but not foolhardiness, so keep your eyes open for any sting in the tail.

Proyet-Season (Emergence)

First Month – Tybi (16 November-15 December)
Sagittarius 23 November-21 December
The Sun enters Sagittarius around 23rd November and leaves around 21st December – the Winter Solstice. A predominantly male sign of Elemental Fire, it is ruled by Jupiter in traditional astrology. Ptolemy wrote in his *Tetrabiblos* [2nd century AD] *'The sign of Sagittarius as a whole is windy but, taken by part its leading portion is wet, its middle temperate and its following part fiery. Its northern parts are windy, its southern moist and changeable.'*

Historically speaking, there is very little with which we can align the constellation of Sagittarius, since its imagery it completely un-Egyptian. The civilisations of the Euphrates-Tigris region identified with the 'Archer' and the two principle deities in the Egyptian pantheon to be associated with arrows are the lioness-headed Sekhmet and Neith.

The 'arrows of Sekhmet' were said to be the cause of widespread disease, illness and pestilence, especially around the time of high summer (the five Epagomenal Days) when people would wear amulets bearing her image for protection. The feast of Sekhmet falls of the 24th November and the text from the Cairo Calendar says: *'The gods are joyful with the offerings of Sekhmet on this day. Repeat the offerings. It will be pleasant to the heart of the gods and the spirits.'* Crossed arrows on a hide shield also formed the sacred emblem of Neith, patron of the Delta city of Sais and one of the national deities of Lower Egypt. The term 'nine bows' was used to refer to the enemies of Egypt, possibly because of the ritual of the physical act of 'breaking the bows' as an analogy for military defeat and/or surrender. The Nine Bows were regularly used to decorate such royal furniture as footstools and throne bases.

Concepts

In the northern hemisphere the Sun occupies Sagittarius as winter falls, though in the southern hemisphere (i.e. Egypt) it is a sign of summer. Here again we are looking at the elements of change and transmutation but with a more balanced overview that one would expect when taking control of a situation. Egyptian god-power in this sphere should be seen as aggressively protective, rather like the symbology of the Emperor in the Tarot. This is the male (i.e. Setian) fiery energy of the Universe; the swift creative energy that produces successful issue. If it is allowed to manifest for too long, however, it burns and destroys. We should not, however, overlook the tremendous creative, or cosmic power, associated with Sagittarius. In astronomical terms we are looking at the hub of the Galaxy and, as such, must take into account the immeasurable Lifeforce emanating from this heavily veiled part of the heavens.

Second Month – Mekhir (16 December-14 January)
Capricornus 21 December-20 January

The Sun enters Capricornus around 21st December and leaves around the 20th January. Its entry marks the Winter Solstice and the shortest day in the northern hemisphere and the Summer Solstice and the longest day in the southern hemisphere. This is a predominantly female sign of Elemental Earth, ruled by Saturn and symbolically represents 'gateways' on both the magical and temporal levels. The constellation was recorded by Ptolemy, although the symbolism of the Babylonian 'goat-fish' is an alien concept in Egyptian mythology – the ram being a more familiar image.

Capricornus is one if the original groups of stars listed by Ptolemy although its mythological associations are not very positive. The nearest in Egyptian imagery is possibly Khnum, the ram-headed god of Elephantine, who is often referred to as a goat because of the shape of the horns. In fact the image is of a flat-horned ram of the species *ovis longipes palaeoaegypticus*, which became extinct around 2000BC.

Another contender is the ram-god Banebdjedet, identified as the 'Goat of Mendes'. Herodotus, the Greek historian, recorded the sacrifice of goats at Mendes, in contrast to the use of sheep elsewhere in Egypt. Egyptologists suggest that he may have mistaken the sacred curved-horned ram (*ovis platyra aegyptiaca*) for a goat. Sacred to Amun, the processional roads to the god's temple were flanked by crio-sphinxes (ram-headed lions). This mis-representation passed into occult lore as the cosmic 'Goat of Mendes', that Eliphas Levi depicted in his celebrated drawing. In both cases the image of each god probably suggests the ram's procreative energy.

Concepts

Ptolemy considered Deneb Algedi to be an important star and if it were overhead at the time of a birth, the child would be blessed with 'great glory, fame, wealth and dignity', providing the rest of the astrological portents were favourable. Here we have the dual meaning of procreative energy, highly influenced by the time of gateways and boundaries (the Solstice). According to the English astrologer, Henry Coley (1676), this sign is *'cold and dry, nocturnal, melancholly, earthy, feminine, solstitial, moveable, cardinal, and a southern signe'*. Like all signs that have a strong duality, it is often difficult to maintain a sense of balance and harmony. This is the point when the Sun begins its journey back to full strength in the northern hemisphere; or winding down in the south. Capricornians are known for their common sense and long-term planning abilities, so this is a time to look far into the future and begin making plans for the year ahead. As you step through the gateway of the old year into the new, use the procreative energies as the driving force to put plans in motion for fruition in the coming months

Third Month – Phamenoth (15 January-13 February)
Aquarius 21 January-19 February

The Sun enters Aquarius around 21st January and leaves around 19th February. This a predominantly masculine sign, that is also ruled by Saturn and aligned with Elemental Air. The sign represents the cleansing, nourishing qualities of water that would have meant a great deal to the ancient Egyptians on both spiritual and temporal levels. The life-giving waters of the Nile played a fundamental part in the religious beliefs of the community as this was seen as the god of Creation pouring the waters of life across the land. The fact that Creation Day falls on the 26th January in Aquarius is highly significant even in modern times – and should be observed as an important festival.

From the historical perspective, perhaps we should look upon the Aquarian stage of the zodiac as being the province of the Egyptian sky-goddess Nut. In popular mythology, Nut and her consort-brother, Geb, were the children of Shu, the air-god, and Tefnut, goddess of moisture. She was one of the personifications of the cosmic elements evolved by the priests of Heliopolis to explain the physical universe. Although in Egyptian art it appears as though Nut is stretching her body with her arms and legs tightly together, the actual concept of the sky-goddess is that her fingers and toes touch the four cardinal points. The usual imagery is that of the goddess arched over the prone earth-god Geb, separated from him by the air-god, Shu. And although the Sun, personified by Egyptian creator-god Atum, was the most important feature in the sky, it was Nut who kept the forces of chaos (Set) from breaking through the sky and engulfing the world. According to *A Dictionary of Egyptian Gods and Goddesses*, it is her body that is the *'firmament dividing the cosmos, that was created by Atum and governed according to his vision of order (person-ified in Ma'at), from the amorphous, primeval merging with which would be tantamount to non-existence'*. In magico-mystical terms, Nut – the Mother of Set – is the firmament, while Set is the uncontrollable cosmic energy of deep space.

Concepts

If it were possible to view the Milky Way from 'above' or 'below', the Galaxy would reveal spiral arms, like a giant Catherine-wheel, with the Sun located near the edge of one of the arms. And we should not lose sight of all this cosmic activity obscured behind the illusion of a veil of peace and harmony, hailed by the 'Dawning of the Age of Aquarius'. More correctly, perhaps we should be looking towards the New Aeon in terms of *broadening* our horizons rather than narrowing our perceptions down to the still-awaited global *entente cordiale* promised by Aquarian Age gurus. A revealing focus for meditation and contemplation is the Star card in Aleister Crowley's *Book of Thoth*, which directly refers to the sign of Aquarius and represents Nut/Nuit, our Lady of the Stars, bearing two cups – one gold, one silver – from which she channels the immortal liquor of life. From the 'star' radiate the curls rays of spiritual light, echoing the actual spiral arms of the Galaxy.

Fourth Month – Pharmuthi (14 February-15 March)
Pisces 20 February-21 March

The Sun enters the tropical zodiac sign of Pisces around 20th February and leaves around the 21st March – the Vernal Equinox. A feminine sign, Pisces is ruled by Jupiter (although some modern astrologers assign Neptune) and Elemental Water. The name for this constellation in most cultures means 'fish' and for the ancient Greeks and Romans its appearance was a sign of improving weather. The 'fish' are positioned so that one sees the end of winter and the other the beginning of spring. The Roman poet, Manilius, wrote *Astronomica* in 1st century CE, around the time of the construction of the Dendera zodiac. *'When the returning Sun courses through the watery stars, then winter's rains mingle with the showers of spring: each sort of moisture belongs in the sign that swims.'*

Fish in ancient Egypt, however, had an ambiguous identity insofar as certain species were the sacred animals of local districts and those who ate them were considered unclean. In fact, the hieroglyph for 'abomination' was a fish. It appears strange that in a country totally dependent on a river, the eating of fish was officially condemned.

On the other hand, there is archaeological evidence of ancient nets, made out of knotted linen cord with lead weights attached, which were closed by pulling a plaited drawstring. Despite this proscription, the people fished often and a good catch was considered to be the welcome gift of the river. Wealthier citizens kept fish in ponds both for ornament and as a source of food.

Hatmehyt was the fish-goddess worshipped in the Delta, particularly in the north-east at Mendes and although a fish-deity is comparatively rare in Egyptian mythology, she appears to have been the 'senior deity' having been in existence when Egypt emerged from the primeval waters.

For most part, the fish is associated with the Osirian legend and the reason for its being deemed as unclean is due to the fact that the fish, Oxyrynchus, consumed the phallus of Osiris, following his dismemberment. Another tradition claims that this particular fish came forth from the wounds of Osiris and was held to be sacred at the town of that name in the Fayum region.

Here we see some provinces regarding particular fish as sacred, so that a fish that was considered taboo in one area could be eaten in another, something which often led to occasional conflict. Other species acted as pilots for the boat of the sun-god Re, warning of the approach of the sinister snake-god Apophis, during the journey through the Underworld.

Concepts

Traditionally, the two Piscean fish represent the sign's dual nature and according to *The New Astrology*, the divisions it embodies between the spiritual and material, between mind and body, and the Piscean individual's ability to face contradictory directions. The Dendera zodiac, however, shows the fishes swimming in the *same* direction. In keeping with its magico-mystical image for bewitchment and illusion *and* the ambiguity of the Egyptian view of the fish, Pisces remains one of the more obscure constellations. Taking into account that Tarot card for the sign is the Moon, we can easily see that Pisces is not to be taken at face value and that there are often hidden depths or two sides to an issue. When the Sun is in Pisces, particularly around the time of the Vernal (Spring) Equinox, we should take the time to reflect on the direction life is taking and see if there isn't some unexpected, or previously undetected path we should be examining. The Piscean concept teaches us to be flexible and open to new suggestions and, most important of all, to retain the ability to dream.

Shomu-Season (Harvest)

First Month – Pakhons (16 March-14 April)
Aries 21 March-20 April

The Sun enters Aries around the 21st March and leaves around the 20th April; this is a masculine sign ruled by Mars and representative of Elemental Fire. Always recognised as the first sign of the zodiac, antiquarians believe that early calendar markers placed Aries at the beginning of the year – which was then around the Winter Solstice. As the centuries rolled by, slowly the stars of Aries receded from the Winter Solstice to move nearer to the Vernal Equinox (spring).'*The sign of Aries as a whole is characterised by thunder and hail. Its leading part is rainy and windy, its middle temperate and the end hot and pestilential.'* [Tetrabiblos, Ptolemy]

The ancient Babylonians, Egyptians, Persians and Greeks all called this group of stars the Ram, and a great deal of attention is devoted to it in the old classic, *Calendars and Constellations of the Ancient World* (1903) by Emmeline Plunkett. Amun, the great god of the Theban Triad (Amun, Mut and Khonsu) is often represented as ram-headed and his magnificent temple at Karnak is approached by an avenue of ram-headed sphinxes. Although sheep were considered to be unclean and an unsuitable food for 'purified' persons, the ram was venerated by the Egyptians from early times.

The earliest of the ram-gods appear to have been based on a distinctive species that sported long, wavy horns, which was the image of the creator-god Khumn from Elephantine and Banebdjedet – 'Lord of Djedet' – of Mendes. A second species, that appeared much later in Egyptian history and with curved horns, is the form often attributed to Amun. At many of the cult centres rams were regularly mummified and buried in the catacombs. Amun is first mentioned in the Pyramid Texts (from the end of Dynasty V) but was almost unknown at the time of the Old Kingdom. His name – which means 'hidden' – appears only four time in the Texts because at that stage of Egypt's history, he was purely a local divinity of Thebes. By the time of the New Kingdom, however, the divinity of Amun was enhanced by interpreting him as a mysterious manifestation of the ancient sun-god of Heliopolis when the image of the god was given the additional symbol of the solar disk.

The Great Temple of Karnak is a testament to Amun's position as supreme god of Egypt by Dynasty XVIII. This vast enclosure contains the spectacular Temple of Amun with its Great Hypostyle Hall is, in most part, the work of Seti I and his son, Ramesses II. Here, religious processions in honour of the god, either carried in state on his sacred boat, or personal encounters between god and pharaoh cover ever column and inch of wall space.

Concepts

This sign is the symbol of great divine strength, although it is a power that is now always evident to the 'unseeing eye'. The ram is not only the ancient symbol of kingship but also of fertility in terms of grand ideas being brought to fruition. The true Arien does not hide his or her light under a bushel and, being ruled by Mars, means that more often than not, they lower their heads and charge – rather than waiting situations out. Mystically, the Arien Ram represents the primordial 'hidden' god of the Egyptians rather than the more modern personification of later dynasties:

Hidden One, no man knoweth his form,
Or can search out his likeness;

He is hidden to gods and men,
And is a mystery to his creatures.
No man knoweth how to know him;
His name is a mystery and is hidden.

Second Month – Payni (15 April-14 May)
Taurus 21 April-21 May

The Sun enters Taurus around 21st April and leaves around 21st May – the sign is ruled by Venus in Elemental Earth. The most famous star in the constellation is Aldebaran (the bull's eye), which rose with the Sun at the Spring Equinox around 3000BC. In classical astrology it was recorded as being one of the most propitious of stars, signifying all the kingly qualities. In Egyptian mythology, the Apis Bull held a very important place and represented harvest – the joyous and fruitful season of the year. According to Ptolemy in the 2nd century AD, *'The part of Taurus nearest the Pleiades was once thought to be marked by earthquakes, strong winds and mist. The part which bordered on the Hyades brought thunder and lightning.'*

Bulls have been worshipped since ancient times as symbols of strength and fertility and the Egyptians were no exception. Their mythology contains two distinct cults – the Apis Bull, the living manifestation of Ptah at of Memphis, and Mnevis, the sacred manifestation of Atum-Re, the Sun-god. The antiquity of the Apis-cult has been traced to shortly after the founding of the Egyptian State (about 3000BC) and it remained an important feature of the Pharaonic funerary rite up until the later periods. The cult centre of Mnevis was at Heliopolis and this solar theology was one of the few state-recognised survivors among the gods during the reign of Akhenaten in Dynasty XVIII.

Cow-goddess also had their place in the Egyptian pantheon – both Hathor and Nut took this form. There is undisputable proof of the former's worship dating from the Old Kingdom and royal ladies from this time took the title of 'Priestess of Hathor'. Nut was referred to as 'the sky-cow' and often had the job of carrying the deceased king on her back to take his place among the stars. In later times, Isis was given the image of wearing a solar disk between cow's horns.

Concept

In ancient Egyptian symbolism, it is '...to the bull triumphantly traversing the sky at night, in the autumn season, that attention is directe' [Calendars & Constellations of the Ancient World] and so we need to use this image for the 'fertilisation' of an idea or project. The bull is a slow, calm, obstinate and tenacious force and it often appears that nothing can stop a Taurian from moving forward. This power, combined with a contemplative spirit offers the perfect symbol of the Earth Element. What should not be overlooked, however, is that Taurus is a *feminine* sign and that Hathor and Nut were powerful protector goddesses in their own right. The female aspect is not lacking in temperament and can be subject to outbreaks of fury. Hathor (as Sekhmet) almost obliterated the human race as the 'Eye of Re'. Or it can be commanding, like Nut when dealing with Set's attempts to impose some other order than her own on the cosmos.

Third Month – Ipt-hmt (15 May–13 June)
Gemini 22 May–21 June

The Sun enters Gemini around the 22nd May and leaves around the 21st June. Ruled by Mercury, this is a masculine sign of Elemental Air. Most ancient cultures have their myths featuring sets of twins to represent conflicting energies or forces and the most predominant in the Egyptian pantheon is the fixed duality of Set and Horus as two sides of the same coin, although in later dynasties, the Osirian cult portrayed them as enemies. In some cases the twins are represented as one male and one female; one may even be responsible for the death of the other. According to Ptolemy, *'Geminians are thoughtful and intelligent in all things, especially in the search for wisdom and religion.'*

The duality of Egypt's most famous twins, Set and Horus, reaches back to pre-dynastic times and refers to the Dyad, or dual-pairing of deities. This term is usually reserved for Egyptian statuary combining images of two gods, but it is a useful magical technique for uniting opposing energies. The other well-known pairs are Re and Atum, both representing opposing images of the same principle; Bast and Sekhmet, which combines the opposing nature of the cat = domestic/untamed; or Isis and Nephthys, who are 'divine sisters'. It can also incorporate the male/female energies as in Osiris and Isis, Mut and Amun and Thoth and Ma'at.

It is important to include the primitive dualism of Horus and Set, simply because this is probably one of the most difficult god-concepts of all – because Set was 'demonised' out of all proportion during the dynastic periods and by successive emerging cultures, who took one look at this strange creature and pronounced it 'devilish'. Academic sources, however, taking a broader overview of the pre-dynastic symbolism of the 'Lord of the Two Lands', have given a much different picture. In *Egyptian Magic,* Dr Christian Jacq describes them as 'brothers who are at the same time both enemies and inseparable, formed into the same being. This dual identity, representing two symbolic tangibilities never ceasing in conflict to maintain supremacy over the Cosmos, is in reality One. The combined knowledge, wisdom and understanding of the [priest] enables him to discern unity in duality.'

Concept

These sentiments can also be expressed as there always being two sides to a story or coin – and that we should always be prepared to examine every aspect of a problem/enterprise before taking action. Because the sign is ruled by Mercury, we must also be prepared for the illusionary aspects that may cloud the judgement because the sign's duality does not necessarily mean harmony. For example, Sekhmet is the 'destroyer of mankind', but she carries out the destruction out of loyalty to the Creator, on whom mankind has turned its collective back. She is responsible for the plague and pestilence that arrives at the hottest time of the year, but the doctors and particularly surgeons were 'Servants of Sekhmet'. The domestic cat, characterised by Bast, can be a playful companion but it is an equally savage hunter. Geminid influences can also be seen as being the opposing forces representing the split between conscious and subconscious.

Fourth Month – *Wp-rnpt* (14 June-13 July)
Cancer 21 June-22July

The Sun enters Cancer around 21st June and leaves around 22nd July. It now marks the Summer Solstice, the longest day in the northern hemisphere; or the Winter Solstice, the shortest day in the southern hemisphere – although New Year is now in the sign of Leo, it was in Aries in pre-dynastic times. Cancer is a feminine sign ruled by the Moon and Elemental Water. By the New Kingdom, the Sun at the Summer Solstice was in the constellation of Cancer; but the seasons had moved around from their original positions due to precession and the numerous re-alignments of the calendar. The image of the crab may, however, be a mistake since it may also represent the scarab beetle – as there is an outward resemblance in the abstract shape between the two creatures – although the scarab is the symbol of the Sun.

In Egyptian myth the crab, like the fish, has a mixed reception. It was sacred in some regions and reviled in others and although fish from both the sea and the Nile were forbidden to the priesthood, they were widely eaten by ordinary folk. Of the *mollusca*, which contains shellfish (i.e. crabs), nothing is known which connects any of them with the religion of Egypt. The scarab, on the other hand, represents one of the most important symbols of dynastic Egypt and also referred to a type of amulet, seal or ring-bezel dating from Dynasty VI until the Ptolemaic period. The scarab seal gets its name from the shape of the scarab beetle, which was personified by Khepri, an aspect of the resurrected Sun-god. The seals, carved from stone, or moulded in faience or glass, were usually carved on the flat underside with inscriptions, with the top being carved in the likeness of the beetle.

Khepri is representative of the Sun-god at dawn on the eastern horizon and so synonymous with rebirth. Inscriptions dating from the Old Kingdom show that this belief was widespread; and many of the beautiful scarabs that have been rediscovered, such as those from the New Kingdom tomb of Tutankhamun that were made of semi-precious stones such as lapis lazuli set in gold.

One of the young king's pectorals in particular stresses the dominance of Khepri the sun-god as well as being a masterpiece of the jeweller's craft: in the centre of the design is a scarab carved from chalcedony combined with the wings and talons of the solar hawk, representing Khepri who, as controller of celestial motion, is shown here pushing the boat of the moon-eye.
[*A Dictionary of Egyptian Gods and Goddesses*]

Concepts

The observation that the scarab beetle emerged, apparently spontaneously, from balls of dung, the Egyptians saw as an association with the process of Creation. On much a grander scale, it has been also suggested that the colossal stone scarabs within temples, represented the temple as the primeval Mound from which the Sun-god emerged to begin the process of cosmogony. Such a scarab is still preserved *in situ* beside the sacred lake in the temple of Amun at Karnak. Here we must think of the crab and scarab as being one and the same – merely a question of interpretation of celestial imagery, since the zodiacal 'house' remains in the heavens in this position, however *we* choose to see it. And, since it falls at the time of the Summer Solstice (the original Egyptian New Year), it remains the symbol of renewal, resurrection and rebirth. This, then, is the time for new beginnings and ventures. Like the ancient Egyptians, it may be a good time to acquire a scarab amulet or talisman to give as a gift, or keep about your person.

The Five Epagomenal or Unlucky Days

The Epagomenal Days fall in the zodiacal house of Cancer from 14th-18th July. This is the point of high summer and the time of widespread disease, illness and pestilence, which were attributed to the 'Arrows of Sekhmet', and so the people would wear amulets of her for protection. These were the five days that divided the old year from the new and were considered unlucky since they were the birthdays of the Children of Nut – Osiris, Horus, Set, Isis and Nephthys who were continuously quarrelling and attempting to murder each other.

The Planets and Lunar Events

Our solar system actually consists of nine known planets (excluding the Sun and Moon) orbiting the Sun. For the ancients, only seven planets (*including* the Sun and Moon) were visible to the naked eye and so early astrological charts assigned a planet to each day of the week and the various zodiacal signs. As we have seen at the beginning of this book, however, according to some texts the ancient Egyptians aligned the planets with the following deities, who do not conform to contemporary planetary attributions:

- Sun with the Creator-god, Atum-Re;
- Moon with Thoth;
- Mars with Horus of the Horizon;
- Mercury with Sebegu (a god associated with Set);
- Jupiter with Horus 'who limits the two lands';

- Venus ('the one who crosses' or 'god of the morning') with either Re or Osiris;
- Saturn with Horus 'bull of the sky'.

Sun

For the Egyptians, the Sun was the focal point of their Universe. From pre-dynastic times, through to the Ptolemaic era, the Sun-god's daily journey across the sky and his descent into the under-world to confront the forces of darkness was at the centre of the Egyptian Mysteries. According to the ancient texts, the Egyptian priesthood offered up prayers to Atum-Re at dawn, mid-day and sunset. From the magical perspective, the ideal time to offer up prayers to Atum-Re would be three hours after sunrise, or three hours after sunset on a Sunday. This is the time suitable for petitioning the Giver of Life for authority, power, dignity, prominence, success in controlling and managing.

Hail to you Re, at your rising, and to you Atum, at your setting. You rise every day, you shine brightly every day, while you appear in glory, king of the gods. You are Lord of the sky and Lord of the earth, who has created the creatures above and those below.

Moon

The Moon is the province of Thoth, the patron of magicians and all learning; he is the record keeper in the Halls of Judgement. As with the symbolism of the Moon, his role is often illusionary and should not be taken on face value. From the magical perspective, the ideal time to offer up prayers to Thoth would be three hours after sunset on a Monday. This is the time suitable for petitioning for contact with inner dimensions, dreams, change, travel, success with people, women and children.

Praise to Thoth, the son of Re, the Moon, beautiful in his rising, Lord of bright appearings, who illumines the gods! Hail to thee,

Moon, Thoth.
[Hymn to Thoth written by Horemheb]

Lunar events

According to the sources given in *Temple Festivals Calendars of Ancient Egypt* by Sherif El-Sabban, provision was made for regular monthly lunar feasts, which celebrated the New Moon and Full Moon. These do appear, however, to be of secondary importance and were celebrated during the day of the New, Half, or Full Moon, not at night. There was also a mid-month feast marked with the symbol of a five-point star inside a quarter circle.

Mars

The red planet was assigned to the falcon-god and symbol of divine kingship, as Harakhti – whose name meant 'Horus of the Horizon'. It refers to the aspect of the god rising in the east at dawn to bathe in the 'field of rushes'. The Pyramid Texts mention the god linked to the sovereign, as the king is said to be born in the eastern sky as Harakhti. As a son of Re, he later became known as Re-Harakhti. From the magical perspective, the ideal time to offer up prayers to Harakhti would be at sunrise or sunset on a Tuesday, although his principle festival was New Year's Day. These are the times suitable for petitioning for being given energy governing aggressiveness, protection, attack and sexual matters.

Free course is given to you by Horus, you flash as the Lone Star in the midst of the sky; you have grown wings as a great-breasted falcon, as a hawk seen in the evening traversing the sky. May you cross the firmament by the waterway of Re-Harakhti.
[Pyramid Texts – Utterance 488]

Mercury

This planet is aligned with Sebegu (a god associated with Set and probably an early translation of Sebek the crocodile-god). This is a protective deity whose origins can be traced back to the early dynasties, although his cult reached its prominence during Dynasty XII and XIII. He is also known as the 'Lord of Bakhu' – the mountain of the horizon. Although on the surface Sebek would appear to relate to more terrestrial energies, the image of the crocodile was an important image in early Egyptian stellar imagery. From the magical perspective, the ideal time to offer up prayers to Sebek would be three hours after sunset on a Wednesday. This is the time for petitioning for magical powers, ingenuity, know-how, duality, cleverness, success in communication, education, trade and travel.

I have come today from out of the waters of the flood; I am Sobk, green of plume, watchful of face, raised of brow, the raging one who came forth from the shank of the tail of the Great One [Neith] who is in sunshine. I have come to my waterways which are in the bank of the flood of the place of contentment, green of fields, which is the horizon.

[Pyramid Texts – Utterance 317]

Jupiter

The planet of Jupiter is assigned to Horus 'who limits the two lands' and may refer to the deity's role as the unifying power between Upper and Lower Egypt.

From the magical perspective, the ideal time to offer up prayers to Horus would be three hours after sunset on a Thursday. This is the time suitable for petitioning for good luck, expansion, health, success in business, law, religion and medicine.

Hail to you, Unique One, who daily endures! Horus comes, the Far-

strider comes, he who has power over the horizon comes, (even) he who has power over the gods ... You traverse the sky in your striding, you include Lower and Upper Egypt within your journeys ...
[Pyramid Texts – Utterance 456]

Venus

The planet Venus has been attributed to Osiris ('the one who crosses') or Re ('god of the morning'). Here we have the symbol of re-birth and/or renewal, which is the province of female/womanly attributes. From the magical perspective, the ideal time to offer up prayers to Re or Osiris would be three hours after sunset, or three hours after dawn on a Friday. This is the time suitable for petitioning for love, graciousness, beauty, success in romance and the arts.

Praise be to Osiris!
Adorations be given unto him!
Smelling of the earth to Un-Nefer!
Prostrations to the ground to the
Everlasting Self-Created Sun-God!

Saturn

The ringed planet is attributed to Horus in his role of 'bull of the sky' – perhaps more aptly aligned with the sacred bull regarded as the physical manifestation of Atum-Re. [Not to be confused with the Apis bull that was the living manifestation of Ptah.]

From the magical perspective, the ideal time to offer up prayers to Horus/Re would be three hours after sunset, or three hours after dawn on a Saturday. This is the time suitable for petitioning for stability, success with time, constriction and the land.

Homage to the O Bull of Re with the four horns.

Thy horn is in the West, they horn is in the East,
Thy horn is in the South, thy horn is in the North.
The meadow of thy horn is the Amenti of the deceased,
Set thou him on his way.
[Unas funerary inscription]

Part Seven

The Egyptian Legacy

May you enter favoured and leave beloved

Those who see the Nile when it surges tremble, the meadows laugh, and the river-banks are inundated. The god's offerings descend, the faces of the men are bright, and the hearts of the gods rejoice.
[Pyramid Texts – Utterance 581]

As we are now aware, the roots of Egyptian wisdom are widespread and dig deep; there's over 4,500 years of concentrated power to provide a vast generator of psychic energy. For the sciolistic who has neither the wit nor understanding to control the unleashing of such immense potency, the repercussions could be grave indeed. As we have seen, Dr Christian Jacq writing on the subject in *Egyptian Magic* likened the recipients of the 'great magic', i.e. the higher priesthood, as being compared to today's atomic scientists. For the Egyptians, this magic was a safeguard against the world descending back into Chaos and the first duty of the classical magician was to dispel negativity and preserve existence. Modern-day magicians are not being pretentious in claiming that magical teachings go back to the earliest antiquity because, in some ways, the Adept places him/herself in direct contact with the 'architect of the universe'.

Each magical act is, by definition, an act of creation with its roots deep in the beginning of the world. The magician remakes it as it was in the beginning, he places the First Time in the present, he restores the world in that time. Magical time is primeval time. In the study of magic we reach for the spark from which all creation sprang.
[*Egyptian Magic*, Dr Christian Jacq]

But what if there are those seekers of Egyptian wisdom who do not wish to explore the cosmos and interact with extra-terrestrial energies? Is there nothing for them in the 21st century?

Not at all. For the seeker who merely wishes to work in harmony with the everyday beliefs and values of ancient Egypt, there *is* much to explore. As Hilary Wilson observes in *People of the Pharaohs*, the structure of Egyptian society was founded on the family unit, and dedicated to the protection of the weakest members so that women and children were both valued and cherished. There was also great importance placed on literacy – which is apparent by the status accorded to the scribe, and *'a scribal education was an absolute necessity for the professional classes, including architects, doctors and administrators'*.

Socialising and humour also played an important part in Egyptian life, and it is a mistake for us to think that every aspect of their daily routine was controlled by austerity and pious behaviour. The Egyptians loved feasting and entertainment; the abundance of their crops was because of the unique contribution of the Nile to agriculture and the rearing of cattle to provide food and drink for the temples and the people. Drunkenness was frequently portrayed, and there is even a record of tomb-builders going on strike because the beer ration hadn't turn up!

In *Wit and Humour in Ancient Egypt*, Patrick F Houlihan tells us that their sense of humour was manifested in a wide range of texts, tomb decorations, illustrated papyri and ostraca. We discover that the workmen added 'touches of comic relief into tomb decoration of the elite, in both picture and word', probably an ancient form of 'Kilroy was here!' Numerous drawings have been discovered featuring the amusing antics of various birds and animals, often engaged in human activities; not to mention the graphic and often slap-stick sexual 'etchings'. As Houlihan concludes:

Increasingly, humour is being taken seriously and is recognised by many scholars as an important way in which a society expresses itself ... Coming to better understand the roles laughter played along the Nile in antiquity provides important insights into the character and humanness of the Egyptian people, helping to bridge the many centuries. It is a refreshing view from the crushing formality that seems to permeate much of the sources for the study of ancient Egypt. This legacy of wit and humour allows us all to further appreciate the brilliance of their remarkable and most fascinating civilisation just a little more.

Applying Ancient Principles to the 21st Century

In *People of the Pharaohs* we also learn that ancient Egyptian family life was remarkable for a leniency that would have been considered progressive in Victorian England. Theirs was a society based on the sanctity of the family, where women's rights and children were well protected. Egyptian women could own and inherit property and even a woman who had been divorced for barrenness would be entitled to take back all the property that she had brought to the marriage. She would also be free to marry again, although this would seem unlikely owing to the great importance placed on producing heirs in Egyptian society.

It was a man's considered duty to marry and produce a large family while still comparatively young. This was largely due to the fact that life expectancy was low; human remains from the Pharaonic period shows the average age to be around 36 years although the nobility tended to live longer (Ramesses II was in his 70s when he died). Thirty-five would have been considered old for a middle-class or noblewoman with childbirth taking its toll; in poorer families, women were lucky if they reached the age of 20!

Children were looked upon as a continuance of the family name and as insurance for the afterlife. If a couple were childless, this gave serious cause for concern. *The Adoption Papyrus* from the reign of Rameses IX cites the marriage of a middle class couple where the wife was barren. Under normal circumstances she would have been divorced to enable the husband to remarry but in this case he did not divorce her but adopted her as his daughter. The couple purchased a slave-girl who then bore the husband children; some years later a young male relative of the original wife was also adopted into the family and married to the eldest daughter of the slave girl. The adoptions allowed the original pair to stay together; the family was 're-invigorated' by the scheme; the first wife became the matriarch of the family and the slave-girl received status by producing children for the family. It also demonstrates that the husband must have had a great love and respect for his first wife.

Despite the penchant of the ruling family to incestuous marriage, the practice was not widespread. Marriage in Egypt was a monogamous affair, with only one woman being recognised as *nebet per*, or 'Mistress of the House'. There is scant evidence that marriage was celebrated by a formal wedding ceremony of either a civil or religious nature. There were long discussions and negotiations between the families involved and there is evidence that sometimes an agreement was drawn up in the form of a legal document. The marriage contract was a formal recognition of the rights to any property – in short, a legal and binding pre-nuptial agreement. The marriage celebrations appear to have consisted of a procession through the streets from the bride's family home to that of her new husband. The parade included a public display of the wedding gifts of household items – and made a public declaration of their union. Often the bride would be 12 or 13 years of age and her husband a couple of years older.

The wife retained ownership of any property she brought with her, and kept her rights of inheritance to her parent's estate: also being entitled to a one-third share of any property acquired during the marriage, which was her 'widow's pension' should she outlive her husband. In the event of widowhood, the remaining two-thirds would be shared equally between all the children of both sexes. Apart from producing an endless supply of children to continue the family line, the wife was also expected to manage the household regardless of its size. A man took on the responsibility for any unmarried or widowed females of the immediate family, while orphaned nephews and nieces would be adopted and brought up with the couple's own children.

From this we can learn to revaluate some of our own social values ... the Egyptian *were* elitist, but they welcomed foreigners settling in their country, while retaining their national identity. The family was all-important ... but so was learning and self-advancement.

Visualisation Techniques

The numerous picture books of ancient Egypt offer up a gateway through which we can step back in time by using visualisation. This is controlled thought projection of a magical journey or scenario in which we *consciously* take part. This technique is used by more experienced practitioners as a springboard for deeper pathworking or meditation. In some traditions, this is referred to as actual pathworking, while others use it purely for relaxation. As a simple exercise, find a large colour picture of an Egyptian temple and study it for a few minutes to set the image in your mind's eye.

Sit or lie down in a comfortable position and try to imagine yourself standing in the Great Court looking towards the temple entrance. The sun is blazing down and there is no shade ... only the shadowed gateway of the

---

pylons that lead to the Inner Court. Beyond the Inner Court there is the distant black rectangle of the temple doorway ... For the moment, you cannot go through the pylon and must stand in the midday heat and silence ... looking towards the sanctuary of your god ... Enjoy the sensations of the scene you have created for a moment before allowing yourself to come back to the present. Try this exercise a few times, and then try to visualise yourself walking through the pylon gateway and into the Inner Court. Try each exercise a few times before going on to the next stage.

When you have completed the exercise, clap your hands to 'break the spell' and treat yourself to a sweet biscuit and hot drink, since this is the most effective way to disperse psychic energy.

The Law

It would be a grave mistake to believe that the land of Egypt was a crime-free society. The Greek historian Diodorus Siculus, visiting the country in the 1st century BC, recorded that there *was* a Pharaonic legal system set out and preserved in eight books but this can only be traced from the Late Period (747BC-332BC). No doubt Egypt had its fair share of crime and, as Joyce Tyldesley comments in *Judgement of the Pharaoh*, human nature being what it is, each social class would have been blessed with its fair share of miscreants and wrongdoers.

Like all things Egyptian, the law was strongly bound up with a code of ethics, closely entwined with the religion. This accepted standard of social behaviour and the clear distinction of right and wrong was presided over by the concept of *ma'at*, with which we are now familiar. As far as Egyptian civil law was concerned, no complete documents have survived and so the information is based on the available fragments of court records, civil contracts, private writings, funerary texts, royal decrees and fictional writing. It would appear that then, as now, society was plagued by theft and violence, but punishment (by today's standards) might appear harsh.

Although Diodorus cites one example of Egyptian law which could be implemented today: *'Those who brought false accusations against others had to suffer the punishment that would have been meted out to the accused had they been found guilty.'* There is also historical evidence of standard 'physical' penalties for specific crimes but these were reserved for the criminal court to dispense. The civil court worked on a system of correction and compensation designed to improve the lot of the victim while depriving the guilty of their assets.

The gold Ma'at pendant mentioned elsewhere in the text, is believed to have been an official insignia, since surviving statues of legal officials of the Late Period show them wearing similar chains and pendants; minor cases would have been tried by the local council of elders. Familiar as we are with the Egyptian love of order, it is quite probable that strict definitions of official appointments existed for all the important positions, each with their own allotted place in the administrative system.

Despite all the beatings, mutilations and executions, we know that the average Egyptian set more store in how they would be judged in the Afterlife when they made their statement of '42 Negative Confessions'. This was, to all intents and purposes, the denial of a list of offences against their neighbours and the gods – an abbreviated version follows:

> *Behold, I have come before you. I have brought you truth. I have foresworn falsehood ... I have not impoverished my neighbours. I have done no wrong in the Place of Ma'at ... I have not deprived the orphan of his property. I have done nothing that is detested by the gods ... I have caused no pain. I have made no one hungry. I have*

caused no one to weep. I have not killed nor have I commanded to kill. I have caused no suffering ... I have not taken the milk from the mouths of children ... I am pure!
[*The Judgement of the Pharaoh,* Joyce Tyldesley]

Personal responsibility and regulation was the social watch-word and meant that an individual could live their life according to their own social conscience.

The Development of Personal Stability

Egyptian law, as ancient as it is, is not a bad standard by which we can live our own lives. True, the penalties might appear a little harsh in our 21st century, politically correct, human-rights obsessed world, but the Egyptians themselves can only be judged according to the lights of their time. If we can go through our lives, conscious of the '42 Negative Confessions' and at the end of the day be able to stand in front of our judges or gods, and say: *'I did what I did, because I believed it to be right at the time,'* then we are living according to our conscience and the Law of Ma'at.

The Medicine

Apart from the post-mortem examination of mummies, the most important source for information on Egyptian medical practice are the surviving medical papyri stored in museums around the world. These texts offer an amazing insight into different categories identified by Egyptian doctors, such as surgical, general medical, rectal diseases, gynaecological, ophthalmic and paediatric techniques together with magical-medical texts and snakebite.

Despite these technical advancements, it must also be understood that not only were the doctors involved in healing – the priests and magicians also had a part to play. And since magic and religion were inseparable in Egypt, both also played a major role in the treatment of the sick. Malign entities or neighbours were believed to be responsible for many diseases and if the cause were thought to be supernatural, then it was logical to look to the supernatural for a cure. Sometimes a spell would be recited and an amulet dispensed; sometimes these would be used in conjunction with conventional medical attention. *'With relatively few effective drugs and operations available, it would be wrong to underestimate the curative value of suggestion and expectation of cure which must have accompanied the use of magic,'* wrote Doctor John Nunn (who is also an Egyptologist), in *Ancient Egyptian Medicine*.

There is ample evidence to show that doctors (*swnw*) were looked upon as important members of society and the names of those preserved for posterity show that they came from noble, if not royal, families. It is also clear that Egyptian doctors were held in high esteem by neighbouring countries, who often sent to Pharaoh asking that a member of the profession be sent immediately to deal with some complaint or ailment. The general impression is that many of the medical papyri were written for doctors who were expected to prepare their own medications although there is the occasional reference to 'then you shall cause one to prepare for him ...' which implies the situation of having someone else preparing remedies other than the doctor.

Dr Lise Manniche, a Danish Egyptologist, has compiled *An Ancient Egyptian Herbal* that shows the ingredients of medicinal preparations were predominantly derived from indigenous plants, trees and fruit. A surprisingly large number of those used have recognised properties very similar to modern herbal medicine. Some remedies were swallowed, some applied as poultices or unguents, while others were used for fumigation or inhalation. Some of the surviving papyri are specialist works but many others contain a wide variety of conditions together with household hints and recipes for cosmetics in similar vein to the 'treasuries' compiled by European housekeepers from the 16th to the 19th centuries.

The Egyptian housewife obviously had her own recipes and cures that would have been handed down from mother to daughter, but the woman's role in medicine appears to have been restricted to wet-nursing. There is no known Egyptian word for midwife and no surviving medical papyri dealing with childbirth but, as Dr Nunn observes, it would be indeed surprising if there were no women who were specially skilled and experienced in this area.

Sympathetic Magic

The Egyptians were skilled in the use of herbs and spices for medicines, cooking, cosmetics, perfumes and many other purposes; some of it involving 'sympathetic magic' – the concept of treating like with like. Simple substitutions for European ingredients in healing and spellcasting can be found in *An Ancient Egyptian Herbal* and *Sacred Luxuries: Fragrance, Aromatherapy & Cosmetics in Ancient Egypt* both by Lise Manniche. For example, Thomas Culpeper's 17th century remedy for treating bruises was a compress of bishops-weed, chervil or Solomon's seal; the ancient Egyptian remedy was roasted garlic in oil, or pounded in salt and vinegar.

Keeping the Faith

The threads of ancient Egyptian influence that weave their way through Western civilisation are many and varied. The continuity of the religion and the revival of the Hermetic Tradition remind us of the antiquity of certain elements within Christian liturgies and beliefs, which connect Western beliefs with something much older. Gnosis, one of the chief forms of syncretism in late classical antiquity, drew on every area of culture in its day, including the *Iliad* and the *Odyssey* – and continued to do so throughout its history. It was a colourful mixture of various religious elements, which lives on today in Theosophy and Anthroposophy.

In other words, these are coherent and consistent threads running through the story of the Egyptian Revival in Western Europe from Classical times to the present day, not to mention the revival emerging later in America. As Dr Curl points out in *The Egyptian Revival*:

> *The influence was absorbed into Graeco-Roman culture and later into European civilisation as a whole. During the Renaissance the Mysteries of Hermes Trismegistus re-emerged in Gnostism and the 'Rosicrucian Enlightenment'. And while the richness of Marian symbolism within the Roman Catholic church clearly owes much to the cult of the Egyptian goddess Isis, the Christian religion itself kept alive many other aspects of Egyptian culture.*

The interest in Egyptian ideas and objects often increased after some spectacular discovery – such as the *Mensa Isiaca* (or Bembine Tablet) or the Rosetta Stone.

Drawings, paintings and a developing appreciation of antiquity brought Egyptian motifs to a wider public throughout Europe. Nevertheless, from Classical times, through the Renaissance to the 18th century, to the revival period after the Napoleonic campaign, the 19th century continued with buildings, furniture, jewellery, etc., offering thousands of variation in the style; and with travel on the increase for the Victorians, strong Egyptian elements also crept into the paintings and literature of the time. By the 20th century, even cinemas and factories acquired the 'Nile style' veneer under the guise of Art Deco architecture – **Egyptomania was here to stay.**

But as Michael Rice observes in *Egypt's Legacy*, the mystery of Egypt is very great. It is so because it is the most creative and enduring expression of the greatest mystery of all, human consciousness.

By defining the archetypes, by giving them form and bringing a new set of concepts into the world, Egypt expanded immeasurably the boundaries of human awareness and, in consequence, of human creativity. Egypt did not invent consciousness but the psychic processes that were at work in the late pre-dynastic period onwards gave rise to the expansion of consciousness and of what it could achieve, on a scale never before apprehended by men.

Although the mythic quality that ancient Egypt conveys is immensely powerful; and despite its plethora of deities, rulers and assorted 'Great Ones', Rice believes it to be an entirely human construct, which should be viewed in a human dimension.

Because the development of ancient Egyptian society so precisely – and so uncannily – replicates the process whereby the individual achieves maturity, it has been possible for the individual, in all ages, to recognise the nature of the experience involved and to associate himself with it.

Expanding Consciousness

Here we allow our minds to register the Egyptian influences that creep into our own everyday lives. If we raise our eyes from the high-street shop fronts and examine the architecture of the upper stories, we may find a whole new world for exploration. The lady chapel of a local church with its image of 'mother and child' is only a thinly

> disguised image of the Egyptian 'Lady of the Starry Heavens'. When we encounter the 'sacrificial god-king' in history and modern paganism, we can relate to the Osirian cult that enveloped later Egyptian thinking. Because of the purity of this ancient wisdom, it means that many of the archetypes we use today in magical practice, have their roots in the Nile Valley. Open up your mind and discover the wonders of an ancient belief that is entering its sixth millennium.

Following the successful absorption of Isis worship into the Roman world, and having combined all the attributes of the other Egyptian gods into this single persona to create the alien but revered figure of the 'most universal of all goddesses', she could hardly have been wished out of existence. As James Curl observes:

Her catholicity and her essential syncretism were absorbed, and Maria Myrionymos took over where her Egyptian forerunner left off. The official ending of Isiac worship did not mean that the cult of the goddess died, for, quite apart from the iconography a number of images of Isis survived in Christian churches for some time with the idea of Isis being identified with the Virgin Mary and child. The merging of the Isiac cult with Christianity in the veneration of the Virgin was a long and subtle process, and the Isiac pictures and images often survived. The great number of churches dedicated to Mary that stand on the sites of Isaea, point to a deliberate absorption of Isiac worship.

Following the direction of Augustine that pagan sites should be rededicated for Christian worship, we find echoes of the building of churches on other hallowed pagan sites throughout

Europe.

Similarly, although an Osiris-Serapis cult developed in Rome, it lacked the appeal and impetus of the Isian cult in order to establish a firm foot-hold. Nevertheless, all the elements of the death of Osiris were grafted into the expanding Christian literature and, together with influence of the Persian god Mithra, the fully formed Son of God, dying for the sins of the world, came into being. This archetypal 'Sacrificial King/Dying God' element has become familiar in multi-cultural myths and legends all over the world.

To fully grasp the extent of this belief, we have to turn to Sir James Frazer's *Golden Bough: 'The practice of putting kings to death either at the end of a fixed period or whenever their health and strength began to fail, the body of evidence which points to the wide prevalence of such a custom is considrable.'* It is possible that primitive Nile cultures did perform such chthonic sacrifices, but by the time of the dynastic kings, the magico-religious system had become much more sophisticated and evolved into a more cosmic culture.

Hermes Trismegistus (Thoth/Tahuti) was always a god of harmony, of reconciliation and transformation, and in his 'modern' role he preaches no rigid dogma – as a result, all Hermeticism is, by its very nature, tolerant and forward thinking. According to *The Egyptian Revival*,

During the 16th and 17th centuries, studies of traditions that had an Egyptian background developed: Hermetic and Cabbalist ideas, with alchemy, achieved expression in the Rosicrucian manifestos. The Renaissance Hermetic Tradition ... gained a new lease of life in the 17th century and Robert Fludd [1574-1637] was an adherent of the philosophy of the 'Egyptian' priest Hermes Trismegistus ... According to Dr Frances Yates [*Giordano Bruno and the Hermetic Tradition*], John Dee is also a key figure in what she calls the 'Rosicrucian Enlightenment' and Giordano Bruno too, made use of

Hermetic themes ... Bruno himself was to die at the stake [1600] for his conviction that the wisdom and magic of ancient Egypt were greater than a repressive orthodoxy that burned dissidents.

Surprisingly, the Jesuits shared certain interests with the Rosicrucians – with Hermetic and occult philosophies forming a considerable part of the *oeuvre* of Athanasius Kircher, whose writings appear to have been used a lot in Jesuit missionary activity. In some instances Rosicrucian symbolism was used by the Jesuits to show that the two Orders shared certain attributes, and further suggesting that the Rosicrucians were a power to be reckoned with. Kircher's philosophy, based on orthodox Roman Catholicism and the teaching of Hermes Trismegistus, claimed that the Egyptians were in the van of metaphysical knowledge, and that it was to Egypt that we should look for the origins of art, science, and religion!

Research into the histories of Rosicrucianism and Freemasonry has been hindered by the enormous amounts of sensational, inaccurate media reporting, and so-called questionable 'occultist' publications. From the 18th century, the 'revival' was particularly associated with a European funerary tradition that was totally divorced from the original Mysteries. Nevertheless, the iconography of European Freemasonry was also steeped in Egyptian design, for Egypt provides the main source of Masonic doctrine, while Masonic tradition holds that Freemasonry is as old as the art and science of architecture, and so there is a debt to Egypt in perpetuality.

The actual founder of 'Egyptian Masonry' was the controversial Count Cagliostro, and by the time he was incarcerated in a papal dungeon, the Egyptian influence had become an integral part of Freemasonry movement. The magical elements, also based on Masonic influences were to dominate the esoteric world from the 18th century to the present day, and we can find references to these in the writings of the Aleister Crowley's *Argentinum Astrum*, the *Ordo Templis Orientis*, the Hermetic Order of the Golden Dawn and the Theosophical Society.

Within the Egyptian Mystery Tradition we are looking at the Elder Gods in Atum-Re, Nut, Thoth, Horus (the Elder) and Set – the gods before the gods of men from the time of *zep tepi*, who are in a different league to the later deities. In other words: *'They are nameless, faceless, devoid of human or earthly attributes, and beyound mundane comprehention'*. We are not really allowed to 'see' them.

In *The Secret Lore of Egypt: Its Impact on the West* by Erik Hornung, he reminds us that esoteric matters have to do with the 'hidden', often deliberately concealed truths

> *...that can be grasped only through intuition or revelations and that elude any and all experimental verification. The esoteric is a way of thinking unto itself, irrational and intuitive, aimed at the overarching unity of nature and the correspondences within it … It lives on the magic of the mysterious, believing itself to be in possession of a higher state of consciousness that remains closed to those who are not 'initiated' into these mysteries.*

No matter how we may think otherwise, as Dr Curl also reminds us, we have to accept the fact that the splendour of Egyptian design and the simplicity of basic Egyptian architectural forms suggest something of an eternal truth and an ageless serenity. A newly discovered awareness of the persistence of Egyptian ideas in religion, art, and iconography creates fresh and enlightening perspectives. **There *is* a sense of continuity from this ancient land.**

> *To consider the survival of the much loved goddess [Isis] and so great a part of the objects and ideas familiar when she was omnipotent in ancient times is enough to emphasise the futilities*

and disagreeable dissonances of the present age. The sense of kinship with a robust and kindly past, in harmony with the moon, the earth, the waters and the sun, is beneficent ... Her presence has been one of the most radiant and tranquil assets of the Christian Church, although she has undergone some subtle metamorphoses, not all of them for the better. Her enchantments have been on the whole been benevolent and affectionate: Egypt is with us still, and we owe a great deal to that ancient land.

But it is not only Isis who has endured – although she carried the seed of the ancient Mysteries to many far-off lands – her brother-consort, Orisis, perpetuated the concept of the Sacrificial King/Dying God, and her son Horus, the Child Saviour. Despite the fact that the image of Set and Nut were submerged beneath this 'holy family', theirs is influence that endures *within* the Mysteries of all esoteric Orders, under whatever guise they may manifest. Atum-Re remains the 'Bornless One', 'the Nameless One', the Creator-God – the Supreme Being that rules the Universe; while in the shadows, Thoth continues to preserve the vast fount of 'hidden' Knowledge, Wisdom and Understanding for the generations to come.

The Final Throw of the Dice

The Sacred Icosahedron

A final magical exercise that bridges the gap between the ancient Egyptians and the modern world is the unique limestone icosahedron now housed in the New Valley Museum in Egypt. Presumed to date from the first century AD it is thought to have been used 'in an oracular procedure' intended to establish which deity would provide help to the petitioner. This icosahedron was influenced by the mixing of cultural and religious traditions of the Graeco-Roman period, and by the names of the gods and the demotic script to the Egyptian tradition.

Formed by 20 equilateral triangles with the 20 divine names written in demotic Egyptian characters on its sides:

1 Amun	11 Bastet
2 Pre	12 Hapy
3 Ptah	13 Triphis
4 Thoth	14 Shai
5 Atum	15 Nephthys
6 Khepri	16 Neith
7 Geb	17 Shepshit
8 Osiris	18 Min
9 Horus	19 Khonsu
10 Isis	20 Mut

It is impossible to say why some of these deities were chosen, but an article in the Egyptian Exploration's *Journal* (Vol 93. 2007) suggests that the deity (or which spell might be used) could be the solution to a problem and identified by throwing the dice. 'An Egyptian might have taken a liking to the Greek form and found it useful to write 20 divine names on it in order to memorise this particular set of deities. While praying he might have moved the die in his hand, rather as is done with a rosary.'

Try to obtain a modern 20-faceted polyhedron from shops that specialise in geology samples, or shops selling polished tumble or palmstones, pyramids and eggs, although they are very rare. Look upon the acquisition of a icosahedron as part of your magical quest, to be inscribed with the names of 20 Egyptian deities of your choosing to use as a prayer stone.

As we have seen throughout *The Atum-Re Revival*, every aspect of life in ancient Egypt was governed by the intimate relationships between the people and their gods. The religion was not a 'way of life' for the Egyptians, 'Life' was their religion. So, in response to travel writer Bob Maddams' original question: *'Was there ever a civilisation more in love with the cult of the dead and the afterlife than the ancient Egyptians?'* The answer is: ' **No! They were more in love with Life.'**

Sources and Bibliography

The Ancient Egyptian Book of the Dead, R O Faulkner (BMP)

The Ancient Egyptian Coffin Texts, R O Faulkner (Arris & Philips)

An Ancient Egyptian Herbal, Lise Manniche (BMP)

Ancient Egyptian Medicine, John F Nunn (BMP)

The Ancient Egyptian Pyramid Texts, R O Faulkner (OUP)

Anthropology, Sir E B Tylor (Watts & Co)

Archaeoastronomy, No 9, (Journal for the History of Astronomy)

Are We Alone? Paul Davies (Penguin)

Astronomy Before the Telescope, ed by Christopher Walker (BMP)

Atlas of the Universe, Patrick Moore (Philips)

Atom, Lawrence M Krauss (Little, Brown)

The Atlantis Syndrome, Paul Jordan (Sutton)

The Book of Nothing, John D Barrow (Cape)

Chronicle of the Pharaohs, Peter A Clayton (Thames & Hudson)

The Complete Astrological Writings, Aleister Crowley (Star)

Confessions, Aleister Crowley (Arkana)

The Cosmic Clocks, Michel Gauquelin (Paladin)

Cosmic Dragons, Chandra Wickramasinghe (Souvenir)

Creation Records, George St Clair (David Nutt)

Daily Life of the Egyptian Gods, Dimitri Meeks & Christine Favard-Meeks (Murray)

Dictionary of Ancient Egypt, Ian Shaw and Paul Nicholson (BMP)

Early Dynastic Egypt, Toby A H Wilkinson (Routledge)

Earth Story, Simon Lamb & David Sington (BBC)

Egypt, K Lange & M Hirmer (Phaidon)

The Egyptian Book of Days, compiled by Mélusine Draco (ignotus)

The Egyptian Book of Nights, Mélusine Draco (ignotus)

Egyptian Magic, Christian Jacq (Aris & Philips)

The Egyptian Revival, Dr James Stevens Curl (Allen & Unwin)

Egypt's Legacy, Michael Rice (Routledge)

Egypt's Making, Michael Rice (Routledge)

Encyclopaedia of the Universe, ed Martin Rees (Collins)

The Eye in the Triangle, Israel Regardie (Falcon)

Exploring Spirituality, Suzanne Ruthven & Aeron Medbh-Mara (Pathways)

God, Time & Stephen Hawking, David Wilkinson (Monarch)

The Golden Bough, Sir James Frazer (Macmillan)

Hecate's Fountain, Kenneth Grant (Skoob)

Hermetica, trans Walter Scott (Solos)

Herodotus, H F Gray (Bell)

The Inner Guide to Egypt, Alan Richardson & Billie Walker-John (Arcania)

Judgement of the Pharaoh, Joyce Tyldesley (Weidenfeld & Nicholson)

The Land of the Fallen Star Gods, J S Gordon (Orpheus)

The Last Three Minutes, Paul Davies (Phoenix)

The Law Is For All, Louis Wilkinson (New Falcon)

Liber Ægyptius, Mélusine Draco (ignotus)

The Magic Furnace, Marcus Chown (Cape)

Magic in Ancient Egypt, Geraldine Pinch (BMP)

Magick, Aleister Crowley (Guild)

The Natural History of the Universe, Colin A Ronan (Doubleday)

People of the Pharaohs, Hilary Wilson (Brockhampton Press)

The Pyramids of Egypt, I E S Edwards (Ebury)

The Observer's Year, Patrick Moore (Springer)

The Occult Sourcebook, Nevill Drury & Gregory Tillett (RKP)

Origins, John Gribbin & Simon Goodwin (Constable)

Osiris & the Egyptian Resurrection, Vol I, trans Wallis Budge (Dover)

Our Cosmic Habitat, Martin Rees (Weidenfeld & Nicholson)

The Oxford Companion to Classical Literature, Paul Harvet (OUP)

The Planets, David McNab & James Younger (BBC)

The Religion of Ancient Rome, Cyril Bailey (OUP)

Rogue Asteroids and Doomsday Comets, Duncan Steel (Wiley)

Sacred Luxuries, Lise Manniche (Opus)

The Secret Lore of Egypt: Its Impact on the West, Erik Hornung (Cornell University Press)

The Secrets of Superstitions, Owen S Rachleff (Doubleday)

The Setian, Billie Walker-John (ignotus)

Starchild, Mélusine Draco (ignotus)

Stardust, John Gribbin (Penguin)

The Stars Above Us, E Zinner (Allen & Unwin)

The Stars and Their Courses, Sir James Jeans (Cambridge)

Starseekers, Colin Wilson (Granada)

Starwatching, David Levy (Collins)

The Thelemic Handbook, Mélusine Draco (ignotus)

Tombs of the Pyramid Builders, Z Hawass (Leiden)

The Universe Next Door, Marcus Chown (Headline)

Wit and Humour in Ancient Egypt, Patrick F Houlihan (Rubicon Press)

AXIS MUNDI
BOOKS

Axis Mundi Books provide the most revealing and coherent
explorations and investigations of the world of hidden or
forbidden knowledge. Take a fascinating journey into the realm
of Esoteric Mysteries, Magic, Mysticism, Angels, Cosmology,
Alchemy, Gnosticism, Theosophy, Kabbalah, Secret Societies and
Religions, Symbolism, Quantum Theory, Apocalyptic
Mythology, Holy Grail and Alternative Views of Mainstream
Religion.